The Economics of Housing Vouchers

STUDIES IN URBAN ECONOMICS

Under the Editorship of

Edwin S. Mills
Princeton University

The Economics of Housing Vouchers

Joseph Friedman

Department of Economics
and Center for Urban Studies
Tel Aviv University
Tel Aviv, Israel
and
Abt Associates Inc.
Cambridge, Massachusetts

Daniel H. Weinberg

Office of Income Security Policy
U.S. Department of Health and Human Services
Washington, D.C.

Academic Press

A Subsidiary of Harcourt Brace Jovanovich, Publishers

New York   London
Paris   San Diego   San Francisco   São Paulo   Sydney   Tokyo   Toronto

ACADEMIC PRESS, INC.
111 Fifth Avenue, New York, New York 10003
CC,

United Kingdom Edition published by
ACADEMIC PRESS, INC. (LONDON) LTD.
24/28 Oval Road, London NW1   7DX

Library of Congress Cataloging in Publication Data
Main entry under title:

The Economics of housing vouchers.

   (Studies in urban economics)
   Includes index.
   1. Rent subsidies--Arizona--Phoenix Metropolitan
Area. 2. Rent subsidies--Pennsylvania--Pittsburgh
Metropolitan Area. I. Friedman, Joseph, Date
II. Weinberg, David H. III. Series.
HD7288.83.E36 1982   363.5'8   82-16262
ISBN 0-12-268360-9

PRINTED IN THE UNITED STATES OF AMERICA

82 83 84 85   9 8 7 6 5 4 3 2 1

To Nurit and Page

Contents

Preface

This book presents an examination of the housing choices of low-income families in two metropolitan areas—Phoenix and Pittsburgh. Some of these households were offered a novel kind of housing subsidy—a housing allowance or housing voucher—in an experimental framework designed to test this approach to demand-side housing assistance. A housing allowance is a direct cash payment made to a needy family, typically based on its income and willingness to find decent housing in the marketplace. A voucher is sometimes suggested as the method to implement this housing assistance strategy.

Three types of housing allowance plans were tested in the Housing Allowance Demand Experiment. One, the "Housing Gap" housing allowance, covered the gap between the cost of modest but decent housing and the fraction of income a household is expected to devote to housing. Housing Gap allowances were conditional subsidies paid only to income-eligible households whose housing met certain health and safety requirements ("Minimum Standards"). As an experimental alternative, the requirement that recipient housing meet these Minimum Standards was replaced by a requirement that housing expenditure exceed a specified "Minimum Rent" level. The second housing allowance type, the "Percent of Rent" housing allowance, offered participants a rebate of a percentage of their rent. Finally, to allow comparisons of housing allowance schemes with income maintenance programs, an "Unconstrained" housing allowance was tested. This type of allowance used the same payment formula as Housing Gap allowances without imposing any housing requirement on participants.

Chapter 1 presents an overview of U.S. housing programs and the dimensions of the U.S. housing problem. The experimental context of our analysis is then described. The rest of the book is divided into three major parts.

The first part investigates the "normal" housing market behavior of low-income households. This investigation of their housing demand uses the housing price reduction resulting from the Percent of Rent allowance to examine their demand for housing. Chapter 2 presents a simple microeconomic model that conceptualizes household behavior and then presents a summary of some of the extant evidence on housing demand. The remainder of the chapter estimates housing demand models for the low-income population in the Demand Experiment, using housing expenditures to measure housing. Chapter 3 then takes a different approach to measuring housing—a hedonic index of housing services that abstracts from particular characteristics of the household or landlord that may affect rent and attempts to measure housing in a more objective manner.

The second major part of the book examines the responses of Housing Gap and Unconstrained households—households receiving an income-based housing subsidy. Chapter 4 presents a model of household behavior that leads to the methodology for estimating experimental effects. The procedure adopted measures household response as a deviation from normal behavior. The models of normal behavior draw on the findings of Chapters 2 and 3. Two types of housing change are examined for Minimum Standards households in Chapter 4—physical housing standards and housing expenditures. Chapter 5 repeats the analysis for Minimum Rent households, and Chapter 6 examines the effect of both kinds of Housing Gap allowance payment on the consumption of housing services (the more objective measure of housing introduced in Chapter 3).

In the final part of the book, Chapter 7, we use our findings, and the findings of other analyses of additional aspects of housing allowances, to focus on the implications of the experimental findings for housing policy. We compare a housing allowance strategy with two other approaches, a pure income-transfer approach and a construction-oriented approach, concluding that none of the three strategies offer *the* one solution to the U.S. "housing problem." After discussing the role a housing allowance program may play in this housing policy triad, we offer some suggested approaches to implementing such a strategy.

The appendixes cover both basic and technical information. After providing more detail on the design and implementation of the Demand Experiment, we offer several technical appendixes that explicate our methodologies in detail and extend the analysis of the main text into additional areas. The final appendix offers some supplementary tables.

Housing vouchers are a particularly timely and important federal housing strategy. The final report of President Reagan's Commission on Housing (1982) has endorsed the concept of housing vouchers as a major element of U.S. housing policy. Similarly, the U.S. Department of Housing and Urban Development (HUD) has sent legislation to Congress in an attempt to create a workable national program of housing allowances (see Congressional Budget Office, 1982). We believe that our book can provide some valuable insights for housing policymakers in both the executive and legislative branches of government as they formulate and consider such an approach.

Similarly, the book would be of interest to all those interested in housing policy, ranging from economists and regional and other social scientists in academia, to housing analysts and HUD, the Congress, and housing lobby groups, and to state and local government housing officials (particularly to those likely to be administering such a program). Others that may find useful information in this book are social scientists interested in the results of one of the largest social experiments ever conducted.

Acknowledgments

This book is the result of 3 years of work on the Housing Allowance Demand Experiment by the authors. It is the condensation of two reports to the Department of Housing and Urban Development (HUD) under a contract to Abt Associates Inc. (AAI) under HUD's Experimental Housing Allowance Program. Without the support and guidance of the members of HUD's Office of Policy Development and Research, the work would not have been possible. The study was carried out under the general and very capable direction of Jerry Fitts and Terry Connell, with the more specific attention of Garland Allen.

The success of the research effort owes a great deal to the careful development of the research design by Stephen Kennedy, Walter Stellwagen, James Wallace, and Helen Bakeman. All were intimately involved in the day-to-day operation of the experiment and the conduct of the research—Kennedy as the overall project director and principal investigator, Stellwagen as the overall quality control reviewer and general statistical advisor, Wallace as the director of research, and Bakeman as deputy project director. Special thanks go to Stephen Mayo, with whom we had numerous discussions on the housing economics involved and who paved the way for several of the analyses we undertook.

Several others contributed to the analyses presented here. Sally Merrill developed the hedonic indices used in Chapters 3 and 6, and Fred Luhmann performed many of the computer programming tasks involved in managing the data processing for the reports. Others too numerous to mention were involved in writing the questionnaires, developing the data base, and providing comments and suggestions along the way. We would also like to thank Clark Abt and Benjamin Chinitz for their support in the early stages of writing this manuscript. Cogent comments and suggestions were provided by Ernst Stromsdorfer and Raymond Struyk, who reviewed the first draft of this book. Of course, none of these individuals or institutions share our responsibility for the analyses reported here.

Even though the initial analysis work was supported by HUD at AAI and one of the authors is now at the U.S. Department of Health and Human Services (HHS), this book was written by the authors in their private capacity. No official support or endorsement by HUD, HHS, or AAI is intended or should be inferred.

The Economics of Housing Vouchers

Chapter 1

Introduction

In the past 50 years, the federal government's role in the housing sector has grown from nearly nil to that of a major participant. This evolution was a response to the perception that the free market failed to respond adequately to the nation's housing needs. Government intervention was needed if the goal of the U.S. housing policy was to be fulfilled. This goal, as stated succinctly in the U.S. Housing Act of 1949, is to "provide a decent, safe, and sanitary living environment . . . for every American."

Although the mix and emphasis of housing policies has varied over time, most programs have been construction-oriented—geared toward increasing the supply of adequate housing. During the 1960s, economists, housing specialists, and the public at large criticized most housing programs as inequitable and wasteful. The programs were considered inequitable because they served only a small fraction of the population eligible for housing assistance and wasteful because the subsidized units were more expensive to build and maintain than similar units in the private housing market. Economists added an inefficiency argument, to wit, that the housing subsidy received was as an in-kind benefit and was therefore valued by the recipients as worth less than its cost to the government. These criticisms led to a revival of the idea of a demand-oriented alternative—a program of housing vouchers called *housing allowances*.

The idea of housing allowances is not new. It was considered but rejected in the formulation of the original Housing Act of 1937. However, in the early 1970s, when the disadvantages of conventional housing programs became increasingly apparent, housing allowances began to be considered a viable policy alternative.

Housing allowances are regular periodic payments made directly to eligible families (or individuals) unable to afford a decent home in a suitable living environment. The amount of the periodic allowance is usually related to a family's size and its income and often to the cost of a standard, existing house or apartment located in a modest neighborhood, as determined in each locality separately. Since the allowance is paid directly to families, they are given the purchasing power to enter the market for decent housing and considerable freedom to select the house or apartment they wish. Recipient families are freed from the direct stigma of welfare assistance or unwarranted restriction on individual choice. The only restriction on the family's choice is the imposition of some basic minimum of housing standards on the unit it occupies. These standards reflect the policymakers' views on what characterizes decent or adequate housing.

A properly designed housing allowance program can meet the policy goals of providing needy families with adequate housing at a price they can afford. Recipients would choose existing units rather than be constrained to specially built subsidized housing. Thus, with a given housing assistance budget, more eligible families could be served by an allowance program than by conventional, more expensive, construction-oriented programs.

Support for housing allowances was far from unanimous. Critics charged that demand subsidies, which do not directly add housing units to the stock of adequate housing, would cause housing price inflation. In addition, doubts were raised about the ability of low-income households to use their allowances effectively in competition for adequate housing units in the marketplace.

In order to determine the effectiveness of a housing allowance-based housing assistance strategy, the U.S. Department of Housing and Urban Development (HUD) established a research program on housing allowances—the Experimental Housing Allowance Program (EHAP). HUD sponsored three experiments, each designed to address a particular cluster of issues:

1. How do households use their allowances?   (Demand Experiment)
2. How does the housing market respond to the allowances? (Supply Experiment)
3. Can existing public agencies adequately administer a program of housing allowances?   (Administrative Agency Experiment)

This book is based on our analysis of household behavior in the Demand Experiment. It describes how families changed their housing in response to housing allowance offers.

THE EVOLUTION OF HOUSING PROGRAMS

Before World War I, public intervention in the housing sector was limited to regulatory measures such as building and occupancy codes to assure minimum standards of safety and health. Large-scale intervention, particularly direct assistance designed to improve housing conditions, is therefore a relatively modern phenomenon.

In the nineteenth century, public concern was concentrated on sanitation, rather than directly on housing. As cities became increasingly populated by poor immigrants, public officials became aware of the severe health problems in densely settled neighborhoods. They proceeded to install or improve water supply and sewage systems. This trend was reinforced in the late nineteenth century as the germ theory of disease gained prominence (Burns and Grebler, 1977, p. 75). Government intervention in housing was extended to include such requirements as sanitary and running water systems and improved ventilation in newly constructed buildings.

Housing conditions that may facilitate the spread of disease have largely been eliminated in the United States. Nevertheless, the continuing public intervention in the housing sector demonstrates that there are additional reasons for public involvement. The two major contemporary rationales for government intervention in the housing sector are housing market imperfections and "merit good" considerations.[1] Imperfections in the housing market arise from "such factors as the fixed supply of land in urban settings, zoning and discrimination which reduce tenant mobility, linkages between location and job availability, lumpiness of housing outlays, credit risks, and so forth" (Musgrave, 1976, p. 215). Furthermore, the existence of externalities in neighborhoods whereby the attributes and living conditions of one dwelling unit can affect the value and living conditions of another also argues for the government to attempt structural remedies for these imperfections.

The basic argument for providing cash assistance to households to be used specifically for housing instead of general cash transfers is based on the belief that housing is a "merit good—a form of consumption which society views more important than allowed for by individual choices" (Musgrave, 1976, p. 215), coupled with the feeling that "the poorest people among us should live in better housing than they are able to afford,

---

[1] The rationales for government intervention in housing have been discussed at length in U.S. Department of Housing and Urban Development, *Housing in the Seventies Working Papers* (1976). See particularly the papers by Weicher, Muth, Musgrave, and DeSalvo.

and that they should be assisted to do so" (Weicher, 1976b, p. 182). In particular, the imposition of building codes to improve the quality of housing increases its cost and places a floor on the rents of such housing. This rent is typically higher than the share of income that families at the lower end of the income scale would freely choose to allocate for housing. Housing subsidies could then be viewed as a way to compensate poor families for the government's actions in limiting their housing choices.

Many approaches have been used to provide housing assistance to low-income households.[2] Subsidies for low-income families began in 1937 when the public housing program was established. Under this program, local housing authorities were empowered to replace slum housing with newly constructed rental housing. The federal subsidy reduced the capital cost of the project by reducing the effective rate of interest paid by the developer. In 1968, the federal subsidy was extended to cover part of the operating costs of public housing projects as well. A second major program was the urban renewal program, established in 1949. This program reduced the costs of building by partially subsidizing land acquisition costs.

To enable the government to work through capital markets, the Federal National Mortgage Association (FNMA) was established in 1938. In their "below market interest rate" program (Section 221.d.2), FNMA lent money at below-market interest rates to private developers agreeing to build moderate-income housing. In 1961, Congress created the "market rate" program (Section 221.d.3). This program allowed loans for apartment projects. It was complemented by the 1965 "rent supplement" program, which allowed the federal government to make rental payments on behalf of tenants to the sponsors of "market rate" housing, thus permitting low-income families to live in conventionally financed (at the market interest rate) housing. Rent supplements covered the difference between 25% of the tenant family's income and the rent. These interest rate programs were succeeded by the Section 236 interest subsidy program.

Since 1961, home ownership has also been subsidized by the federal government. The subsidy program extended loans to buyers who were perceived to have high default probabilities. In 1968, the Section 235 program introduced subsidies for home purchase using the same formula as did the Section 236 program.

Practically all federal housing programs came under criticism by the late 1960s and the early 1970s as being too costly, not working as desired, or not serving enough eligible families. At that time, a major shift in policy

---

[2] This description of U.S. housing programs is based on Weicher (1976b).

was undertaken to focus on the demand side of the housing market, by giving subsidies directly to families. This approach was in sharp contrast to the supply-oriented programs in which subsidies were in effect tied to specific units. The Housing and Urban Development Act of 1965 added two programs—the rent supplement program and the Section 23 leased-housing program—which moved in the direction of the housing allowance by giving beneficiaries more flexibility in choosing the places they could live and by making the value of the subsidy depend on a family's income. The Section 23 housing program allowed Public Housing Authorities to lease existing private dwelling units and subsidize low-income households to live in them. One potential expansion of this program was to provide housing allowances—to directly enable eligible households to purchase adequate housing in the private market. The households themselves would then be responsible for finding apartments and negotiating with landlords.

One step toward such an unrestricted system of housing subsidies was the 1974 revision of the Section 23 program—retitled Section 8. The Existing Housing portion of the Section 8 program focused on households as objects of the subsidy and permitted them to locate suitable units by themselves, but the government retained some control over location and assisted in lease negotiation, with payment going directly to the landlords. (The two other parts of the Section 8 program are known as "New Construction" and "Substantial Rehabilitation" and retain a supply-side orientation.)

Housing allowances, though not a new idea, having been examined by Congress in some way for more than 40 years (see Hamilton, 1979, pp. 3–4), may be viewed as representing a further step in the direction of demand-side housing subsidies. As mentioned earlier, housing vouchers were considered but rejected in formulating the Housing Act of 1937. They were reconsidered in the Taft Subcommittee hearings on postwar housing policy in 1944, in designing the Housing Act of 1949, and in the 1953 report by the President's Advisory Committee on Government Housing Policies and Programs.

In 1968, the President's Committee on Urban Housing (the Kaiser Committee) argued in favor of a housing allowance and recommended that the government undertake an experiment to determine whether a housing allowance program would be feasible and worthwhile. Housing allowances were thought to have several potential advantages. Housing allowances could be less expensive than some other kinds of housing programs because they permit utilization of existing sound housing and they are not tied to new construction. Housing allowances could also be more equitable. Because no new units have to be built, more eligible households can be served by a housing voucher program than by a new construction program of the same dollar size.

In addition, the amount of the allowance can be adjusted to changes in income without forcing the household to change its residence. To obtain better housing than is required to qualify for the allowance, households may also, if they desire, use their own resources, either by paying higher rent or by searching for housing more extensively. As long as program requirements are met, housing allowances offer households considerable choice in selecting the housing most appropriate to their needs. In contrast to traditional housing assistance programs that provide a specific type of housing in a given location, housing allowance recipients are free to choose where they live. They may choose to locate near schools, near friends or relatives, or to break out of racial or socioeconomic segregation. They may also choose the type of building they live in—single or multifamily. Finally, housing allowances may be less costly to administer. Because program administration need not involve supervision of every detail of participant housing, the burden of obtaining housing that meets essential requirements is shifted from program adminstrators to participants.

The recommendations of the committee inspired preliminary analytic efforts, and small-scale demonstrations were conducted by the Model Cities agencies in Kansas City, Missouri, and Wilmington, Delaware. The Housing and Urban Development Act of 1970 called for HUD to carry out a major investigation of housing allowances; under this mandate HUD initiated the Experimental Housing Allowance Program (EHAP). Of the three experiments initiated, only the Demand Experiment was designed to examine the effects of alternative formulations of the housing allowance on the behavior of households offered an opportunity to participate. The Demand Experiment was also the only one to follow the model of prior social experimentation, by including control groups and drawing heavily on the design of the income maintenance (negative income tax) experiments.[3] Neither the Supply nor the Administrative Agency experiments included a control group and should, therefore, more correctly be called demonstration projects.

THE U.S. HOUSING PROBLEM

There is a widespread perception by the American public that there is a housing problem. Furthermore, it is believed that the problem can and

[3] See, for example, Rossi and Lyall (1976).

should be ameliorated by federal intervention. Frieden and Solomon (1977, pp. 82–85) characterize housing-deprived households as households who occupy dwelling units that are physically inadequate, overcrowded, excessively costly, or in an inadequate neighborhood environment. Using their criteria and data from the 1973 Annual Housing Survey, they concluded that 16.8 million of a total of 69.3 million households (24%) suffered housing deprivation. Using only their first three criteria (physical inadequacy, overcrowding, and excessive cost), there were still 12.8 million housing-deprived households (18%).

These figures do represent an improvement from 13.1 million and 15.3 million housing-deprived households in 1970 and 1960, respectively. Frieden and Solomon assert that the problem of housing deprivation is changing from one of physical inadequacy to one of excessive cost. In 1960, the proportion of housing-deprived low-income households in physically inadequate units to those in adequate units but paying more than 25% of their annual income for rent was almost three to one (71% in physically inadequate units, 24% in adequate but excessively costly units, and 5% in overcrowded units). In contrast, by 1973 the proportion was approximately even (49%, 47%, and 4%, respectively).

Martin Levine (Congressional Budget Office, 1978) developed alternate measures of housing need, again based on the three-way classification used by Frieden and Solomon: physical deficiencies, overcrowding, and excessive housing cost.[4] He concluded that in 1976 7.7% of all occupied dwelling units were physically inadequate, 4.6% of units were overcrowded (more than 1.0 persons per room), and 46.6% of all renters paid too much (more than 25% of family income) for rent. Of course, as shown in Table 1-1, some families are subject to more than one deficiency. The table provides a cross-classification of U.S. households in 1976 by categories of housing deprivation. Overall, 11.1 million (65.5%) of all lower- and moderate-income renters and 6.7 million (35.9%) of lower- and moderate-income homeowners experienced some form of housing deprivation.

Analysts have disagreed about the implications of these trends for housing policy. For example, Levine emphasized the continuing existence of physically inadequate housing while Weicher (1976a) concluded that "we are probably very close to meeting the national housing 'goal of a decent home,' as it was originally envisioned in 1949." In any case, a consensus had begun to emerge that there was more of a need for rent relief than for physical improvements in housing.

---

[4] The use of neighborhood conditions to indicate inadequacy is a fairly recent development, made possible only through use of information collected by the Annual Housing Surveys. Based on household reports on aspects of neighborhood blight, this data offered the possibility of extending the definition of housing deprivation.

Table 1-1

Incidence of Multiple Housing Needs in 1976 (Households in Thousands)

| Tenure and housing condition[a] | Income-eligible for federal housing assistance | | | | | | Ineligible for housing assistance[d] | |
| | Rental and home ownership assistance[b] | | Home ownership assistance only[c] | | Total | | | |
	Number of households	Percentage	Number of households	Percentage	Number of households	Percentage	Number of households	Percentage
Renters								
Not in Need	4,590	30.7	1,304	61.0	5,894	34.5	7,505	83.0
Living in inadequate housing and/or overcrowded; not paying more than 25% of income for housing	1,916	12.8	311	14.6	2,227	13.0	984	10.9
Both living in inadequate housing and/or overcrowded and paying more than 25% of income for housing	1,811	12.1	40	1.9	1,851	10.8	47	0.5
Paying more than 25% of income for housing; not in inadequate housing or overcrowded	6,618	44.3	481	22.5	7,099	41.6	501	5.5
Homeowners								
Not in need	9,046	60.9	2,986	76.1	12,032	64.1	26,205	89.7
Living in inadequate housing and/or overcrowded; not paying more than 25% of income for housing	1,311	8.8	308	7.9	1,619	8.6	1,282	4.4
Both living in inadequate housing and/or overcrowded and paying more than 25% of income for housing	408	2.7	2	0.7	434	2.3	60	0.2
Paying more than 25% of income for housing; not in inadequate housing or overcrowded	4,088	27.5	603	15.4	4,691	25.0	1,655	5.7

Source: Congressional Budget Office (1978), Table 13.

a A unit is classified as physically inadequate if it has at least one of the following conditions: (1) the absence of complete plumbing facilities; or (2) the absence of complete kitchen facilities; and/or if the unit had two or more of the following conditions: (3) three or more breakdowns of 6 or more hours each time in the heating system during the last winter; (4) three or more times completely without water for 6 or more hours each time during the prior 90 days, with the problem inside the unit; (5) three or more times completely without flush toilet for 6 or more hours each time during the prior 90 days, with the problem inside the unit; (6) leaking roof; (7) holes in interior floors; (8) open cracks or holes in interior walls or ceilings; (9) broken plaster or peeling paint over greater than one square foot of interior walls or ceiling; (10) unconcealed wiring; (11) the absence of any working light in public hallways for multi-unit structures; (12) loose or no handrails in public hallways in multi-unit structures; (13) loose, broken, or missing steps in public hallways in multi-unit structures. Households with greater than 1.0 persons per room are classified as overcrowded.

b Very-low and low-income households.

c Moderate-income households.

Table 1-2
Housing Adequacy of Demand Experiment Enrollees (1973)

	All low-income households	Poverty households	Nonpoverty low-income households
Percentage in			
Clearly inadequate units	43%	56%	30%
Questionable units	26	24	27
Apparently adequate units	31	19	43
Sample size	(3357)	(1697)	(1670)

Source: Budding (1980), Figure 2-2.

Note: All households enrolled in the Demand Experiment were low-income, with the eligibility limit determined by family size and the allowance plan enrolled in.

In contrast, Budding (1980) discovered that these conclusions substantially misrepresent the housing needs of low-income households, especially those low-income households with incomes below the poverty line.[5] Budding used survey information on the preexperimental housing conditions of households enrolled in the Housing Allowance Demand Experiment to classify housing units as clearly inadequate if they were structurally unsound, had unvented gas heaters, rats, inadequate fire exits, incomplete plumbing or kitchen facilities, no heat, seriously damaged interior surfaces, inadequate electrical services, or needed major repairs (to obtain working plumbing, adequate light and ventilation, or adequate ceiling height). Units that were rated as being unsound or needing major repairs, but without having a specific deficiency noted, and units with deficiencies that could be temporary (such as nonworking plumbing) were designated as questionable units.

The results of his analysis, shown in Table 1-2, are startling. Of all enrolled households, *43%* lived in clearly inadequate units, as compared to the 13% found by Levine. Another 26% lived in units of questionable quality, while only 31% were in units that were apparently adequate. Among households with incomes below poverty level, the situation was even worse—*56%* were in clearly inadequate units; 24% were in questionable units; and only 19% were in apparently adequate units.

The second form of housing deprivation analyzed by Budding was

[5] The discussion of Budding's findings is based on Kennedy (1980).

overcrowding. Concerns about crowding have shifted over time from questions of family privacy and health, involving several families crowded into one unit, to issues of individual privacy involving too little space per person within the unit. HUD regulations define a unit as crowded when there are more than two persons per bedroom. Budding developed a somewhat more sophisticated and more complex measure that took into account the ages and sexes of household members.

The two measures do give different incidences of crowding, as shown in Table 1-3. Overall, the percentage of households in crowded units is 23% under the two persons per room standard and 27% under the household composition standard. More important is the strong relationship between crowding and household size. At least two-thirds of large households (with five or more members) were overcrowded while only one-quarter of three- and four-person households were overcrowded. The high incidence of crowding persists across a wide range of incomes. Among large households, crowding exists for more than half the households with incomes up to twice the poverty level. Among smaller households, the incidence of crowding is substantially greater than 25% only for households with incomes below the poverty line.

The final form of housing deprivation considered by Budding was excessive rent burden. Households in physically adequate and uncrowded

Table 1-3
Overcrowding of Demand Experiment Enrollees

Household size	More than two persons per bedroom	Not enough bedrooms for privacy[a]	Sample size
1 or 2[b]	0%	0%	1376
3 or 4	24	26	1291
5 or more	68	80	700
All households	23	27	3367

Source: Budding (1980), Table 3-2.

[a] The number of bedrooms needed under this measure is defined as one bedroom for every two household members, with the added requirement that unrelated roomers and boarders (adults and children) and teenage children of opposite sexes not have to share a bedroom.

[b] Crowding is definitionally impossible for one- or two-person households.

Table 1-4
Rent Burden of Demand Experiment Enrollees by Poverty Status

	All low-income renters	Incomes below poverty	Incomes above poverty
Percentage with rent burdens greater than 25% of income	68	79	58
Percentage with rent burdens greater than 40% of income	28	43	14
Sample size	3367	1697	1670

Source: Budding (1980), Figure 3-5.

housing are often regarded as housing-deprived if they obtain their housing at the cost of failing to meet other basic household needs. The most frequently used criterion for excessive rent burden, both in analysis and legislation, is spending more than 25% of income for housing.[6] Rent burdens of over 25% were quite common among the low-income renters enrolled in the Demand Experiment. As indicated in Table 1-4, over two-thirds of all enrollees had rent burdens in excess of 25% of income, while 28% had rent burdens of more than 40%. Not surprisingly, households with incomes at or below poverty were more often suffering excessive rent burdens, and especially very high rent burdens.

Budding's analysis makes it clear that, in the U.S. in the early 1970s, there was still a substantial *housing* problem, as distinct from an *income* problem. A general income support program could ameliorate or even eliminate the problem of excessive rent burden but would not necessarily have much of an effect on the problem of inadequate housing. On the other hand, a properly designed housing voucher program could reduce the incidence of both problems. The different impacts of housing allowances and general income support are examined later in the book.

THE HOUSING ALLOWANCE DEMAND EXPERIMENT

As stated earlier, to address the issues associated with establishing an efficient and equitable U.S. housing strategy, HUD initiated a series of housing experiments. The experiment examined in this book, the Housing

[6] Despite its common use, the 25% criterion for reasonable rent burdens is essentially arbitrary. Lane (1977) indicates that the figure first arose from the practice in certain mill towns, where workers were charged one week's pay a month for company-supplied housing. Thereafter, it seems to have become a widely used but unsubstantiated rule of thumb.

Allowance Demand Experiment, was designed to address issues of feasibility, desirability, and appropriate structure of a housing voucher program by measuring how individual households would react to various allowance formulas and housing standards requirements. The Demand Experiment was operated simultaneously in two sites—Allegheny County, Pennsylvania (Pittsburgh), and Maricopa County, Arizona (Phoenix)—and involved approximately 1200 experimental and 500 control households in each area for a 3-year period. The experimental sites, Pittsburgh and Phoenix, were selected on the basis of their growth rates, rental vacancy rates, degree of racial concentration, and housing costs. These sites were chosen to provide contrasts between an older, more slowly growing eastern metropolitan area and a newer, relatively rapidly growing western metropolitan area. In addition, Pittsburgh has a substantial black minority and Phoenix a substantial Hispanic minority population.

Analysis was based on data collected from households during their first 2 years after enrollment in the experiment. The experimental programs were continued for a third year in order to reduce confusion between participants' reactions to the experimental offers and their adjustment to the phaseout of the experiment. During their last year in the experiment, eligible and interested households were aided in entering other housing programs.

There were four basic treatment plans under which households were enrolled: Housing Gap, Unconstrained, Percent of Rent, and Control.[7] Households in Housing Gap plans were offered payments designed to bridge the gap between the cost of modest, existing standard housing and the fraction of income that a low-income household could reasonably be expected to spend on housing. The formula used was

$$S = C - bY, \tag{1}$$

where S is the amount of the allowance payment; C is the basic payment schedule, varied experimentally and by household size and site; b is the benefit reduction rate (the rate at which the allowance is reduced as income increases); and Y is household disposable income.

The Housing Gap allowance plans were constrained in the sense that households received an allowance only if they occupied a unit that met the

---

[7] The basic design and analysis approach is presented in Abt Associates Inc., *Experimental Design and Analysis Plan of the Demand Experiment*, August 1973, and in Abt Associates Inc., *Summary Evaluation Design*, June 1973. Details of the operating rules of the Demand Experiment are contained in Abt Associates Inc., *Site Operating Procedures Handbook*, April 1973. See Appendix I for more details.

program's housing requirements, described further in the following pages. In contrast, the Unconstrained plan offered households payments based on the same formula as in the Housing Gap plan but without a housing requirement. This plan resembled a general income support program, except that the payment amount was determined by need for housing expenses rather than need for all household expenses.

Percent of Rent plans offered households rent rebates in the form of cash payments equal to a fixed fraction of their monthly rents. Households in these plans had no housing requirements to meet. Their payment was tied directly to the amount spent for housing. Finally, the group of Control households did not receive any housing allowance payment but received a $10 monthly cooperation payment for providing the same information as experimental households. They served as a comparison group against which to estimate the effect of different allowance plans.

The Demand Experiment was designed not only to evaluate the impact of a Housing Gap allowance program but also to evaluate a variety of possible alternative plans within such a program. The experiment included 11 different Housing Gap allowance plans, testing three levels for the basic payment schedules, three values for the benefit reduction rate, and two types of housing requirements—Minimum Standards and Minimum Rent. The three basic payment schedules tested were proportional to C^*, the estimated cost of modest, existing, standard housing for various household sizes in each metropolitan area.[8] The value of the benefit reduction rate b varied around 0.25 (corresponding to typical payment formulas in conventionally subsidized housing).

To receive payments, households under the Minimum Standards requirements had to occupy units that met certain physical quality standards for the dwelling unit and had a minimum number of rooms per person. This sort of requirement has been used in existing housing programs such as Section 23 and Section 8. Such physical housing requirements necessitate housing inspections, which are costly to the government and may impose inconvenience on both tenants and landlords. As a possible less costly alternative, a Minimum Rent requirement was tested. Minimum Rent plans required households to spend at least a certain minimum amount for housing in order to receive allowance payments. Two minimum rent levels were tested, $0.7C^*$ and $0.9C^*$ (where C^* was the estimated cost of standard housing).

Households in the Percent of Rent plans had no specific requirements to meet as their payment was tied directly to rent: A household's allow-

---

[8] The value of C^* varied by household size and site and was established from estimates given by a panel of housing experts familiar with the sites.

Housing Gap: Payment = $C - bY$

		HOUSING REQUIREMENTS			
b value	C level	Minimum Standards	Minimum Rent Low ($0.7C^*$)	Minimum Rent High ($0.9C^*$)	No requirement (Unconstrained)
$b = 0.15$	C^*	Plan 10			
	$1.2C^*$	Plan 1	Plan 4	Plan 7	
$b = 0.25$	C^*	Plan 2	Plan 5	Plan 8	Plan 12
	$0.8C^*$	Plan 3	Plan 6	Plan 9	
$b = 0.35$	C^*	Plan 11			

Percent of Rent: Payment = aR

$a = 0.6$	$a = 0.5$	$a = 0.4$	$a = 0.3$	$a = 0.2$
Plan 13	Plans 14-16	Plans 17-19	Plans 20-22	Plan 23

Control:

With housing information	Without housing information
Plan 24	Plan 25

Symbols: C^* = Basic payment level varied by household size and site
         Y = Net income
         R = Rent
         a = Percentage of rent subsidized
         b = Rate at which the housing gap allowance was reduced
             as income increased

Figure 1-1. **Allowance plans tested.**

ance payment was proportional to the total rent. The payment formula was

$$S = aR \qquad (2)$$

where R is rent and a is the fraction of rent paid by the allowance. Five values of a ranging from $a = 0.2$ to $a = 0.6$ were tested in the Demand Experiment, and the value of a remained constant once a household had been enrolled in order to aid experimental analysis.[9]

Figure 1-1 illustrates the 17 experimental and 2 control treatment

[9] In a national Percent of Rent program, a would probably vary with income or rent, or both.

groups in the Demand Experiment design. The first nine plans included three variations in the basic payment level, C ($1.2C^*$, C^*, and $0.8C^*$), and three variations in housing requirements [Minimum Standards, Minimum Rent Low ($0.7C^*$), and Minimum Rent High ($0.9C^*$)]. The value of b (the rate at which the allowance was reduced as income increased) was 0.25 for each of these plans. The next two plans had the same level of C (C^*), used the Minimum Standards housing requirement, but used different values of b (in the tenth plan the value of b was 0.15, and in the eleventh plan, 0.35). Eligible households that did not meet their housing requirement were still able to enroll. They received full payments whenever they met the requirements during the 3 years of the experiment. Even before meeting the housing requirements, such households received a cooperation payment of $10 per month as long as they completed all reporting and interview requirements.

The twelfth plan was unconstrained; that is, it had no housing requirement. This unconstrained plan allowed a direct comparison with a general income-transfer program. All the households in the various allowance plans had to meet a basic income eligibility requirement. This limit was approximately the income level at which the household would receive no payment under the Housing Gap formula, ($C^*/0.25$).

Analysis of the impact of the housing allowance on housing consumption was based on the first 2 years of experimental data. Thus, the key sample size is the number of households in the experiment at the end of the first 2 years. The enrollment and 2-year sample sizes are shown in Appendix Table IV-10 and are composed of households that were still active, in the sense that they were continuing to fulfill reporting requirements.

Chapter 2 _____

The Demand for Rental Housing

Housing allowances increase household income. Consequently, housing allowances should induce recipients to increase their consumption of goods and services in general, and housing in particular. During the early policy debates on the effectiveness of a housing allowance strategy, it was argued that the increased demand for housing, if concentrated in one sector of the housing market (such as rental housing meeting a particular housing standard), might cause inflation in the price of housing in that sector. Such an increase would, in turn, have a dampening effect on the demand for housing. The exact magnitude of a household's housing demand response to changes in income and prices depends upon the demand function for housing. This function depicts the quantitative relationship between housing demanded on the one hand, and the various characteristics of the household and the housing market that determine demand on the other. During the planning phase of the Demand Experiment (in the early 1970s), there was considerable uncertainty over what this function looked like. This uncertainty led to the inclusion of the Percent of Rent component in the experiment to make it possible to estimate relevant demand parameters.[1]

The demand for housing discussed here is the demand for the consumer good "housing services." Note that this demand is distinct from the demand for the asset (investment good) "housing stock." The concept of housing services is crucial to the understanding of the analysis; therefore an explanation follows.[2] A dwelling unit (including the land on which it

_____

[1] The Housing Assistance Supply Experiment was designed to measure inflationary effects. Rydell (1979) found that at the two Supply Experiment sites (Green Bay, Wisconsin, and South Bend, Indiana), no such effects were detected.

[2] This explanation is based on Olsen (1969).

stands) represents an amount of housing capital stock. Landlords are investors who buy and sell housing services to consumers. Consumers, at least those who rent their housing, are not typically in the market for housing stock. Rather, they are in the market for housing services—the flow of services yielded during any period of time by the capital stock embodied in the dwelling unit.

When consumers buy housing services, they get not only the dwelling unit but also many neighborhood amenities including accessibility to employment, shopping centers, and various municipal services (schools, fire protection, garbage collection, etc.). Although landlords do not directly control the provision of these other services, their cost is reflected in the rents that tenants pay. These costs are embodied in rent both because the type and quality of these services, as well as the property taxes charged by the local government, influence the price of land on which the dwelling unit stands and, therefore, its purchase price and the rents charged to cover costs (including normal return on investments). In contrast to tenants, homeowners have the dual role of landlords and tenants. They are the owners of the housing stock represented by their house and at the same time they use the housing services yielded by that stock. We are concerned here only with renters and therefore ignore investment aspects of housing consumption.

The Percent of Rent plans were included in the Demand Experiment in an attempt to overcome a major obstacle faced by analysts of the demand for housing services. Separate observations on prices and quantities of housing services are not normally available. Instead, one usually observes only the unit's rent, which may be thought of as the price per unit of housing services p_H times the quantity of housing services H: $R = p_H H$.

Households in Percent of Rent plans received housing allowances in the form of a rent rebate S equal to a fixed fraction a of their gross housing expenditures (including utilities) R:

$$S = aR. \tag{1}$$

The household's net housing expenditure R_n thus consisted of the difference between its gross expenditure and the rebate,

$$R_n = R - S = (1 - a)R. \tag{2}$$

For a given quantity of housing, then, the net outlay for Percent of Rent households was

$$R_n = (1 - a)R = (1 - a)p_H H. \tag{3}$$

Thus, the rent rebate can be viewed as having reduced the effective price of housing to recipients from p_H to $(1 - a)p_H$.

Experimental variation in the price of housing was achieved by randomly assigning households to groups with different percentages of rent rebated, ranging from 20% to 60% for experimental households and zero for control households. As is shown later, this variation enabled estimation of the relationship between housing price and housing demand. The natural variation in the incomes of households in the sample enabled the estimation of the relationship between income and housing demand.

A MICROECONOMIC MODEL OF HOUSING DEMAND

In this section, we introduce a few concepts of the microeconomics of housing demand and explain how the proportional rent rebates affect household behavior.

Assume that households normally consume the quantity of housing services (H) and nonhousing goods (Z) that maximizes household utility $U(H, Z)$, subject to the budget constraint

$$Y = p_H H + p_Z Z \tag{4}$$

where Y is household income; P_H is the price of housing (thus $p_H H$ is rent); and p_Z is the price of nonhousing goods.

Figure 2-1 represents this diagrammatically with a hypothetical household choosing to consume an amount of housing services H_0 and an amount of nonhousing goods and services (including savings) Z_0 (determined from the budget constraint). The indifference curves show the combinations of housing and nonhousing goods needed to maintain a given level of utility. A key assumption is that indifference curves are concave from above—as housing consumption is reduced, an increasing amount of nonhousing goods is needed in order to leave the household equally satisfied.

Any increase in income (such as receipt of a regular cash allowance payment) would move the budget line outward, inducing the household to consume more housing (H_1) and more nonhousing goods (Z_1), see Figure 2-1(a). Alternatively, a reduction in the relative price of housing from (p_H/p_Z) to $[(1 - a)p_H/p_Z]$, pivots the budget line outward, again inducing the household to increase housing consumption, see Figure 2-1(b). The extent of these changes in consumption depends on two factors: the size of the change in income or price and the responsiveness of the household to such changes. This responsiveness reflects the tastes of the household for the particular good in question and is often expressed as an elasticity of demand—the percentage change in consumption resulting from a given percentage change in income or in price.

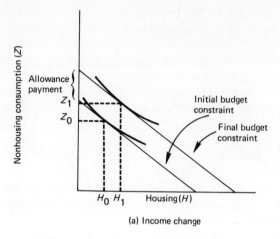

(a) Income change

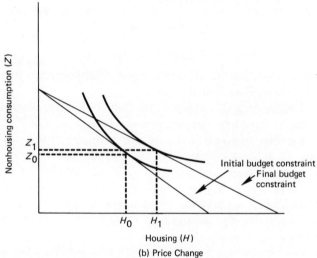

(b) Price Change

Figure 2-1. **Effect of price and income changes on desired housing consumption.**

The functional relationship between the desired amount of each good chosen and household income and prices is termed a demand function. One way this demand function for housing services can be expressed is as

$$H = H(Y, p_H, p_Z). \tag{5}$$

In addition to income and prices, other variables may also affect housing demand. For example, different demographic groups may have different relative preferences for housing versus other goods and services.

The exact impact of a housing allowance on housing consumption depends on the recipient's relative valuation of housing and nonhousing goods, as reflected by the demand function for housing. The theory of consumer demand does not suggest a specific form for the demand function, and the choice of the functional form is usually based on empirical considerations. Two different specifications are used here to investigate the response of Percent of Rent households to the rent rebates in order to gain insights into the sensitivity of the estimates to the exact specification. Demand functions then form the basis for an examination of the Housing Gap housing allowances in Chapters 4–6. Both specifications of the demand function for housing examined here relate the quantity of housing demanded to a consumer's income and housing prices. The first is the log-linear demand function, which has been widely used in empirical studies of housing demand. The second is a linear expenditures function.

Since the rent rebate offered Percent of Rent households in effect reduced the price of housing they faced, their response to the rent rebate is measured by the price elasticity of demand for housing. The price elasticity of demand, n_p, is defined as the ratio of the percentage change in quantity demanded to the percentage change in housing price. Similarly, the income elasticity of demand, n_y, is defined as the ratio of the percentage change in quantity demanded to the percentage change in income. These elasticities can be expressed mathematically as

$$n_p = \frac{\partial H/H}{\partial p_H/p_H} = \frac{\partial \ln(H)}{\partial \ln(p_H)},$$

and   (6)

$$n_Y = \frac{\partial H/H}{\partial Y/Y} = \frac{\partial \ln(H)}{\partial \ln(Y)}.$$

If the price and income elasticities are constant, the demand function is log-linear and can be expressed mathematically as[3]

$$\ln(H) = b_0 + b_1 \ln(Y) + b_2 \ln(p_H),$$ (7)

where b_0 is a constant and the coefficients b_1 and b_2 are, respectively, the income and price elasticity of demand for housing.

[3] In this equation, p_z is normalized to equal unity. The log-linear demand function could be written

$$\ln(H) = b_0 + b_1 \ln(Y/p_z) + b_2 \ln(P_H/p_z)$$
$$= [b_0 - (b_1 + b_2) \ln(p_z)] + b_1 \ln(Y) + b_2 \ln(p_H).$$

If p_z is unobservable and differs across sites, then the estimated constant term will differ as well.

Equation (7) can be written in terms of rental expenditures rather than the abstract "quantity of housing services" by recognizing that rental expenditures equal the product of price and quantity ($R = p_H H$). For a log-linear demand equation, this is done by adding the logarithm of price to both sides of the equation:

$$\ln(R) = \ln(p_H H) = b_0 + b_1 \ln(Y) + (1 + b_2) \ln(p_H). \qquad (8)$$

Equation (8) expresses the logarithm of housing expenditures, $\ln(R)$, as a linear function of the logarithms of income and of the relative price of housing.

The log-linear demand function has several advantages which explain its popularity in empirical work. It is simple to estimate using Ordinary Least Squares (OLS) regression; its parameters may be easily interpreted as (constant) price and income elasticities; and only the constant term is affected by changes in the units of measurement. Thus, general price inflation is easily accommodated in estimation by permitting the intercept, b_0, to change over time. This attribute greatly facilitates comparisons over time and across cities. On the other hand, restricting the price and income elasticities to be constant may be unwarranted, and the function itself cannot be derived from a known direct utility function.

Equation (8) includes one important variable, p_H, which is not observable on the household level.[4] However, because of the experimental variation in prices due to the proportional rent rebates, it is not necessary to observe p_H. As was shown previously, the price of housing faced by Percent of Rent recipients was changed by the rent rebates from p_H to $(1 - a)p_H$. Substituting $(1 - a)p_H$ for p_H in Eq. (8) gives

$$\ln[(1 - a)p_H H] = b_0 + b_1 \ln(Y) + (1 + b_2) \ln[(1 - a)p_H]. \qquad (9)$$

Equation (9) can be rearranged as

$$\ln[(1 - a)p_H H] = [b_0 + (1 + b_2) \ln(p_H)] + b_1 \ln(Y) + (1 + b_2) \ln(1 - a). \qquad (10)$$

Equation (10) is in terms of net rent. Subtracting $\ln(1 - a)$ from both sides yields an equation in terms of gross rent:

$$\ln(p_H H) = [b_0 + (1 + b_2) \ln(p_H)] + b_1 \ln(Y) + b_2 \ln(1 - a). \qquad (11)$$

---

[4] As discussed later, several researchers have circumvented this problem by using the Bureau of Labor Statistics housing budget indices computed on a metropolitan basis as a proxy for housing price. However, Polinsky (1977) has shown that such a proxy is theoretically likely to lead to biased estimates of both income and price elasticities.

Equation (11) contains the unobservable variable, p_H, the price of housing services. To estimate the equation, it must be rewritten in terms of observable variables only, and a stochastic error term e added

$$\ln(R) = b_0' + b_1 \ln(Y) + b_2 \ln(1 - a) + e, \qquad (12)$$

where

$$b_0' = [b_0 + (1 + b_2) \ln(p_H)].$$

If the price of housing p_H varies across locations, the constant term b_0' will also vary since it is a function of p_H. If p_H varies within sites, variations around the mean are included in the stochastic term e. As long as Y and $(1 - a)$ are independent of the unobserved variable p_H, unbiased estimates of the parameters of Eq. (12) may be obtained using OLS regression. Indeed, in the Demand Experiment, households were assigned to the different rent rebate plans (including the plan $a = 0$, the Control group) at random, assuring that the a level is stochastically independent of the unobserved price p_H. Likewise, there is no reason to believe that income is significantly correlated with the overall unit price of housing services.[5]

A useful alternative to the log-linear function is the linear expenditure function which expresses rent as a linear function of income and price:

$$R = A + BY + Cp_H. \qquad (13)$$

For the linear expenditure function, income and price elasticities are not constant, but vary with both price and income. The price elasticity is

$$n_p = \frac{-(A + BY)}{A + BY + Cp_H}, \qquad (14)$$

and the income elasticity is

$$n_Y = \frac{BY}{A + BY + Cp_H}. \qquad (15)$$

---

[5] The Percent of Rent plan with a 60% rebate was only offered to households in the lower third of the income distribution of the eligible population, while the 20% rebate plan was only offered to the households in the upper two-thirds. Since income is included as a variable in the demand equations, this will not bias the results.

Some models of residential location have implied that p_H and Y are negatively correlated (that is, higher income households pay less per unit of housing than lower income households). If that were the case, b_1 would be misestimated. This particular objection is not applicable here, since those location models separate locational attributes from housing services. In this analysis, the commodity housing includes location and accessibility. Secondly, if minorities pay more for a given housing unit than do nonminorities, then income Y and p_H may be correlated because income and race are usually correlated. Merrill (1980), however, found no evidence of any large price differentials due to race or ethnicity in the Demand Experiment sites.

Both the income and price elasticities approach unity (in absolute value) as income rises. In contrast to the log-linear demand function, the linear expenditure function can be derived from a known utility function. This utility function is the Stone–Geary utility function, which is written as

$$U(H, Z) = (H - x_1)^b(Z - x_2)^{1-b}, \tag{16}$$

where b, x_1, and x_2 are parameters, $0 < b < 1$, $H \geq x_1$, and $Z \geq x_2$.

When this utility function is maximized subject to the budget constraint [Eq. (1)] and is normalized by setting the price of the composite good Z equal to one ($p_Z = 1$), the equilibrium demand function is[6]

$$H = x_1 + (b/p_H)(Y - p_H x_1 - x_2). \tag{17}$$

In terms of rental expenditures, Eq. (17) becomes

$$R = p_H H = p_H x_1(1 - b) + b(Y - x_2), \tag{18}$$

which is identical to Eq. (13), where $A = -bx_2$, $B = b$, and $C = (1 - b)x_1$. Moreover, in contrast to the log-linear form, since this function is derived

---

[6] The demand function is derived by taking the log of the utility function [Eq. (16)] and defining the Lagrangian

$$L = b \ln(H - x_1) + (1 - b) \ln(Z - x_2) + m(Y - p_H H - p_Z Z).$$

The first order conditions are

$$\frac{dL}{dH} = \frac{b}{H - x_1} - mp_H = 0 \tag{i}$$

$$\frac{dL}{dZ} = \frac{1 - b}{Z - x_2} - mp_Z = 0 \tag{ii}$$

$$\frac{dL}{dm} = Y - p_H H - p_Z Z = 0 \tag{iii}$$

From (i) and (ii),

$$\frac{b}{p_H(H - x_1)} = \frac{1 - b}{p_Z(Z - x_2)}$$

or

$$b(p_Z Z - p_Z x_2) = p_H H - p_H x_1 - b(p_H H - p_H x_1).$$

This can be rewritten as

$$p_H H = p_H x_1 + b(p_H H + p_Z Z - p_H x_1 - p_Z x_2).$$

Finally, using (iii):

$$H = x_1 + (b/p_H)(Y - p_H x_1 - p_Z x_2),$$

which yields Eq. (17) when p_Z is set equal to one. Thus, equilibrium rent ($p_H H$) can be interpreted as some minimum ($p_H x_1$) plus a constant fraction b of income above some minimum amount (known as supernumerary income).

directly from a utility function, it satisfies the theoretical constraints on demand functions within certain ranges (see Phlips, 1974).[7]

Since the underlying utility function is defined only for values of H greater than or equal to x_1 and Z greater than or equal to x_2, the parameters x_1 and x_2 have often been interpreted as minimum subsistence levels of housing and nonhousing goods. This interpretation is untenable if the x's are negative, as will be true if the price elasticity of demand is greater than one (in absolute value). Alternatively, the parameters x_1 and x_2 can be viewed merely as parameters that affect the shape of the household demand function.

Rent rebates can be introduced in a way identical to the log-linear case. Replacing p_H with $(1 - a)p_H$ in Eq. (13) yields (recall that $R = p_H H$)

$$(1 - a)p_H H = A + BY + C(1 - a)p_H. \qquad (19)$$

Dividing both sides of Eq. (19) by $(1 - a)$ yields

$$R = p_H H = A[1/(1 - a)] + B[Y/(1 - a)] + C' + e. \qquad (20)$$

where

$$C' = Cp_H.$$

The term $1/(1 - a)$ in Eq. (20) enables estimation by OLS regression of all the parameters of the 2-good Stone–Geary utility function (b, x_1, and x_2) using individual household data.[8]

---

[7] The potential usefulness of the theoretical link to individual utility functions is largely lost in estimation. The constraints on the coefficients are those for the utility function—that for every household, $0 < b < 1$, $H \geq x_1$, and $Z \geq x_2$. These restrictions may in theory be maintained for every observation in either of two ways. First, if taste are assumed to be the same for all households (so that the stochastic term represents disequilibrium housing expenditures), then parameters can be restricted so that no income and price observation yields a predicted expenditure level less than $p_H x_1$. Alternatively, a (restricted) stochastic distribution of parameters could be specified. Neither of these procedures is attempted in this book.

[8] Introduction of the rent rebates also modifies the formulas for the price and income elasticities of demand. The price elasticity becomes

$$n_p = \frac{-(A + BY)}{A + BY + C'(1 - a)}$$

and the income elasticity

$$n_Y = \frac{BY}{A + BY + C'(1 - a)}.$$

EVIDENCE FROM RECENT EMPIRICAL
ESTIMATES OF HOUSING DEMAND[9]

This section presents some recent empirical evidence on price and income elasticities of demand for rental housing. For the most part, housing demand analyses have ignored the role of housing price in influencing demand, choosing instead to focus on the role of income. The major reason for this focus is the difficulty of constructing accurate and generally applicable indices of housing price and the lack of time-series measurements of household housing demand under different housing prices.

The difficulties of measuring the price of housing are more severe than those of measuring the prices of most consumer goods. There is no single price of housing. The difference in cost of a 1-bedroom unit between two cities may not reflect the difference in cost for a 4-bedroom unit in those two cities. Most recent housing demand analyses that attempted to estimate price elasticities have relied on aggregate data from the City Worker's Family Budgets established by the Bureau of Labor Statistics (BLS). However, since the BLS budget is estimated only for a particular housing type, the index based on it may be unrepresentative or even misleading concerning price differences in housing in general.[10]

In addition, the type of household (as defined by household size, composition, or income, for example) that occupies the prototypical BLS unit may differ from place to place or over time, due to, among other things, differences in the price of housing. In this case, measurement errors in the price index may be systematically related to household characteristics. Unless such factors are explicitly accounted for in estimated demand relationships, the estimated price elasticity of housing demand based on the BLS index will subsume the effects of such household characteristics on housing demand and may produce misleading results.[11]

One further limitation of conventional housing price indices is that they typically apply to entire metropolitan areas and consequently fail to account for housing price variations within those areas. There is growing evidence that intracity price variations may be considerable, relative to between-city variations, as a result of geographical or ethnic submarkets,

[9] This section was adapted from a paper by Mayo (1981).

[10] The "rent shelter component of the (City Worker's) Budget refers to an unfurnished five-room unit (house or apartment) in sound condition and with a complete bath, a fully equipped kitchen, hot and cold running water, electricity, central or other installed heating, access to public transportation, schools, grocery stores, play space for children, and location in residential neighborhoods free from nuisances" (Gillingham, 1975).

[11] For a more extended discussion of this problem, see Mayo and Fenton (1974), especially pp. 7–22. See also Polinsky (1977).

racial price discrimination, and spatial variation in land prices and rental unit operating expenses. Not only have such price variations been identified, but households have been found to adjust their housing consumption patterns rationally to intra-area price variations (see particularly Straszheim, 1975; King, 1972). By ignoring such variations, conventional housing price indices are subject to what may be considerable measurement error, thereby raising the possibility that extant estimates of price elasticities of housing demand are biased.

The inadequacies of conventional price indices provide an explanation for the wide variation in price elasticity estimates among studies that have used similar or even identical data but different empirical specifications of housing demand functions or different sets of explanatory variables. For example, three recent analyses have relied on data from the same panel survey, the Panel Study of Income Dynamics (PSID), administered by the University of Michigan Survey Research Center, and all have used BLS "rent shelter component" data as the basis for housing prices (Carliner, 1973; Fenton, 1974; Lee and Kong, 1977). The major differences among the analyses are due to the different explanatory variables (other than housing price) included in their estimated demand functions.

The analyses produced strikingly different results. Carliner found that in no alternative demand function specification was the estimated price elasticity for renters significant at a high level; estimated magnitudes ranged from -0.1 to $+0.02$, depending on the specification. Fenton, on the other hand, observed uniformly significant price elasticity estimates ranging from -0.7 to -1.9 depending on which of several socioeconomic groups was being considered, and he estimated the price elasticity for the entire renter population at -1.27. Furthermore, Lee and Kong estimated statistically significant price elasticities of -0.6 for renters in two alternative specifications of housing demand functions. Of the three, the Lee and Kong specification does the best job of attempting to account for potential biases in their estimate of the price elasticity. Yet the results of these three analyses with nearly identical basic data seem to indicate that the specification of the housing demand function appears critical in influencing estimated price elasticities.[12]

Several other studies have found price elasticities of about -0.7.

---

[12] The estimated income elasticities are generally quite similar among the three analyses, despite some differences in specification. Carliner (1973) estimated income elasticities from about 0.4 to about 0.5 for renters, depending on the functional form and the definition of income. Fenton's (1974) income elasticity estimates also centered on the 0.4 to 0.5 range for most socioeconomic groups. Lee and Kong (1977) estimated income elasticities ranging from about 0.3 to 0.7 for renters (depending on the income definition and estimation method); for their most carefully specified model, they obtained an estimate of about 0.5.

DeLeeuw (1971), using BLS price data and 1960 Census data on renters, estimated a price elasticity of about -0.7 but conceded that the true value could be as high as -1.5, as a result of simultaneous determination of housing prices, quantities, and rents. Nelson (1975) reproduced deLeeuw's analysis using 1970 Census data and found a price elasticity for renters of about -0.7.[13] One review of empirical analyses of housing demand (Polinsky, 1977) concluded that although biases on price and income elasticities may be serious in most extant analyses, by correcting for such biases a price elasticity of housing demand for homeowners on the order of -0.75 is obtained. Despite Polinsky's analysis, there appears to be little consensus on an appropriate value for the price elasticity of housing demand. The disparate results of the three analyses of the PSID data (Carliner, 1973; Fenton, 1974; Lee and Kong, 1977) illustrate most dramatically the range of uncertainty that surrounded the subject of housing price elasticity, particularly for renters.

Experimentally created variations in housing prices—the result of rent rebates offered Percent of Rent households—have the potential of reducing that uncertainty considerably for three main reasons. First, the percentage price reduction applies to all housing equally. Thus the price of every unit the household could rent is rendered by the same proportion, so that the effect of a proportional change in prices can be estimated without having to know the base price of housing or whether this price varies among households. Second, assignment of households to the Percent of Rent rebate groups was random, so that the housing price variation created by the rebate should not be correlated with household characteristics that influence housing consumption, thereby eliminating one of the more serious problems associated with using conventional housing price indices in demand studies.[14] Third, the range of price variations resulting from the subsidy is large relative to variations in such housing price indices as the BLS index; thus housing consumption responses may be estimated over a broader range of prices than has been typical of nonexperimental analyses.

In contrast to the price elasticity, the relationship between income and housing consumption has received considerable attention. An important

[13] Nelson (1975) found a price elasticity for homeowners of about -0.3. Other analyses of housing price elasticities for homeowners have estimated values of -0.3 (Carliner, 1973), -0.8 to -0.9 (Maisel *et al.*, 1971), and -0.7 to -0.8 (Muth, 1971). The last two analyses were based on Federal Housing Administration data on individual homeowners, and the first on the PSID.

[14] As noted previously, because measurement errors in conventional price indices are likely to be systematically related to household characteristics, their use in estimating demand functions can result in biased price elasticity estimates.

review article (deLeeuw, 1971) cited several analyses that estimated income elasticities greater than one (indicating that housing consumption is highly sensitive to income changes) and only one analysis that found an income elasticity less than one (Lee, 1968). Since deLeeuw's review, however, many analyses have indicated income elasticities less than one, and no recent analysis has indicated an income elasticity for renters even approaching one. Some analyses, in fact, have indicated income elasticities as low as 0.1 and 0.3 (Kain and Quigley, 1975; Nelson, 1975). Several others have indicated income elasticities from 0.4 to 0.6 (Carliner, 1973; Fenton, 1974; Lee and Kong, 1977; Mayo, 1973; Straszheim, 1975).

The major source of the discrepancies between the results of the analyses reviewed by deLeeuw and of subsequent analyses is the level of aggregation of the data. Nearly all of the analyses cited by deLeeuw used data aggregated to at least the Census tract level, and most were based on Standard Metropolitan Statistical Area (SMSA) averages. The subsequent analyses have been based on individual household data. Three recent analyses have indicated that biases in estimated income elasticities may be severe as a result of using aggregate data. In one (Maisel *et al.*, 1971), demand functions were estimated for homeowners using Federal Housing Administration data—first for individual households and then for SMSA averages of the same households. The disaggregated data produced an income elasticity estimate of about 0.45, whereas the SMSA-average data produced an elasticity of about 0.9.

Polinsky (1977) argued that aggregation of the data and misspecification of demand relationships combine to account for the differences between income elasticity estimates using household data and those using aggregated data. He suggests that an appropriate value for the income elasticity is about 0.75, although the figure could be higher for homeowners and lower for renters. Nelson (1975), using data on individual households, estimated income elasticities (for renters) of about 0.28. When individual data were grouped randomly, income elasticity estimates were about 0.35. When they were grouped according to Census tracts, income elasticities were about 0.76—an increase of about 170% over estimates using individual data.[15]

Estimated income elasticities may also be biased by errors in measuring household income. In particular, if households make decisions about

---

[15] There may be biases in estimates from household data as well. Polinsky (1977), for example, argues on theoretical grounds that many such estimates of income elasticities are biased as a result of improper specification of housing price, that is, by using a metropolitan areawide index instead of an observation-based one. Since analysis of the Demand Experiment data used observation-based price variation, this is not a concern here.

housing expenditures on the basis of expectations concerning income to be received over a long period of time rather than on the basis of current income, then some measure of permanent or normal income will be more appropriate than current income to use in estimating demand functions (see Friedman, 1957). Use of a short-term income measure would then be likely to underestimate the income response, in that changes in short-term income would lead to housing changes only as they lead to changes in long-term (permanent) income. In general, analyses that have used household data to estimate demand functions have attempted to estimate income elasticities with respect to permanent income rather than (or in addition to) elasticities with respect to current income. The methods used have varied greatly and have generally tended to be somewhat ad hoc. Two alternate income measures are examined in this book—current income and income averaged over 3 years, the latter chosen to approximate normal income.[16]

EXPENDITURE CHANGES FOR PERCENT OF RENT HOUSEHOLDS

As described previously, rent rebates provide an incentive to increase rental expenditures by reducing the effective price of housing to recipients. Thus, recipients of the rebates would be expected to increase housing expenditures relative to control households during the experiment. As shown in Table 2-1, the average increase in rental expenditures for recipients was higher than that for control households at both sites. Percent of Rent households increased their housing expenditures by an average of 26% in each site, while control households had a smaller increase—18%.

These figures suggest that the rent rebate did indeed induce Percent of Rent households to increase their housing expenditures and that households were sensitive to the price of housing. A straightforward, but crude, way of measuring the expenditure response induced by the allowances is the amount by which recipient households' rent increases exceed that of Control households. Table 2-1 indicates that the experimentally induced change in housing expenditures, net of the normal increases represented by Control households (due in part to inflation), averaged 8 percentage points in each site. The average price reduction attributable to the rent rebate was approximately 40%. Consequently, a rough estimate of the

---

[16] An additional measure of permanent income—one based on income predicted from an instrumental variable regression using socioeconomic characteristics—was tested, but it gave results similar to the average income measure.

Table 2-1
Monthly Housing Expenditures

TREATMENT GROUP	Mean housing expenditures		Mean change in housing expenditures		Sample size
	At Enrollment	At Two Years	Amount	Percentage[a]	
			Pittsburgh		
Percent of Rent households	$114	$139	$25	26	(385)
Control households	115	133	18	18	(289)
			Phoenix		
Percent of Rent households	132	162	30	26	(280)
Control households	128	145	17	18	(252)

[a] Percentage change is defined as the mean of the ratio of the change in rent to the rent at enrollment.

price elasticity of housing expenditures is the ratio of these two numbers or −0.20 (that is, for every 10% decrease in price, housing expenditures increased by about 2%). These crude comparisons of expenditure changes indicate that housing demand is somewhat (but not very) responsive to income and price incentives. More accurate estimates of the demand elasticities are presented next.

ECONOMETRIC ESTIMATES OF DEMAND PARAMETERS

Table 2-2 presents the price and income elasticities in the total sample of Percent of Rent and Control households, as estimated using both the log-linear and the linear expenditure functions.[17] The price elasticity point estimates from the log-linear form for the total sample are about −0.18 in

[17] Two income variables were used in estimation of the demand parameters—a current income measure and a permanent income measure (3-year average income). Since theoretical arguments suggest that response to the average income measure is more closely related to household behavior, average income will be presented in the text. (The current income estimates are presented in Appendix IV.)

Table 2-2
Price and Income Elasticity Estimates for the Overall Sample

Demand function	Pittsburgh	Phoenix
	Price elasticity	
Log-linear	-0.178 (0.038)	-0.234 (0.049)
Linear[a]	-0.164 (0.042)	-0.213 (0.051)
	Income elasticity[b]	
Log-linear	0.333 (0.028)	0.435 (0.032)
Linear[a]	0.291 (0.021)	0.377 (0.024)
Sample size	(674)	(532)

Note: Standard errors in parentheses; t-statistics all significant at
the 0.01 level.

[a] At mean income and price (mean monthly household income is $417 for
Pittsburgh and $434 for Phoenix; mean Price is 0.75 for Pittsburgh
and 0.77 for Phoenix).

[b] Three-year average income is used here as a measure of permanent income.

Pittsburgh and -0.23 in Phoenix; the income elasticity estimates from the
log-linear specification are about 0.33 in Pittsburgh and 0.44 in Phoenix.
Since under the linear specification the elasticities vary with price and
income, the numbers presented for comparison represent derived linear
price and income elasticities as computed from the estimated parameters
of the linear demand function using the mean monthly income and mean
relative price, $(1 - a)$, for the sample. That the linear and log-linear
estimates are so close at the mean for the low-income Demand Experiment population suggests that, if a single elasticity estimate is needed, the
log-linear demand function provides a reasonable approximation for the
mean of the sample and, therefore, will be focused on for much of the rest

of this chapter. For some applications, one should nevertheless realize that the log-linear price elasticity estimate may be affected by the level and distribution of income in the sample used for estimation.

The entire sample of renter households may not be the best sample to use in order to estimate the demand functions. The theory underlying the housing demand and expenditure functions discussed earlier was based on the household's choice of optimal, utility-maximizing amounts of housing. However, the expenses of search and moving that usually precede adjustments of housing consumption to changed household circumstances may be significant. Households may not adjust immediately to correct imbalances in their consumption of housing and nonhousing goods. Thus, unless they have moved recently, they may not be consuming their desired amount of housing; the actual amount of housing they consume may differ from the amount implied by their demand function. (A more complete discussion of the role of housing disequilibrium in residential mobility is presented in Appendix V.)

If renters generally adjust their housing by moving, then households that did not move would be expected to show little change in housing expenditures in response to the rent rebates. As these households move, they may respond more like the households that moved during the experimental period. Thus, estimates for movers may provide a better estimate of the underlying demand function and the eventual response to a rent rebate than would estimates based on the entire sample. This suggests that it is desirable to estimate a separate demand function solely for movers.

The idea that the psychological and financial costs of moving may lead some households to consume apparently nonoptimal amounts of housing for long periods of time raises several other issues relevant for the estimation of demand functions. For example, households may attempt to base their current housing purchases on their best notion of what their income and prices are likely to be over some period of time. In particular, they might either adjust slowly to the price changes offered by the Percent of Rent rebates or they might discount these rebates because the rebate was offered for only 3 years. These factors would suggest that the responses observed during the experiment would be lower than the eventual response to a permanent program. On the other hand, households that move may be those having the greatest responsiveness to price changes and hence the greatest incentive to adjust their housing. This would mean that the responses of movers would tend to overestimate the eventual response to a permanent program. These and other issues in the analysis are discussed in Appendix II, where it is shown that they do not in fact pose serious problems in using mover households to estimate household responses to changes in price and income.

Table 2-3 presents the elasticities estimated for the sample of house-holds that moved between enrollment and 2 years after enrollment. The site similarity is striking; the estimated price elasticities for the two sites are −0.21 in Pittsburgh and −0.22 in Phoenix, and the estimated income elasticities are identical: 0.36. Indeed, one demand equation can be esti-mated for the entire mover sample (pooling the sites). As shown in Table 2-4, the price elasticity estimated by a pooled log-linear regression with different site intercepts is −0.22, and the income elasticity is 0.36, both significantly different from zero at the 0.01 level.

THE EFFECT OF DEMOGRAPHIC VARIABLES

Different demographic groups may have different relative preferences for housing versus other goods and services. Furthermore, policy interest

Table 2-3
Price and Income Elasticity Estimates for the Movers Sample

Demand Function	Pittsburgh	Phoenix
	Price elasticity	
Log-linear	−0.211 (0.063)	−0.219 (0.059)
Linear[a]	−0.222 (0.069)	−0.198 (0.061)
	Income elasticity[b]	
Log-linear	0.363 (0.052)	0.364 (0.042)
Linear[a]	0.375 (0.038)	0.330 (0.029)
Sample size	(236)	(292)

Note: Standard errors in parentheses; t-statistics all significant at the 0.01 level.

[a] At mean income and price (mean monthly household income is $417 for Pittsburgh and $434 for Phoenix; mean Price is 0.75 for Pittsburgh and 0.77 for Phoenix).

[b] Three-year average income is used here as a measure of permanent income.

Table 2-4

Price and Income Elasticity Estimates for the Movers Sample (Pooled Sites)

	Elasticity estimate
Price elasticity (log-linear)	-0.216
	(0.043)
95% confidence interval	[-0.301, -0.131]
Income elasticity[a] (log-linear)	0.364
	(0.033)
95% confidence interval	[0.299, 0.429]
Sample size	(528)

Note: Standard errors in parentheses; t-statistics significant at the 0.01 level.

[a] Three-year average income is used here as a measure of permanent income.

is often focused on certain demographic groups, in particular, minority or elderly households. Thus the influences of demographic variables on the price and income elasticities are investigated further in the following pages.

The data collected during the Demand Experiment enabled a detailed characterization of each household in terms of its demographic attributes. A combination of statistical tests, consideration of sample sizes, and judgment was used to reduce the relevant demographic characteristics to two statistically significant and policy-relevant variables: minority status and household composition. Minority status indicates whether the head of the household is a member of a minority group (black in Pittsburgh, and black or Hispanic in Phoenix). Household composition indicates whether the household is an elderly single person, is a single head of household (with children or other family members present), or is a couple (with or without children). These three types of households are referred to as single-person, single-headed with others present, and couple, respectively.

To determine the importance of the demographic characteristics, the sample was stratified into subsamples defined by combinations of these variables. The results of this investigation are discussed shortly for the sample of movers. Because the results for the log-linear and the linear equations are very similar, only the former are discussed.

Under this approach, each demographic group is allowed to have different price and income elasticities. Each equation was estimated for white and minority households, for single-person households, households headed by a couple, and households headed by a single person with others present. In addition, each equation was estimated for subsamples created by combining the minority and the household composition criteria. These equations were used to test hypotheses of homogeneity of elasticities among the groups via variance-ratio tests. (The full equations are presented in Appendix IV.)

In Pittsburgh, minority and white households were the same with respect to their equilibrium demand for housing. This similarity is indicated by an insignificant variance-ratio test statistic (see Table 2-5). In Phoenix, minority and nonminority households appear to have had different equilibrium demand equations. A variance-ratio test for homogeneity of elasticities, given different minority intercepts, rejects the hypothesis of homogeneity. Minority households in Phoenix had much lower price and income elasticities than did white households. Note also that, while the estimated elasticities for Hispanic households were lower than for any other group and not significantly different from zero, their error of estimate was too large for a conclusive finding.

In Pittsburgh, dummy variable regression indicated that intercepts may vary among the three household types. Examination of the elasticity estimates reveals large differences among elasticities by household type (see Table 2-6), and test statistics reject the homogeneity assumption. Households headed by a couple have the largest elasticities with respect to income (0.61) and with respect to price (−0.36). Pairwise comparisons of the elasticities among the three demographic groups show that the only significant difference is between the income elasticities for single-headed households and couples in Pittsburgh. In Phoenix, the hypothesis of homogeneity of the demand elasticities by household type cannot be rejected; no group appears more responsive than another to price and income changes.

Pooling the sites was statistically possible for the complete mover sample. Although the preceding individual examination of the two sites identified somewhat different demographic patterns of demand response in each site, variance-ratio tests cannot reject the hypothesis that the two sites are homogeneous with respect to price and income elasticities when the sample was stratified by either race or by household composition (allowing for site-specific intercepts). Table 2-7 presents these estimated elasticities. Furthermore, once the samples of both sites are pooled, homogeneity across demographic groups is rejected for race/ethnicity but not for household types (despite the wide variation in coefficients among the different groups). It appears that minorities have smaller responses to

Table 2-5
Price and Income Elasticities by Minority Status

Household group	Pittsburgh			Phoenix		
	Price elasticity	Income elasticity	Sample size	Price elasticity	Income elasticity	Sample size
All households	-0.213*** (0.064)	0.359*** (0.053)	(234)	-0.219*** (0.060)	0.370*** (0.043)	(285)
Nonminority households	-0.210*** (0.069)	0.386*** (0.057)	(196)	-0.287*** (0.068)	0.431*** (0.047)	(185)
Minority households[a]	-0.204 (0.179)	0.212 (0.148)	(38)	-0.179* (0.105)	0.177** (0.083)	(100)
Black households	—[b]	—[b]		-0.255 (0.217)	0.224 (0.168)	(28)
Hispanic households[c]	—	—		-0.137 (0.122)	0.133 (0.101)	(72)

Note: Standard errors in parentheses.

[a] A variance-ratio test could not reject the hypothesis of homogeneity between white and minority households in Pittsburgh [F(2,227) = 0.50] but could in Phoenix [F(2,279) = 4.42].

[b] Minority households in Pittsburgh are all black.

[c] A variance-ratio test could not reject the hypothesis of homogeneity between Hispanic and black households in Phoenix [F (2,94) = 0.49].

   * t-statistic significant at the 0.10 level.
  ** t-statistic significant at the 0.05 level.
 *** t-statistic significant at the 0.01 level.

Table 2-6

Price and Income Elasticities by Household Composition

Household group	Pittsburgh			Phoenix		
	Price elasticity	Income elasticity	Sample size	Price elasticity	Income elasticity	Sample size
All households	-0.213*** (0.064)	0.359*** (0.053)	(234)	-0.219*** (0.060)	0.370*** (0.043)	(285)
Single-person households	-0.077 (0.069)	0.274*** (0.057)	(33)	-0.245*** (0.068)	0.480*** (0.047)	(32)
Single-headed households with others present	-0.156* (0.092)	0.165 (0.102)	(98)	-0.128 (0.087)	0.342*** (0.072)	(121)
Households headed by a couple	-0.364*** (0.096)	0.613*** (0.090)	(103)	-0.327*** (0.100)	0.383*** (0.083)	(132)

Note: Standard errors in parentheses. A variance-ratio test could not reject the hypothesis of homogeneity among household types in Pittsburgh [$F_{(4,225)}$ = 3.20] but could in Phoenix [$F_{(4,277)}$ = 1.62].

* t-statistic significant at the 0.10 level.

*** t-statistic significant at the 0.01 level.

Table 2-7

**Price and Income Elasticity Estimates for Pooled Sites
by Demographic Characteristics**

Household group	Price elasticity	Income elasticity	Variance-ratio F-statistic[a]	Sample size
All movers	−0.217*** (0.044)	0.366*** (0.033)	0.017	(519)
White households	−0.249*** (0.048)	0.413*** (0.036)	0.437	(381)
Minority households	−0.182** (0.089)	0.184*** (0.071)	0.023	(138)
Single-person households	−0.175 (0.116)	0.426*** (0.083)	0.723	(65)
Single head of household with others	−0.137** (0.063)	0.294*** (0.058)	0.999	(219)
Households headed by a couple	−0.327*** (0.070)	0.468*** (0.061)	1.665	(235)

Note: Standard errors in parentheses. Variance-ratio tests indicate
        that, once pooling across sites is performed, pooling across house-
        hold types is possible [F(6,507) = 1.90] but pooling across races is
        not [F(3,511) = 9.170].

[a] Testing site homogeneity allowing site-specific intercepts.

 ** t-statistic significant at the 0.05 level.

*** t-statistic significant at the 0.01 level.

price and income changes than do nonminorities. This effect is especially marked in Phoenix. In addition, while there is evidence of differences in elasticities across household types in Pittsburgh, these are not significant for the pooled-site estimates or for Phoenix alone.

DYNAMIC MODELS OF HOUSING DEMAND

The basic idea in using the sample of movers to estimate the equilibrium demand for housing is simple—households faced with the costs of moving and other transactions do not adjust their housing consumption to a disequilibrium instantaneously. In other words, if an unforeseen change in the desired level of housing consumption occurs, the household will evaluate the benefits to be gained from adjusting housing and nonhousing consumption against the transactions costs and will make an adjustment only when the benefits from such an adjustment exceed the costs (see, for example, Muth, 1974; Quigley and Weinberg, 1977; Weinberg *et al.*, 1981; Appendix V).

The existence of transactions costs will cause lags in adjustment between the actual and the desired or equilibrium levels of housing. Thus, in a random sample of households, some will consume their desired housing, while others may consume either more or less housing than they desire. The observation that households may be in housing disequilibrium for long periods of time, and the corollary that short-term response to a change in circumstances may differ from the long-term response, have led Hanushek and Quigley (1979) and Mayo (1977), among others, to describe the dynamic behavior of housing demand as a stock adjustment process. However, as is shown below, because of some econometric problems, such an interpretation of the dynamic adjustment of housing consumption may be misleading.

In its simplest form, the stock adjustment model of demand assumes that: (*a*) households have some desired level of spending for particular goods or services; (*b*) the desired level is determined by exogenous influences, such as income and tastes; and (*c*) when desired and actual levels of spending differ, households adjust expenditures so as to close this gap at some fixed rate. Solving the model produces a time path of actual expenditures as they adjust toward their desired levels.[18] Applied to rental expenditures, the model, in its log-linear version, may be stated mathematically as

$$\ln(R_t) = \ln(R_{t-1}) + w[(\ln(R_t^*) - \ln(R_{t-1})] \\ = w \ln(R_t^*) + (1 - w) \ln(R_{t-1}) \tag{21}$$

where $\ln(R_t)$ is log rental expenditures in period t, $\ln(R_{t-1})$ is log rental expenditures in period $t - 1$, $\ln(R_t^*)$ is log desired rental expenditures in period t, and w is an adjustment parameter.

If the adjustment parameter equals one, then actual expenditures adjust instantaneously and completely to discrepancies between desired and actual expenditures. If $0 < w < 1$, the adjustment is "incomplete" or "partial"; actual expenditures will approach the desired level asymptotically.

---

[18] See Johnston (1972), pp. 300–320, or Intriligator (1978), pp. 235–248, for a detailed description of this model.

In most applications of the stock adjustment model, levels of desired consumption or expenditures are presumed to be unobservable, yet determined by observable variables. For example, one could express desired expenditures as

$$\ln(R_t^*) = a + b \ln(Y_t) + c \ln(P_t), \tag{22}$$

where Y_t is income in period t, and P_t is the relative price of housing in period t. Equation (22) is, in principle, no different from the static demand function, Eq. (8). In fact, the only theoretical contribution of the stock adjustment model to the static framework is that it hypothesizes a particular process by which a disequilibrium between desired and actual expenditures is resolved.

A stock adjustment model is typically estimated by substituting into Eq. (21) the function of observable variables determining R_t^* [Eq. (22)] for R_t^* itself, as did Mayo (1977). The equation estimated is therefore

$$\ln R_t = aw + bw \ln(Y_t) + cw \ln(P_t) + (1 - w) \ln(R_{t-1}) + v_t, \tag{23}$$

where v_t is a stochastic error term.

Alternatively, if a population thought to be in housing equilibrium can be found, R_t^* can be predicted by estimating Eq. (8) using a sample of this population, as in Hanushek and Quigley (1979) and in this chapter.

The basic problem with the stock adjustment model is that it assumes that "on average, households adjust to their equilibrium positions by closing the gap between actual and desired housing at a constant rate" (Hanushek and Quigley, 1979, p. 92). However, both Mayo and Hanushek and Quigley reject this interpretation on the grounds that, because housing adjustments may involve large search and moving costs, the notion of incremental adjustment to equilibrium is inappropriate. Since repeated moves within a short period of time are costly, households may decide to adjust to equilibrium either completely or not at all. Consequently Hanushek and Quigley interpret their adjustment parameter, w, as "the average propensity to respond"—the proportion of households that will either move or improve their housing within a given time period. Similarly, Mayo interprets the adjustment parameter as the probability that a randomly selected household makes a full adjustment to its desired level of spending within a given period. Since "the average propensity to respond" or "the probability of making full adjustment" are characteristics of populations, it is not clear why they should be used to estimate demand parameters using individual households which are either in equilibrium or disequilibrium. A model that may be correct when applied to grouped data is not necessarily correct when applied to household level data.

Given these interpretations, the usefulness of the stock adjustment model becomes questionable. A more direct method of obtaining the demand parameters is available. If after a move households consume their desired (equilibrium) quantity of housing, then the long-term demand parameters may be estimated by selecting a sample of recent movers. Furthermore, aside from the problem of interpreting the parameters of Eq. (23), there is also an econometric problem in estimating them because of the presence of a lagged dependent variable, R_{t-1}, in the equation.

It is well known that serial correlation in the error terms of each household in 2 consecutive years is almost inevitable. There may be several reasons for such serial correlation; the most obvious of which is that some unobservable variables determining behavior, such as taste for housing, will remain more or less constant over a span of years when households are observed over time. The existence of serial correlation implies that, if the true model is

$$\ln(R_t) = a + b \ln(Y_t) + c \ln(P_t) + e_t, \qquad (24)$$

with

$$e = p e_{t-1} + u_t \qquad (25)$$

where e_t is the error term in time t, u_t is random error, and p is the serial correlation coefficient, then combining Eqs. (24) and (25) gives

$$\ln(R_t) = a(1 - p) + b(1 - p) \ln(Y_t) + c(1 - p) \ln(P_t) + p \ln(R_{t-1}) + u_t. \qquad (26)$$

Because Eqs. (23) and (26) are mathematically identical, it is very difficult to distinguish between them, particularly if the true model is a combination of the two. As a result, in the econometric analysis that follows, we specify the model as

$$\ln(R_t) = A + B \ln(Y_t) + C \ln(P_t) + D \ln(R_{t-1}) + e_t. \qquad (27)$$

In the presence of serial correlation in Eq. (27), $\ln(R_{t-1})$, which includes e_{t-1}, will be correlated with e_t. If the serial correlation is positive, the OLS estimate of the parameter D will be biased upward, and the estimates of the parameters A, B and C will be biased downward. Consistent estimates of the parameters can be obtained if 2-Stage Least Squares (2SLS) is used.[19] To use 2SLS, however, one needs to find instrumental variables that are correlated with $\ln(R_{t-1})$ but are uncorrelated with e_t. Unfortunately, such variables rarely exist. For almost every potential instrumental variable one might argue is correlated with $\ln(R_{t-1})$, the variable is also correlated

---

[19] The use of 2SLS in situations that involve lagged dependent variables and serial correlation was suggested by Griliches (1967).

with e_{t-1} and, therefore, e_t. For the subset of households in the Demand Experiment that moved during the experiment, one variable, length of residence at the initial residence, L_{t-1}, meets the requirement. For such households, L_{t-1} was correlated with the initial premove rent, R_{t-1}, but uncorrelated with the post move rent, R_t, and is therefore also uncorrelated with e_t.

Use of movers alone prevents us from making a direct test of the stock adjustment frameworks proposed by Hanushek and Quigley and Mayo. Nevertheless, it can give us an indication of the importance of serial correlation and consequently the likelihood of their misspecifications of the dynamic adjustment process. As was su⁻ ⁻ested previously, movers are likely to have made a complete adjus⁻ ⁻ ⁻ ⁻o housing equilibrium. Thus, for them, the estimate of the co⁻ ⁻ould be zero in the absence of serial correlation. If OLS ⁻stimation and there is serial correlation, then according ⁻ ⁻ne coefficient estimate is equal to the serial correlation c⁻ ⁻thermore, 2SLS estimation of this model should purge th⁻ ⁻of serial correlation.

The empirical results ar⁻ ⁻ in Table 2-8. When OLS is used,

Table 2-8
Dynamic Demand Parameter Estimates for Mover Households

Independent Variable	Pittsburgh		Phoenix		.Pooled Sites	
	OLS	2SLS	OLS	2SLS	OLS	2SLS
Constant	2.668***	2.888*	1.977***	2.588***	2.236***	2.739***
	(0.268)	(1.799)	(0.225)	(0.869)	(0.170)	(0.715)
Phoenix Dummy	–	–	–	–	0.068***	0.120***
					(0.024)	(0.024)
Income	0.247***	0.323***	0.220***	0.321***	0.222***	0.323***
	(0.045)	(0.042)	(0.033)	(0.034)	(0.028)	(0.026)
Price	-0.204***	-0.197***	-0.178***	-0.212***	-0.194***	-0.208***
	(0.059)	(0.060)	(0.050)	(0.053)	(0.039)	(0.039)
Lagged Rent	0.289***	0.185	0.470***	0.269	0.401***	0.214
	(0.058)	(0.381)	(0.048)	(0.180)	(0.037)	(0.150)
R^2	0.28	NA	0.42	NA	0.37	NA
Standard error of estimate	0.07	0.07	0.07	0.08	0.07	0.07
Sample size	(236)	(236)	(291)	(291)	(527)	(527)

Note: NA is not available.
  * t-statistic significant at the 0.10 level.
*** t-statistic significant at the 0.01 level.

the estimate for the coefficient D is highly significant, approximately equal to 0.3 in Pittsburgh and 0.5 in Phoenix. When 2SLS is used, however, D is not significantly different from zero. The comparison of the OLS and the 2SLS estimates of D implies considerable serial correlation. In addition, the price and income elasticities obtained from 2SLS estimates are very similar to those reported in Table 2-3. The evidence, therefore, does not suggest the superiority of the dynamic model and is consistent with viewing the complete adjustment model estimated earlier for movers as an adequate theoretical description of the behavior of low-income renters. This finding, therefore, contradicts the findings of Hanushek and Quigley (1979) and Mayo (1977), both of whom ignored the possibility of serial correlation.

CONCLUSION

This chapter has presented new evidence on price and income elasticities of housing demand based on individual household data. Comparable results were obtained from two different demand functions—log-linear and linear expenditures functions. The results demonstrate that both price and income elasticities of demand are not constant over a range of prices and incomes or across demographic types. The evidence indicates that low-income households change their housing consumption very little in response to income and housing price changes. A 10% increase in income or a 10% reduction in the price of housing induces a change in housing expenditures of *less* than 4%. More precisely, our estimates show that in both Pittsburgh and Phoenix a 10% reduction in the price of housing would result in only a 2.2% increase in housing expenditures; a 10% increase in household's average income would result in only a 3.6% increase in housing expenditures.

Minorities make smaller changes in housing expenditures in response to changes in the price of housing or income than do nonminorities. The percentage change in housing expenditures resulting from a given percentage change in household income is estimated to be about half as large for minority households as for nonminority households, while the percentage change in response to a price change is estimated to be three-fourths that of nonminority households. There is no consistent evidence of important differences in response among other demographic groups. A variety of other demographic factors were tested, including the age, sex, and education of the head of household, as well as the size and composition of the household. Of these, only household composition proved significant when the sites were analyzed separately, and even this variable was not significant for estimates based on the combined sites.

The chapter also argued that the equilibrium demand for housing can best be estimated when only recent movers are included in the sample. Evidence was developed that suggests that dynamic stock adjustment models of housing demand are inappropriate for estimating the equilibrium demand functions of individual households.

Chapter 3 _____

The Demand for Housing Services

The previous chapter discussed the demand for housing and the effects of proportional rent rebates on housing consumption solely in terms of housing expenditures. That focus was based on the implicit assumption that the household was buying a single homogeneous commodity called housing services. Each dwelling unit is presumed to yield some quantity of housing services during each period of time. As long as all consumers in a given housing market face the same price of housing services, and as long as this price does not vary during the analysis period, analysis of housing expenditures is akin to analysis of housing services.

The alternative to viewing the housing market as a market in which housing services are bought and sold is to view it as the market in which households value various characteristics of the dwelling units (different combinations of rooms of different size and function, quality, location, etc.). Characterizing each dwelling unit type as a separate commodity becomes extremely cumbersome. Quigley (1976) attempted such an approach, classifying housing into 18 residential types (three structure types by two quality levels by three interior size measures). Even this approach clearly required substantial simplifying assumptions about what a household values in choosing a dwelling unit. An alternative approach to comparing different dwelling units is to find some method that measures the units in some common way. The method typically used is that of hedonic indices, which weight each characteristic by its importance in determining the unit's rental (or market) value. Such an index results in a dollar amount of housing, interpretable as housing services (see, for example, Follain and Malpezzi, 1979; King, 1972).

47

AN EXPLANATION OF HEDONIC INDICES[1]

The assertion that an apartment renting for $200 provides double the amount of housing services provided by a $100 apartment is similar to the assertion that the $200 food bundle contains twice as many groceries as a $100 food bundle. Just as the $200 grocery bundle does not necessarily contain two of every item in the $100 bundle, the $200 apartment may have a different mix of housing characteristics from the $100 apartment.

The concept of hedonic indices of housing was developed to enable comparisons among different housing units. Where houses are identical in all but a single feature, comparison is simple. A 4-bedroom house, for example, clearly contains more housing than an otherwise identical 3-bedroom house. Comparison becomes more difficult when dissimilar units are compared. It is not obvious whether a 3-bedroom unit with three baths represents more housing than a 4-bedroom house with two baths. In order to compare the two houses, we need to determine the relative value of a bathroom to a bedroom. For the grocery bundle, since all individual items have clearly marked prices, the more expensive bundle represents *more* groceries because the money used to buy the expensive bundle could be used to buy the less expensive bundle and there would still be money left over to buy more groceries. Comparisons of different housing units are unfortunately more complicated since the prices of the individual features which comprise a housing unit are not directly observable.

The assumption underlying the hedonic approach is that the rent or value of a housing unit comes directly from the quantity and types of characteristics it contains and that the market prices of these housing characteristics can be estimated by pooling information from many dwelling units via multivariate regression analysis between rents and dwelling characteristics.[2] The result of the regression is a set of implicit prices which measure the value of each dwelling and neighborhood characteristic for the time period and geographical area from which the sample of

[1] The following discussion is based, in part, on Follain and Malpezzi (1979).

[2] The hedonic methodology was first developed by Court (1939) and was later revived by Griliches (1971). The hedonic approach to the analysis of consumption rests on the assumption that goods may be disaggregated into sets of basic characteristics, and that the characteristics of the particular good, rather than the good itself, constitute the arguments of the consumer's utility function (see Lancaster, 1971). As summarized by Griliches (1971), the parametric version of the hedonic technique asserts the existence of a "reasonably well-fitting" relation between the price of the composite commodity, for example "housing services," and the levels of its characteristics (the various dwelling unit characteristics and neighborhood and locational attributes). The coefficients that result from estimation of this relationship, usually by a regression, are referred to as the shadow, or implicit, prices of the characteristics.

dwellings is drawn. For example, the regressions might determine that an extra bathroom adds 10% or adds $20 to a dwelling unit's rent. Prices of the housing characteristics may differ among areas or over time. Moreover, it should be realized that these prices do not contain information about the underlying relationships of demand for and supply of housing characteristics but only about their interaction (see Rosen, 1974).

More formally, the theory of hedonic indices suggests the following general hedonic specification:

$$R = f(\mathbf{S}, \mathbf{L}, \mathbf{N}), \tag{1}$$

where R is rent, $\mathbf{S}$ are structural characteristics, $\mathbf{L}$ are locational characteristics, and $\mathbf{N}$ are neighborhood characteristics. Regression estimates of a properly specified function can provide estimates of the coefficients of this expression. The relationship between housing characteristics and rent is, however, not likely to be the same for all types of households in all types of situations. It is well documented that some households or groups of households pay more than other groups for apparently similar housing. Almost everyone who has searched for a house or an apartment is aware that similar units in similar locations sometimes rent for different amounts. Thus, by careful and extensive shopping, or sometimes just by luck, a household can obtain its unit at a rent lower than the market average.

Likewise, long-established tenants may pay lower rents because they are known to the landlord as good tenants, or because long-term residency may reduce landlord's costs, or simply because it is easier for landlords to raise rents when a unit turns over. Others may pay lower rent because of a particular relationship with the landlord (for example, a relative). Finally, discrimination against racial or ethnic minorities may result in price differentials with the minority group paying more or less than the majority group for comparable housing.[3] Thus, the basic hedonic relationship should be modified to reflect these cases:

$$R = f(\mathbf{S}, \mathbf{L}, \mathbf{N}, \mathbf{T}), \tag{2}$$

where $\mathbf{T}$ are tenant characteristics which affect the housing prices such a consumer would face.

---

[3] Becker (1957) argued that even in segregated conditions, prices would equalize across black and white submarkets. Other theorists have suggested that whites will pay higher prices to maintain segregated conditions (see Bailey, 1966; Muth, 1969; Pascal, 1970, for example). Still others have argued that segregated housing is maintained by collusion and other restrictions rather than market prices, with the result that blacks pay higher prices (see Haugens and Heins, 1969; Kain and Quigley, 1975; for example). See Mieszkowski (1980) for a review of the literature on housing market segregation.

HEDONIC INDICES FOR THE DEMAND
EXPERIMENT SITES

Hedonic indices for the Demand Experiment sites were estimated by
Merrill (1980). They are discussed briefly later, using excerpts from her
report.[4] As already suggested, hedonic indices give a dollar value for the
amount of housing services provided by a unit, and this value can be
interpreted as the expected or average market rent of a unit with given
location, size, and other physical characteristics. The hedonic housing
services index was derived by regressing the logarithm of rent on housing
unit and neighborhood characteristics and on tenure conditions at enrollment:

$$\ln(R) = a + \mathbf{Xb} + \mathbf{Tc} + w, \tag{3}$$

where $\mathbf{X}$ is a vector of housing unit, locational, and neighborhood charac-
teristics [$\mathbf{S}$, $\mathbf{L}$, and $\mathbf{N}$, in Eqs. (1) and (2)]; $\mathbf{T}$ is a vector of tenure characteristics, such as length of residence in the unit and whether the landlord
lives in the building; a,$\mathbf{b}$,$\mathbf{c}$ are vectors of regression coefficients; and w is a
stochastic error.

Appendix Tables IV-8 and IV-9 present Merrill's estimated hedonic
functions. The housing attributes included in the hedonic equations explain 66% of the variance of the log of rent in Pittsburgh and 80% in
Phoenix. These results compare very favorably with the explanatory
power obtained in other studies that used individual dwelling unit data.
The included variables represent all major components of the housing
unit—tenure conditions, dwelling unit quality, dwelling unit size, neighborhood quality, and accessibility. Within most component groups, a
broadly descriptive set of variables is significant. Dwelling unit descrip-
tors include basic facilities (such as heat or kitchen facilities), additional
features (such as air-conditioning or appliances), and the surface and
structural quality of walls, ceilings, and floors. Neighborhood quality is
described by the immediate neighborhood (the "block face" of the unit);
by the housing and the socioeconomic characteristics of the census tract;
and, for aggregations of census tracts, by numerous measures of amenities
and public services as perceived by those enrolled in the Demand Experiment.

As might be expected, the hedonic regressions for Pittsburgh and
Phoenix are different. Different variables are included and the coefficient
values of included variables often differ substantially. The basic reason for

---

[4] See Merrill (1980) for a more detailed explanation of the procedures used in estimation
of these indices.

this difference is that the two housing markets differ markedly. Phoenix residents generally have lived in their units for less time, reflecting higher mobility rates. Phoenix units are also generally newer (about half the average age of Pittsburgh units) and more often have features associated with newer units, such as a dishwasher, a garbage disposal, or a stove or refrigerator included with the unit. In addition, Phoenix units tend to have fewer and somewhat smaller rooms, somewhat higher average ratings for surface and structural quality, and higher overall evaluator ratings. The better fit achieved in Phoenix probably reflects its greater homogeneity; the Pittsburgh housing stock is generally older and is divided into many more well-defined neighborhoods than the Phoenix housing stock.

These indices are used to divide actual rent into three components: the average market value of housing services consumed, the value of conditions of tenure, and a residual. The log of the average dollar value of the amount of housing services consumed by a household in period t, $\ln(Q)$, was estimated by multiplying the vector of the dwelling unit, neighborhood and location characteristics of the household's period t housing, $\mathbf{X}$, by the vector of hedonic weights, $\hat{\mathbf{b}}$ (the estimator of the implicit market prices of the housing attributes at enrollment). That is, $\ln(Q)$ is estimated as

$$\ln(Q) = \hat{a} + \mathbf{X}\hat{\mathbf{b}}. \qquad (4)$$

Since the same vector of hedonic weights $\hat{\mathbf{b}}$ is used to predict *each* time period's housing services, changes in estimated housing services occurred only because of changes in some or all of the characteristics of the household's housing. Similarly, the value of tenure conditions, $\ln(Z)$, is computed as

$$\ln(Z) = \mathbf{T}\hat{c}. \qquad (5)$$

The difference between the log of actual rent and the value of the the hedonic index plus the effect of tenure conditions is the estimate of the hedonic residual:

$$\hat{w} = \ln(R) - [\ln(Q) + \ln(Z)]. \qquad (6)$$

DEMAND FUNCTIONS FOR HOUSING SERVICES

The major motivation for estimating demand equations using a hedonic index as the dependent variable is the possibility that the rent rebates could have affected the shopping behavior of recipients. The hedonic residual w indicates whether a unit is over- or underpriced. A negative w

indicates that the unit's rent is lower than the market average rent for a similar unit, so that the unit may be considered a bargain. On the other hand, a positive w indicates that the unit's rent is above the market rent for similar units, so that the unit may be considered a bad deal. In this context, efficient shopping for rental housing may be viewed as looking for units that are bargains. However, because of the rent rebates, recipients were paying less out-of-pocket than the normal market rent, since their net payments were reduced by 20–60% (depending on the particular rent rebate plan in which they were enrolled). For example, for a household with a 50% rent rebate, finding a unit that rents for $10 more or less than another makes only a $5 difference in the out-of-pocket cost to the household. Thus, as long as the search for bargains requires effort, Percent of Rent households might be expected to have shopped for new housing less vigorously than Control households. This can be tested by estimating the effects of rent rebates on the purchase of housing services and comparing these effects with the effects already estimated for housing expenditures.

The estimates of price and income elasticities for both expenditures and the hedonic index using the sample of mover households are presented in Table 3-1. In Phoenix, the income elasticity estimates are almost the same for expenditures and housing services; in Pittsburgh, the income elasticity of housing services is slightly lower than that for expenditures, but their 95% confidence intervals substantially coincide. Rather striking differences are evident in the price elasticity estimates, however. The estimated price elasticity for housing services in Phoenix is close to zero and insignificant. In Pittsburgh, the estimated price elasticity of housing services is only one-half of the estimated price elasticity of expenditures. These results suggest that, in response to a decrease in the price of housing, households increased their housing services by less than their expenditures. Moreover, in Phoenix the change in housing services for Percent of Rent households was no larger than for similar Control households.

Several explanations are possible for these results. A rent rebate program such as a Percent of Rent allowance that provides no *direct* incentive for households to increase their housing quality may lead to inefficiency in shopping behavior. Households would no longer be paying the full market price for each additional unit of housing services and would possibly be happy to reduce their search effort and accept less housing services per dollar than the market provides on the average. On the other hand, the estimated hedonic index may be subject to several types of specification bias. For example, if important attributes of the housing unit were omitted from the estimating equation, the index would not adequately reflect the unit's housing services, and the estimated price and income elasticities for housing services might be biased downward from the true elasticities.

Table 3-1

Comparison of Price and Income Elasticities Estimated Using Housing Expenditures and a Hedonic Index of Housing Services

Elasticity estimates	Pittsburgh	Phoenix
Income elasticity		
Expenditures estimate	0.338***	0.353***
	(0.054)	(0.046)
Hedonic estimate	0.226***	0.375***
	(0.047)	(0.043)
Price elasticity		
Expenditures estimate	−0.230***	−0.215***
	(0.065)	(0.064)
Hedonic estimate	−0.113**	−0.045
	(0.057)	(0.060)
Sample size[a]	(214)	(257)

Note: Standard errors in parentheses.

[a] Sample sizes differ from those presented in Chapter 2 due to the extra data requirements for the hedonic index.

** t-statistic significant at the 0.05 level.

*** t-statistic significant at the 0.01 level.

Next, if the housing markets in Pittsburgh or Phoenix were segmented, that is, if different groups of households (central city versus suburban residents or blacks versus whites, for example) faced different housing prices, the same set of relative prices for the housing attributes estimated by an overall hedonic index may not be applicable to all submarkets. Finally, the attribute weights estimated during the baseline period may not be applicable after 2 years due to changing market conditions or, more likely, to decisions made by movers to rent units in areas unlike those included in the original sample.[5]

These issues can be addressed in a formal framework. As described previously, the hedonic housing services index was derived by regressing

[5] The housing units of all enrolled households were used to estimate the hedonic index. The sample is not a random sample of all dwelling units since those households all had low or moderate incomes. Furthermore, census tracts with low concentrations of rental units (less than 5% of housing units) were excluded from the sampling frame. These tracts might possibly have had rental units with higher average quality.

rent on housing unit and neighborhood characteristics and on conditions of tenure at enrollment: $\ln(R) = a + \mathbf{Xb} + \mathbf{Tc} + w$. When rent at 2 years is predicted using the estimated coefficients, the estimated residual, $\hat{w}$, may represent omitted quality variables, omitted tenure variables, experimentally induced shopping inefficiency, and luck or other random effects.

Several hypotheses can be tested to determine the correct interpretation of the estimated residual. If the residual involves some omitted quality (i.e., quality unmeasured by the variables included in the index), then it should be positively correlated with household income and possibly with household satisfaction. If the residual reflects changes in shopping behavior, then the search behavior of Percent of Rent households should show some differences from Control households. These specification issues have been assessed in detail by Merrill (1980) in the development of the hedonic index, and by Kennedy and Merrill (1979) in analysis of the index's behavior over the experimental period. The next section summarizes some of these analyses and provides some hypotheses concerning the reasons for the differences in the elasticity estimates for expenditures and housing services.

ANALYSIS OF THE HEDONIC RESIDUAL

If the hedonic residual contains *only* omitted quality items, then analysis of housing quality should examine the sum of the hedonic index and the residual ($a + \mathbf{Xb} + w$) rather than just the index alone. On the other hand, if the residual does not consist solely of omitted quality, then analysis of the price response should take account of possible shopping inefficiencies as well.

If the hedonic residual includes some omitted quality, then it should be positively related to the household's satisfaction with its dwelling unit (to the extent that satisfaction is positively related to the level of housing quality). If, on the other hand, the hedonic residual is due largely to price effects rather than omitted quality, the association with satisfaction is expected to be negative—that is, that satisfaction increases as the amount of quality relative to expenditures increases (and the residual gets smaller). To test these hypotheses, the change in hedonic quality and the change in the hedonic residual over the 2 years of the experiment were each regressed on the change in dwelling unit satisfaction for Control households. The results showed that the change in quality and satisfaction had a significant and positive relationship in both sites. On the other hand, in both Pittsburgh and Phoenix, satisfaction and the hedonic residual have a negative relationship (which is significant only in Pittsburgh). Thus, it seems that the hedonic residual is *not* solely due to omitted quality items.

Similar hypotheses were tested concerning the relationship of search effort to quality and price effects. If the hedonic residual reflects price differences, then a diligent search will result in a better deal (more quality per dollar) than would a haphazard search. If this theory is true, then the hedonic residual will be negatively associated with search effort. This test would not be very powerful, however, because there is some evidence that some households who do not search at all obtain good deals by luck—being referred to a unit by friends or relatives (Vidal, 1980), for example. Tests were conducted accounting for this "windfall search" as well as for a more active search, using the number of days spent searching for housing as a measure of search effort.[6] Increased search time does in fact result in getting a better deal, that is, more quality per dollar of expenditures in both Pittsburgh and Phoenix.

Part of the smaller increase in housing services relative to expenditures for Percent of Rent households in both Phoenix and Pittsburgh may be due to conscious decisions to use less effort in searching for a new unit. Since there is a significant association between increased search time and obtaining more housing services per dollar of expenditures, if Percent of Rent households search less than Control households, then the price discount will have a smaller effect on their housing services than on their expenditures. There is some weak evidence that a decrease in search effort occurred—Percent of Rent movers spent fewer days looking for a unit than did Control movers, although not significantly so (on average 97 versus 119 days in Pittsburgh, and 34 versus 46 days in Phoenix).[7]

Another approach to analyzing the residual is direct estimation of demand for the residual and for the housing services and tenure components. During the develoment of the hedonic index, extensive analysis of the residual was carried out using the entire enrolled sample (see Merrill, 1980). The hedonic residuals and the percentage deviation of predicted and actual rent were regressed on household income, race, household size, and age and education of head of household. The major hypothesis tested was the following: If important quality attributes were omitted, there would be a significant positive relationship between the residual and income and, perhaps, education. The income coefficients were in fact significant but were extremely small in both Pittsburgh and Phoenix.

A series of similar models have been estimated for Percent of Rent households and Control households that remained in the experiment for 2 years. In logarithmic form, Eq. (3) becomes

$$\ln(R) = \ln(Q) + \ln(Z) + \ln(e) \tag{7}$$

---

[6] See Kennedy and Merrill (1979) for additional details.
[7] See Table 3-5.

where

$\ln(Q) = (\hat{a} + \mathbf{X}\hat{\mathbf{b}})$ the hedonic index of housing services abstracting from tenure characteristics,

$\ln(Z) = \mathbf{T}\hat{\mathbf{c}}$, the value of tenure characteristics, and

$\ln(e) = \hat{w}$, the stochastic error.

If each component of Eq. (7) [$\ln(Q)$, $\ln(Z)$, and $\ln(e)$], is regressed on the logarithms of price and income, Eq. (7) implies that the sum of the price (or income) elasticities for Q, Z, and e will equal the price (income) elasticity of R:[8]

$$n_R = n_Q + n_Z + n_e. \tag{8}$$

These elasticities may be estimated using log-linear regressions; they are summarized in Table 3-2. In Pittsburgh, both the price and income elasticities of housing services are smaller than the respective expenditure elasticities. The difference is almost entirely accounted for by the hedonic residual and not by the tenure characteristics. Since there is a significant positive income elasticity for the residual in Pittsburgh, it becomes plausible to assume that the residual in that site at least partially represents omitted quality variables (recall that the R^2 for Pittsburgh's hedonic equation was 0.66, lower than Phoenix's fit, 0.80). The presence of a significant price elasticity for the residual in both sites suggests that price differences due to shopping effects are also present in the residual.

The ratio of the elasticities can also provide some information on the relative importance of omitted quality and price effects. As stated earlier, the significant income elasticity of the hedonic residual in Pittsburgh suggests that, at that site, the hedonic residual does include some omitted quality. In this case, the estimated price and income elasticities based on the hedonic index would underestimate the true elasticities of housing services; at least part of the change in the hedonic residual w would represent real changes in housing in addition to the changes reflected by the index, $\ln(Q)$. Friedman and Weinberg (1980a) estimate this partial

---

[8] From Eq. (7),

$$\frac{\partial \ln(R)}{\partial \ln(p)} = \frac{\partial \ln(Q)}{\partial \ln(p)} + \frac{\partial \ln(Z)}{\partial \ln(p)} + \frac{\partial \ln(e)}{\partial \ln(p)},$$

and these elasticities are the estimated coefficients of log-linear demand functions for R, Q, Z, and e. Actually, since the rent definition used for the hedonic analysis and the rent definition used for the housing consumption analysis are slightly different, there is another term representing this adjustment. The adjustment has no impact on any of the findings reported here (see Table 3-2).

Table 3-2
Price and Income Elasticity Estimates for Rent Components

	Pittsburgh		Phoenix	
Dependent variable	Price elasticity	Income elasticity	Price elasticity	Income elasticity
Rent	-0.230*** (0.065)	0.338*** (0.054)	-0.215*** (0.064)	0.353*** (0.046)
Hedonic index	-0.113** (0.057)	0.226*** (0.047)	-0.045 (0.060)	0.375*** (0.043)
Hedonic residual	-0.159*** (0.047)	0.089** (0.039)	-0.193*** (0.048)	-0.021 (0.034)
Tenure characteristics	0.027** (0.013)	0.019* (0.010)	(0.017 (0.011)	0.001 (0.008)
Definitional difference[a]	0.016 (0.013)	0.004 (0.010)	0.005 (0.007)	-0.002 (0.005)
Sample size	(214)		(257)	

Note: Standard errors in parentheses.

[a] Difference between the analytic rent variable used for the expenditure analysis and that used in the derivation of the hedonic index.

*   t-statistic significant at the 0.10 level.

**   t-statistic significant at the 0.05 level.

*** t-statistic significant at the 0.01 level.

effect.[9] Since the total price elasticity of housing services is the sum of the hedonic elasticity and the elasticity of omitted items, the implied overall price elasticity for housing services in Pittsburgh is −0.158. Since the expenditures price elasticity is −0.230, this implies a shopping effect of −0.072; that is, only about two-thirds of the expenditure increase induced by the Percent of Rent plans in Pittsburgh went to increase housing services, while the other one third represents either shopping inefficiency (reduced quality per dollar of expenditure) or reduced search effort.

[9] The estimate is based on using the ratio of income elasticities for the hedonic index and the residual to indicate the proportion of omitted quality that is in the residual.

In contrast, the evidence in Phoenix seems most consistent with viewing the hedonic residual solely as a price effect (representing changes in shopping behavior) and not as omitted quality.[10] The income elasticity estimates are the same for the hedonic index and rent, and zero for the residual. Almost all of the difference in price elasticity estimates is found in the residual.

Thus, it appears that in Phoenix the rent rebates did not induce any significant increase in the consumption of housing services of recipients, but rather, only a change in their shopping behavior. On the other hand, the residual in Pittsburgh represents both some omitted quality and some price behavior changes and indicates a significant household response.

DEMOGRAPHIC STRATIFICATION

As was seen in Chapter 2, expenditure elasticities differ among certain demographic groups. Stratification by household composition was indicated in Pittsburgh, and stratification by race was indicated in Phoenix. Since expenditures elasticities were not uniform across demographic groups, housing service elasticities probably will not be either. Tables in Appendix IV present the hedonic regression estimates cross-classified by demographic characteristics for movers. Variance ratio tests indicate that, as for expenditures, price and income elasticities differ by household composition in Pittsburgh but not in Phoenix (see Table 3-3). The overall estimated housing services price elasticity for Pittsburgh movers is -0.11 (significantly different from zero at the .05 level).

The estimates for the different types of households vary a great deal. The price elasticity of housing services was insignificant for single-person and single-headed households. In contrast, the price elasticity is -0.25 for households headed by a couple (still smaller than the expenditures estimate for that group of -0.36, although within that estimate's 95% confidence interval). The housing services income elasticities are much closer to each other. The largest estimate is again that for households headed by a couple: 0.49 (again within the 95% confidence interval of the expenditures estimate for that group of 0.61). Indeed, all the estimated housing services elasticities by household type fall within the 95% confidence intervals of the corresponding expenditures estimates.

In contrast to housing expenditures where racial stratification was important only in Phoenix, this stratification yields significant differences at

---

[10] In Phoenix, the income elasticity of the residual is small, negative, and not significantly different from zero. Therefore, no adjustment in the Phoenix housing services elasticity is indicated.

Table 3-3

Housing Services Elasticities by Household Composition

Household group	Pittsburgh			Phoenix		
	Price elasticity	Income elasticity	Sample size	Price elasticity	Income elasticity	Sample size
All households	-0.113** (0.057)	0.226*** (0.047)	(214)	-0.045 (0.060)	0.375*** (0.043)	(257)
Single-person households	-0.118 (0.168)	0.241 (0.163)	(32)	-0.366** (0.197)	0.464*** (0.101)	(29)
Single-headed household with others present	-0.038 (0.085)	0.181* (0.095)	(87)	0.045 (0.081)	0.416*** (0.067)	(111)
Households headed by a couple	-0.246*** (0.080)	0.489*** (0.076)	(95)	-0.121 (0.098)	0.365*** (0.082)	(117)

Note: Standard errors in parentheses. A variance-ratio test could reject the hypothesis of homogeneity among household types in Pittsburgh [$F(4,205) = 6.27$], but could not in Phoenix
[$F(4,248) = 1.69$].

*   t-statistic significant at the 0.10 level.

**   t-statistic significant at the 0.05 level.

*** t-statistic significant at the 0.01 level.

both sites for housing services (see Table 3-4). Minority households have an insignificant and positive estimated price elasticity in both sites, while nonminority households even in Phoenix (which has an insignificant overall elasticity) have a negative and significant price elasticity. On the other hand, minority households have zero or very low price and income elasticities (though the estimated housing services income elasticity for Phoenix minority movers is very close to the expenditures estimate and is significant at the .10 level). When minority households in Phoenix are further divided into black and Hispanic groups, it is clear that it is the Hispanic households that did not increase their expenditures in response to these changes. Furthermore, the fit for this group for both expenditures and housing services is very poor ($R^2 = 0.02$ and $R^2 = 0.03$, respectively).

Apparently, then, the estimated equations do not describe the behavior of Hispanic households, in particular, very well. The price and income elasticity estimates for minority households in Phoenix, particularly for Hispanic households, suggest that these households did not respond to the Percent of Rent rebates by increasing their consumption of housing services or their housing expenditures. One possible explanation for this lack of response is that minority households face market barriers that either prevent them from purchasing an average amount of housing services per dollar of additional expenditure or prevent them from entering areas with higher rent and higher quality units. If minority households face a different structure of housing attribute prices due to market segmentation or only have access to a limited range of housing choices (perhaps due to racial or ethnic discrimination) then use of a hedonic index with implicit attribute prices based on the full sample would misestimate the actual housing services consumed by minorities.

A series of tests to assess market segmentation were made during the development of the hedonic index (Merrill, 1980). In Phoenix, separate equations were estimated for nonminority and Hispanic households, and comparison of these regressions did not indicate the existence of market segmentation.[11] (There were too few black households in Phoenix to estimate a separate submarket index for them.) Use of this submarket hedonic index does not change the results for any group; bias due to misestimated attribute prices is apparently not responsible for the insignificant housing services price and income elasticities in Phoenix.

Two alternate potential explanations for the elasticity differences between Hispanic and nonminority households deserve attention. First, quality variables may be omitted from the hedonic index which are systematically associated with the purchases of Hispanic households but not

---

[11] Although overall differences were minor, several important implicit prices, particularly for space, did differ.

Table 3-4
Housing Services Elasticities by Minority Status

Household Group	Pittsburgh			Phoenix		
	Price elasticity	Income elasticity	Sample size	Price elasticity	Income elasticity	Sample size
All households	-0.113** (0.057)	0.226*** (0.047)	(214)	-0.045 (0.060)	0.375*** (0.043)	(257)
Nonminority households	-0.143** (0.057)	0.269*** (0.048)	(180)	-0.129** (0.065)	0.440*** (0.045)	(168)
Minority households[a]	0.067 (0.201)	-0.012 (0.151)	(34)	0.023 (0.106)	0.154* (0.085)	(89)
Black households	—b	—b	—b	-0.138 (0.218)	0.159 (0.165)	(27)
Hispanic households[c]	—	—	—	0.116 (0.121)	0.100 (0.102)	(62)

Note: Standard errors in parentheses.
a A variance-ratio test rejected the hypothesis of homogeneity between white and minority households in both Pittsburgh [F(3,208) = 3.48] and in Phoenix [F(3,251) = 16.96].
b Minority households in Pittsburgh are all black.
c A variance-ratio test did not reject the hypothesis of homogeneity between Hispanic and black households in Phoenix [F(3,083) = 1.07].

*   t-statistic significant at the 0.10 level.
** t-statistic significant at the 0.05 level.
*** t-statistic significant at the 0.01 level.

61

of nonminority households. Second, minority Experimental households may have searched less than minority Control households, possibly due to discrimination.

It is not at all clear which potential omitted variables, if any, might be systematically associated with minority or Hispanic housing consumption. Investigation of several possibilities, as reported in Kennedy and Merrill (1979), resulted in the conclusion that such omissions would not bias the price elasticity estimate sufficiently to make it zero. Furthermore, since income is not significantly related to the hedonic residual in Phoenix for Hispanic movers, even at 2 years after enrollment, the evidence of systematic bias due to omitted variables seems rather slim.

The last hypothesis concerns the effect of search effort on obtaining an amount of housing services per dollar of expenditure. As previously suggested, part of a smaller increase in housing services relative to expenditures for Experimental households in both Phoenix and Pittsburgh may be due to a conscious decision on their part to use less effort in searching for a new unit. Hispanic movers who received rent rebates did spend significantly fewer days searching (28 days) than did Hispanic Control movers (76 days); see Table 3-5.

In summation, there is a general pattern of reduced shopping effectiveness in Phoenix. That is, Experimental households apparently worked less hard to find housing bargains than they would have in the absence of a subsidy. The extent of this shopping effect is similar for all demographic groups (with the possible exception of some single-person and single-headed households). There is also some evidence of reduced effectiveness in Pittsburgh, but it is much smaller than the reduction in Phoenix. Minorities in Phoenix, and especially Hispanic households, showed little or no real change in housing or rent in response to the rent rebates. No clear reason for this lower response—with the possible exception of reduced search effort—has been found. Indeed, the error of estimate for this group is large enough that the very low response estimates could simply reflect stochastic error. Furthermore, in contrast to housing expenditure functions, variance-ratio tests reject the possibility of pooling the sites, even when the combined housing services function includes a site-specific intercept. The hypothesis of homogeneity across sites of the demand for housing services was rejected for all mover households and for the mover subsamples stratified by race.

CONCLUSION

The housing services response of Percent of Rent households to the price discount offered to them was smaller than the expenditures re-

Table 3-5
Search Effort for Last Move

Household group	Mean search time (days)		Mean number of units seen		Mean number of calls made		Sample sizes	
	Percent of Rent households	Control households	Percent of Rent households	Control households	Percent of Rent households	Control households	Percent of Rent households	Control households
Pittsburgh								
All movers	97	119	6.6	7.8	13.2	16.0	143	102
Nonminority movers	97	117	6.6	7.3	13.5	16.4	118	82
Black movers	98	129	6.5	9.8	12.1	14.3	25	20
Phoenix								
All movers	34	46	6.3	6.2	10.2	8.1	162	140
Nonminority movers	31	37	7.1	7.6	12.6	10.4	108	90
All minority movers	40	62	4.8	3.7	5.5	4.0	54	50
Hispanic movers	28	76[a]	4.4	4.5	6.0[b]	5.4	40	31

[a] t-test comparing means of Percent of Rent and Control Hispanic households significant at the 0.05 level (one-tail test), t = 1.81.

[b] t-test comparing means of white and Hispanic Percent of Rent households significant at the the 0.05 level (one-tail test), t = 1.74.

63

sponse. This was true not only for all movers but also for most demographic groups as well. Even allowing for the fact that hedonic indices may
not fully reflect all real changes in the amount of housing services, it still
appears that about one-fifth of the increased housing expenditure by nonminority Percent of Rent households in Pittsburgh went for increased
spending above levels usually needed to purchase the level of housing
services that they actually obtained. The comparable figure in Phoenix is
one-half. This finding prompted further investigation into the nature of the
hedonic index.

There is evidence that some quality components were omitted from the
Pittsburgh hedonic index. As a result, there is only weak evidence for
shopping inefficiency for that site. In Phoenix, however, there was little
evidence of omitted quality, implying that Percent of Rent households
shopped inefficiently there and received less housing services per dollar
than Control households. This shopping effect was much the same for all
demographic groups except possibly single-person and single-headed
households.

In addition, it appears that single-headed households and minorities
had little real change in housing in response to the Percent of Rent offers.
This was especially marked for Hispanic households in Phoenix. They
also appear to have had little or no change in expenditures. These low
response levels may, however, reflect measurement imprecision due to
the relatively small sample sizes rather than a genuine difference in behavior.

Chapter 4 _____

The Effect of Minimum Standards Housing Allowances on Housing Consumption

The analyses of the preceding chapters found that low-income families have low price and income elasticities of housing demand. These findings imply that an income support program that simply increases families' incomes while imposing no housing requirements is likely to induce only very modest increases in housing consumption and expenditures. However, the Housing Gap form of housing allowances was paid only to households that met particular housing requirements. Consequently, the response to such allowances may well be larger than to an otherwise similar cash transfer program. The following three chapters analyze the effect of Housing Gap housing allowances on the housing expenditures and services of recipients.

It is the housing requirements used in the Demand Experiment that distinguish the Housing Gap allowance plans from general income support schemes and tie the allowance payment to housing. Household income and composition determined who was eligible to enroll in the program, but only enrolled households that met the housing requirements could receive allowance payments. The housing requirements thus played a central role in influencing household responses to the allowance program.

The effect of a housing allowance on the housing consumption of recipients, at least in theory, would be different from the effect of an unconstrained income transfer. Therefore, the housing consumption effect of constrained housing allowances should be evaluated not only relative to what housing consumption would have been without the allowances, but also relative to what housing consumption would have been if the allowances were unconstrained.

MEETING A PHYSICAL HOUSING
REQUIREMENT

One criterion for evaluating the effectiveness of housing allowances is the induced reduction in the incidence of substandard housing and over-crowding, or, conversely, the increased incidence of meeting some physical housing standard, such as the experiment's Minimum Standards requirement.

Figure 4-1 is a representation of the actual behavior of households enrolled in the Minimum Standards plans and of Control households over the course of the experiment in terms of meeting the Minimum Standards requirement. In both sites, almost 80% of the households remaining active in the experiment for the full 2 years lived in housing that did not meet the Minimum Standards at enrollment (78% in Pittsburgh and 80% in Phoenix). Nearly all households that met the Minimum Standards requirements in their enrollment units continued to do so over the course of the experiment.

One indicator of program impact is the percentage of households that did not meet the Minimum Standards at enrollment but met them after 2 years in the program. Figure 4-1 shows that of such Minimum Standards households, 32% in Pittsburgh and 49% in Phoenix improved their housing over the 2 years to meet the requirements. Not all of the increase in the number of households who met the housing requirements may be attributed to the incentive provided by the allowance offer, however. Examination of Control households' experiences in meeting the Minimum Standards indicates that meeting the requirements is a normal phenomenon that would occur even without a program, although with different intensity. (It should be emphasized, however, that Control households were not told about the housing requirements, were not required to meet any, and were probably not even aware of their existence.) Data on Control households give information on how the housing of nonrecipients changed during the experiment in response to such nonexperimental factors as inflation, other changes in local economic conditions, and normal changes in household circumstances.

The change in the probability of meeting the Minimum Standards at 2 years for a household not meeting them at enrollment was estimated using a logit function which expressed the probability of meeting the standards as a function of household characteristics and program variables. This function was used to compute the probability of meeting the Minimum Standards for both a Control and an Experimental household (using the same mean household characteristics). Because Experimental households may have left the program differentially more often than Control house-

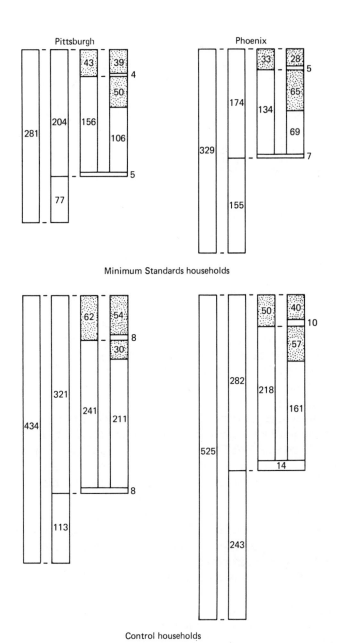

Figure 4-1. **Participation of Minimum Standards and Control households.**

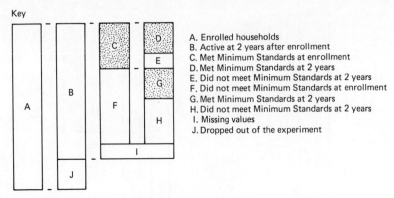

Figure 4-1. (continued)

holds, a second sample was used to estimate an alternative probability function. The latter sample included not only the households remaining in the program for the full 2 years but also households that voluntarily dropped out. Since there is no observational data on their housing at 2 years, it is assumed that they would have continued not meeting the requirement. Consequently, this second sample gives a lower bound estimate of the experimental effect on the probability of meeting Minimum Standards, since this assumption is clearly too conservative given the actual experience of Control households.

The comparisons of the probabilities for a typical household suggest that the program had a sizeable effect on the probability of meeting the Minimum Standards (see Table 4-1). The probability of meeting the requirements for an active Minimum Standards household was 20 percentage points higher in Pittsburgh and 28 percentage points higher in Phoenix than the probability for a comparable Control household. The probabilities based on the expanded sample also indicate that Minimum Standards households have a larger probability of meeting requirements, although the size of the effect is reduced when the extreme assumption about the behavior of dropouts is made.

The experience of households in the Unconstrained plan illustrates the effect of the allowance income alone, without the imposition of housing requirements. Examination of Table 4-1 indicates that the estimated probability of meeting Minimum Standards for the Unconstrained households was essentially the same as that of Control households in Pittsburgh but somewhat higher than that of Control households in Phoenix, although this difference was not statistically significant. In any case, the probability of meeting Minimum Standards for Unconstrained households was lower

Table 4-1

Probability of Initially Nonparticipating Households Meeting the Minimum Standards Requirements Following Enrollment

Treatment type	Pittsburgh	Phoenix
Control households	0.096	0.241
Unconstrained households	0.106[b]	0.325[b]
Minimum Standards households		
Computed using active sample only	0.298[c]	0.523[c]
Computed using active sample plus voluntary dropouts (lower bound estimate)[a]	0.229[c]	0.370[c]

Note: These probabilities are evaluated at the means of the independent variables.

[a] This is a special sample that includes Minimum Standards households that dropped out of the program for voluntary reasons. It is assumed that these households maintained their enrollment housing requirement status.

[b] Logit coefficient indicates probability not significantly different from that of Control households at the 0.10 level.

[c] Logit coefficient indicates probability significantly different from that of Control households at the 0.01 level.

than even the lower bound estimate for the effect on Minimum Standards households.

The Minimum Standards measure is one possible gauge of housing quality, but it is a flawed one at best. Because the measure simply classifies housing into two discrete categories—standard and substandard—it makes no distinction between a dilapidated or deteriorating unit and one barely failing the standard, or between a unit just passing the standard and one of high quality. In an attempt to resolve this problem, Budding (1980) created another measure of housing adequacy for units in the Demand Experiment. His method, mentioned in Chapter 1, also derived from the individual housing evaluations performed for each dwelling unit, classified units into one of three categories:

1. If there was clear evidence that a dwelling unit contained one or more serious housing deficiencies, the unit was classified as clearly "inadequate."

2. If the unit passed every one of the indicators intended to measure serious housing deficiencies and received an overall evaluator rating consistent with such a classification, the unit was classified as at least minimally "adequate."
3. If the unit was neither clearly inadequate nor adequate, the unit was classified as "ambiguous" or "questionable."

Budding's measure was designed to reflect general housing policy concerns. It was intended to be used to classify units as inadequate if they have one or more serious deficiencies. An ambiguous category accounts for cases where either the exact nature or the importance of the deficiency is not clear. The dichotomies "adequate/not adequate" and "inadequate/not inadequate" thus provide a range of possible program standards. Because of the ambiguous category, Budding's measure will tend to understate to some degree both the number of households in inadequate housing and the number of households in adequate housing. (It should be noted that the adequacy and the Minimum Standards measures are quite similar. Only a few items used in the adequacy measure were not included in some way in the Minimum Standards measure.)

Table 4-2 presents the induced change in the probabilities of occupying an adequate and an inadequate unit at 2 years after enrollment. These probabilities were based on logit function estimates similar to those used to construct Table 4-1 and were evaluated at the mean of the independent variables. Of all households meeting the Minimum Standards at enrollment, the probability that a Minimum Standards household was living in adequate or in inadequate housing 2 years after enrollment was no different from the probability for a typical Control household. On the other hand, Phoenix Minimum Standards households that did not meet requirements at enrollment were significantly more likely than similar Control households to be living in adequate housing at 2 years and were significantly less likely than similar Control households to be living in inadequate housing. No difference was found for these households in Pittsburgh.

Part of this effect was due simply to the allowance payment— Unconstrained households in Phoenix were significantly less likely than Control households to be living in inadequate housing at 2 years, as well, and were somewhat more likely than Control households in both sites to be living in adequate housing. Overall, the estimated effects for Unconstrained households appear to be about the same as the effects for Minimum Standards households who did not meet requirements at enrollment in both sites and for both categories of housing adequacy. This finding suggests that the effect of Minimum Standards requirements was very specific. In comparison with Unconstrained households, imposing Mini-

Table 4-2

Change in the Probability of Living in Adequate Housing

Household Group	Change in probability of living in:	
	Minimally adequate housing	Clearly inadequate housing
	Pittsburgh	
All Minimum Standards households	+ 4	- 2
Did not meet Minimum Standards at enrollment	+ 6	0
Met Minimum Standards at enrollment	+ 1	-13
All Unconstrained households	+ 8	- 3
	Phoenix	
All Minimum Standards households	+11**	-14***
Did not meet Minimum Standards at enrollment	+13**	-18***
Met Minimum Standards at enrollment	- 2	- 1
All Unconstrained households	+10	-22***

Note: The changes are measured as deviations from the probability for Control households, evaluated at the mean of the independent variables. Significance is of the logit coefficient contrast with similar Control households.

**   t-statistic significant at the 0.05 level.

*** t-statistic significant at the 0.01 level.

mum Standards requirements increased substantially only the probability of meeting those explicitly imposed requirements; there was no significant difference even for the closely related alternatives defined by Budding's categories.

Categorical measures such as Minimum Standards and adequacy are but one aspect of housing consumption. The next section develops a model for looking at continuous measures of housing consumption (housing expenditures and housing services).

A MODEL OF HOUSEHOLD BEHAVIOR

Household response to a constrained housing allowance offer can be analyzed using the same microeconomic model of consumer behavior used in Chapter 2. In such a model, the conditional nature of the offer will have a profound effect on household response. This can be seen as follows. Assume, as in Chapter 2, that households normally consume the quantity of housing services H and nonhousing goods Z that maximizes household utility $U(H, Z)$, subject to the budget constraint

$$Y = p_H H + p_Z Z \tag{1}$$

where Y is household income, p_H is the price of housing (thus $p_H H$ is rent); and p_Z is the price of nonhousing goods.

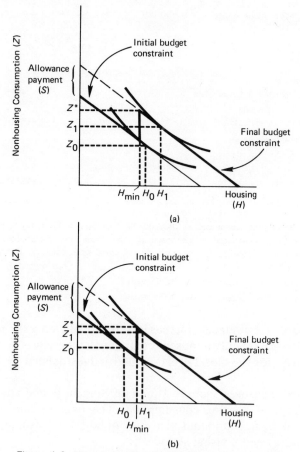

Figure 4-2. **Allocation of the allowance payment to housing.**

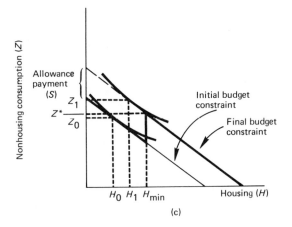

Key: H_{min} = minimum housing requirement
 H_0 = initial housing consumption
 H_1 = hypothetical post-subsidy housing consumption
 Z^* = consumption of nonhousing goods and services
 associated with consumption of H_{min}
 Z_0 = initial consumption of nonhousing goods and services
 Z_1 = hypothetical consumption of nonhousing goods and
 services associated with consumption of H_1

Figure 4-2. (continued)

Figure 4-2 represents this diagrammatically with a hypothetical preenrollment household choosing to consume H_0 quantity of housing and Z_0 quantity of nonhousing goods. Receipt of an unconstrained allowance payment (S) would move the budget line outward, inducing the household to increase consumption of both housing and nonhousing goods to H_1 and Z_1, respectively. However, a Housing Gap housing allowance is received only if the household's housing consumption is greater than some minimum level, represented as H_{min}, which is the quantity of housing services implied by the minimum housing standards.

The response to the allowance offer depends on the relationship among H_{min}, H_0, and H_1. Three cases are illustrated. In Figure 4-2(a), initial housing consumption exceeds H_{min}, and the household automatically receives the allowance payment. These households can treat the payment simply as additional income. The change is indicated as the move from H_0 to H_1. If the income elasticity of demand is low, the change in housing consumption (the difference between H_1 and H_0) will be small. For example, using the income elasticity estimate of 0.36 (from Chapter 2), a housing allowance that increases income by 30% will induce only about a 10% increase in housing consumption.

Figure 4-2(b) illustrates a second case. This household would normally consume an amount of housing of less than H_{min} and would not normally meet the housing requirement. If it were to receive the allowance payment, however, the income-induced increase in housing would be sufficient for the household to meet the requirement. Such households, like those in the previous case, are in effect unconstrained by the requirement and are also free to treat the payment just as they would additional income. As in the previous case, the housing allowance will induce only a modest increase in housing consumption.

The final case is illustrated by Figure 4-2(c). A household whose housing consumption would be less than H_{min} even with receipt of an unconstrained allowance payment is constrained to allocate more of the allowance payment to housing than it normally would. Because it is required to make a nonoptimal allocation, its benefits from the program are lower than the overall benefits it could have under an unconstrained allowance offer. [Note that the indifference curve that passes through the point (Z^*, H_{min}) is lower than the indifference curve that passes through the point (Z_1, H_1)]. Nevertheless, as long as the household's utility with the allowance payment and the nonoptimal consumption of housing is larger than the household's utility without the allowance, the household should choose to participate in the program. That is, the household should participate as long as

$$U(H_{min}, Y_0 + S - p_H H_{min}) > U(H_0, Y_0 - p_H H_0). \tag{2}$$

For some households, however, the payment will not be large enough to compensate for the required nonoptimal allocation of their income to housing and nonhousing goods. Such households would not in theory participate in a program that requires them to consume more housing than they desire.[1] The households that do participate will have the largest increase in housing in response to the program when they fall into case (c). (Under case [c], households must increase their expenditures by more than they would in response to the additional income from the allowance alone, and hence by more than they would if they were effectively unconstrained, as in cases [a] and [b].)

For an individual household, the change in housing thus depends on the size of the allowance payment and the relationship between their enrollment housing and the housing requirements level. The average change for a group of households will also be affected by the proportions of participating households that fall into cases (a), (b), and (c). Two factors in particular complicate this model. First, H_{min} is not well defined for the

---

[1] See Kennedy and MacMillan (1980) for further analysis of the participation decision.

Minimum Standards requirement. This requirement merely requires that the household's dwelling unit have certain specified features that reflect health, safety and space requirements. While units that meet the Minimum Standards requirement do, on average, rent for more than those which do not, it is possible for a household to meet the Minimum Standards requirement while reducing its housing expenditures.

In summary, the experimental program did not require households that already met the housing requirements at enrollment to alter their housing in any way. In particular, they were not required to spend any part of their allowance payment on improvements to their housing. As long as they continued to meet the requirements, they could treat that allowance payment like any other income.[2] Although the housing requirements did not force households that already met them to consume more housing, the requirements still acted as a lower bound. Households could not reduce their housing below required levels without losing their allowance payments. Thus, even for households that already met the requirements at enrollment, the requirements may have kept average housing expenditures above normal levels by discouraging some households from reducing their expenditures.

It seems reasonable to suppose, therefore, that households that met the requirements at enrollment would divide the housing allowance between housing and nonhousing expenditures in much the same way they would divide any other additional income. The analysis in Chapter 2 on the way low-income households allocate additional income to housing expenditures suggests that in this case only a small proportion of the housing allowance would be used to increase housing consumption.

Households that did not meet the requirements at enrollment faced a very different situation. These households could receive the allowance payment only after they modified their housing to meet the housing requirements. The program did not dictate how households should modify their housing—they could arrange with their landlords to fix their enrollment units; they could fix their enrollment units themselves; or they could move to another unit that passed the housing requirements. Households choosing to move or upgrade their units to meet the requirements would generally be expected to spend a larger part of their allowance payment on increased housing expenditures than households that already met the housing requirements at enrollment.

___

[2] Actually, program rules permitted allowance payments to continue to a recipient non-mover household whose unit no longer passed the housing requirement at an annual inspection. In an established program, payments would be discontinued if a unit no longer met the program standards. If the household moved, however, its new unit had to meet the Minimum Standards in order for the household to continue to receive allowance payments.

ACTUAL CHANGES IN HOUSING CONSUMPTION

The preceding discussion indicated that a household's response to a Housing Gap allowance offer is likely to depend in a critical way on whether they met the Minimum Standards requirement when they enrolled in the program. Households that already met the requirement at enrollment were not required to alter their normal housing consumption pattern and could treat the allowance payment essentially like any other additional income. The allowance payment was on average a 20% increase in the income of Minimum Standards households that met the Minimum Standards requirement in both their enrollment and 2-year units. Using the income elasticity estimated in Chapter 2 for movers of 0.36, this suggests that, when these households move, their housing expenditures would normally increase by about 7% (beyond normal increases such as those due to inflation). To the extent that not all households move, the overall average increase would be smaller. (The behavior of Control households indicates that almost all the households that met Minimum Standards at enrollment would normally have continued to meet them over the 2 years of the experiment, see Figure 4-1.)

The response of households that met the Minimum Standards only after enrollment is more complex because this group includes households that would normally have met the requirements (see Figure 4-2[b]) and households that were induced to meet the requirements (see Figure 4-2[c]). The basic difficulty in estimating the allowance-induced changes in housing consumption for this group is the inability to determine which households belong to which case. The behavior of Control households indicates that at least one-third of the Housing Gap households who only met the standards after enrollment would also have done so normally. Furthermore, an unknown number of other households would have met the requirement if they had been given additional allowance income as an unconstrained transfer.

Therefore, the group of households that met the standards only after enrollment contained both households whose behavior was similar to that of Housing Gap households that already met the requirements at enrollment (responding only to the additional allowance-provided income) and households that were induced by the allowance offer to meet the requirements. The response of those households induced to meet requirements is likely to be larger than that implied by increased income alone, because, simply to meet the requirements, they had to increase their expenditures by more than they normally would have.

The observed changes in housing expenditures between enrollment and

2 years after enrollment for Minimum Standards and Control households are summarized in Table 4-3. The changes in rent for Control households that already met the housing requirements at enrollment and continued to meet them during the experiment suggest that in Pittsburgh, normal increases (that is, those not induced by the experimental program) amounted to 14%, while in Phoenix they amounted to 12%. These changes are not very different from estimated 2-year rates of rent inflation: 15% in Pittsburgh and 10% in Phoenix (see Merrill, 1980, p. 140). The percentage rent increases for Minimum Standards households in the same category were only slightly higher—16% in Pittsburgh and 13% in Phoenix. The tabular comparison thus suggests that the experiment induced households that already met the requirements at enrollment to increase their housing expenditures by only 1–2 percentage points. These rather small increases in expenditures for households who met requirements at enrollment imply that most of their allowance payment was used to increase nonhousing consumption (and thus to reduce the high fraction of income spent on rent by this group).

The experimentally induced change in rent for Minimum Standards households that met the housing requirements only after enrollment cannot be estimated directly from the rent changes for the Control and Experimental households shown in Table 4-3. Using those data directly would underestimate the induced change, since, as discussed earlier, the group of Minimum Standards households that only met the requirements after enrollment consists of two different groups of households—one that would have met the requirements even without a program and one that was induced to meet the requirements by the allowance offer. The normal change for the group can be approximated, however. Average normal rent change for households that would normally have met the requirements may be inferred from the change for Control households that only met requirements after enrollment. Average normal rent changes for households that were induced to meet the requirements may be inferred from the changes for Control households that would normally not have met the requirements (i.e., Control households that did not meet the requirements during the experimental period). Average normal rent changes for Minimum Standards households that met the requirements only after enrollment can then be computed as the weighted average of the changes for the two Control groups (those meeting the standards after enrollment and those never meeting them), using the proportion of households that normally met the requirements and the proportion of households that were induced to meet them as the weights.

Using this approximation method, the computed normal rent changes

Table 4-3

Mean Housing Expenditures for Minimum Standards and Control Households

Household group	Mean housing expenditures		Change in housing expenditures		Sample size
	At enrollment	At Two years	Amount	Percentage[a]	
Pittsburgh					
All households that met Minimum Standards requirements at two years					
Minimum Standards households	$119	$142	$23	24	(87)
Control households	132	154	22	22	(83)
Households that did not meet requirements at enrollment					
Minimum Standards households	114	142	28	31	(49)
Control households	127	155	27	23	(29)
Households that met requirements at enrollment					
Minimum Standards households	125	140	16	16	(38)
Control households	135	154	19	14	(54)
Phoenix					
All households that met Minimum Standards requirements at two years					
Minimum Standards households	135	170	34	35	(91)
Control households	144	168	24	23	(89)
Households that did not meet requirements at enrollment					
Minimum Standards households	128	170	42	44	(64)
Control households	140	173	33	33	(50)
Households that met requirements at enrollment					
Minimum Standards households	150	166	16	13	(27)
Control households	150	163	13	12	(39)

for Minimum Standards households meeting the standards after enrollment are 20% in Pittsburgh and 23% in Phoenix.[3] The implied experimentally induced change in rent above normal expenditures is therefore 9% in
Pittsburgh and 17% in Phoenix.[4] These figures, which are based on
straightforward comparison of means, are fairly close to the more carefully computed estimates to be developed later.

In summary, the data in Table 4-3 suggest that households that already
met the housing requirements at enrollment did in fact behave much as
they would have without the requirements and that therefore the allowance had only a small impact on their housing expenditures. On the other
hand, in both sites, the derived changes above normal for households that
only met the requirements after enrollment show that the change in expenditures was much larger than the change for Control households.
Thus, the responses of the two groups of households do, in fact, appear to
be very different. Indeed, the change for the subset of households induced
to meet housing standards is likely to be much larger than the overall
average for the group of households that met requirements after enrollment.

The simple estimates just discussed neglect many nonexperimental differences between Experimental and Control households. The next section
presents an econometric technique for estimation of program effects that
adjusts for these differences.

ECONOMETRIC ESTIMATION

Methodology

Experimental effects are measured under the assumption that the actual
housing expenditures of Minimum Standards households at 2 years after

---

[3] The formula used for computing the normal rent change is

$$\frac{P_c \, \Delta R_M^c + (P_e - P_c) \, \Delta R_{NM}^c}{P_e} = \left(\frac{P_c}{P_e}\right) \Delta R_M^c + \left(1 - \frac{P_c}{P_e}\right) \Delta R_{NM}^c$$

where P_c is the proportion of Control households that did not meet requirements at enrollment that met them at 2 years, P_e is the proportion of Minimum Standards households that
did not meet requirements at enrollment that met them at 2 years, ΔR_M^c is the percentage rent
change for Control households that met requirements only after enrollment, and ΔR_{NM}^c is the
percentage rent change for Control households that did not meet requirements at enrollment
or at 2 years after enrollment. The proportion (P_c/P_e) is interpreted as the normal probability
of Housing Gap households that did not meet requirements at enrollment meeting them at 2
years after enrollment.

[4] Computed as the ratio of actual expenditures at 2 years, R_A, over enrollment expenditures, R_0, to normal expenditures at 2 years, R_N, over enrollment expenditures, minus one:

$$\frac{(R_A/R_0)}{(R_N/R_0)} - 1.$$

enrollment R_A can be separated into two parts—the normal housing expenditures that would have been made in the absence of the experiment R_N, and an additional amount that is induced by the experiment, R_X. Thus,

$$R_A = R_N + R_X \tag{3}$$

where R_A is actual expenditures 2 years after enrollment; R_N is normal expenditures 2 years after enrollment; and R_X is the experimental effect on expenditures.

The experimental effect can be measured either as the difference between actual and normal expenditures or as their ratio:

$$\frac{R_A}{R_N} = \frac{R_N + R_X}{R_N} = 1 + \frac{R_X}{R_N}. \tag{4}$$

Since log-linear functions proved useful in analyzing housing demand in response to the experimental rent rebates for households enrolled in the Percent of Rent plans (as was shown in Chapter 2), and for convenience, throughout this and the following chapters the experimental effect is measured as a percentage change.

Experimental effects are estimated under the assumption that the ratio of actual to normal housing expenditures is functionally related to experimental variables and a random error, specifically as

$$R_A/R_N = \exp(\mathbf{X}\mathbf{b} + e), \tag{5}$$

or

$$\ln(R_A/R_N) = \ln(R_A) - \ln(R_N) = \mathbf{X}\mathbf{b} + e \tag{6}$$

where $\mathbf{X}$ is a vector of experimental variables; $\mathbf{b}$ is a vector of experimental effects; and e is a random error term. The coefficients $\mathbf{b}$ of Eq. (6) may be interpreted as the median percentage change in rent associated with a change in the relevant variable in $\mathbf{X}$.[5]

The logarithm of a household's normal housing expenditures has been estimated by the procedure described in Appendix III using the sample of Control households.[6] That appendix indicates that there is a possibility that the estimated experimental effect for Housing Gap households may be biased since only recipients were selected for analysis. However, for

---

[5] Since log rent is used, the estimated median percentage change is computed from the actual effect $\hat{b}$ as $\exp(\hat{b}) - 1$ with standard error $\exp(\hat{b}) \times \{[\exp(\hat{s}^2)]^2 - \exp(\hat{s}^2)\}^{1/2}$ where $\hat{s}$ is the estimated standard error of $\hat{b}$ (see, for example, Hastings and Peacock, 1975, p. 84). Friedman and Kennedy (1977, Appendix V), showed that the mean would differ from the median for this sample by *at most* one-half percentage point.

[6] Percent of Rent households were not used in this estimation to preclude the possibility that misspecification of the price effect could lead to misprediction of normal rent.

Minimum Standards households, the estimated selection bias, using either of the methods presented in Appendix III, is statistically insignificant and close to zero.[7] That is, once household characteristics and the initial condition of the household's housing unit are taken into consideration in the prediction of normal rent, a further correction for selection bias appears unnecessary. Therefore, the effects of the Minimum Standards plans were computed as the mean of the difference between actual and predicted log rent.[8]

Overall Results

The estimated effects on the expenditures of Minimum Standards households are presented in Table 4-4. The effect for all recipient households is statistically significant only in Phoenix where the increase in expenditures was 16.2% above normal (the effect in Pittsburgh, 4.3%, is significant only at the 0.15 level). Stratifying the sample according to the enrollment unit's status with respect to the Minimum Standards requirement confirms that while the allowance had little or no effect on households living in units that already met the requirements at enrollment, it did significantly affect households whose units met the Minimum Standards only after enrollment. For the group that met Minimum Standards after enrollment, the median increase in rental expenditures was 7.5% above normal in Pittsburgh and 23.6% above normal in Phoenix; both increases are statistically significant.

There are at least three potential reasons for the large difference in the estimated effects between the two sites: different initial housing conditions in the two sites, differences in the way the payment was used in the two sites, and differences in the size of the allowance payment itself between the sites. The first reason seems to provide at least a partial explanation for the site differences. One measure of the amount that households not meeting requirements at enrollment had to pay to obtain standard units is the difference between the ratio of enrollment rent to C^*, the estimated cost of standard housing. A comparison between the ratio for the households that did not meet the standards at enrollment with the ratio for households that met the standards shows that this difference was much larger in Phoenix than in Pittsburgh. This difference suggests that Phoenix households that did not meet the requirements had to make larger changes in expenditures simply to obtain standard housing than did similar Pittsburgh households.

---

[7] A third method, described in Friedman and Weinberg (1981b) also finds no important selection bias for these households.

[8] The results corrected for selection bias are presented in Appendix III.

Table 4-4
Increase in Housing Expenditures above Normal for Minimum Standards and Unconstrained Households

	Pittsburgh		Phoenix	
Household group	Median percentage change in expenditures	Sample size	Median percentage change in expenditures	Sample size
All Minimum Standards recipients	4.3 (2.7)	(84)	16.2*** (3.9	(90)
Did not meet requirements at enrollment	7.5** (3.9)	(47)	23.6*** (5.4)	(63)
Met requirements at enrollment	1.1 (3.5)	(37)	–0.7 (3.8)	(27)
Unconstrained recipients	2.6 (3.1)	(59)	16.0*** (5.6)	(37)

Note: Standard errors in parentheses.
** t-statistic significant at the 0.05 level.
*** t-statistic significant at the 0.01 level.

Another possible explanation for the difference in behavior between the sites is that the allowance payment was viewed differently at the two sites. This could happen if the administration of the experiment was not exactly identical in the two sites. Alternatively, households' planning horizons in the two sites could have been different. Since program participants knew that the allowance program would last for only 3 years, it is possible that they viewed the allowance income differently from their other, nonexperimental income. The analysis presented in Chapter 2 found that the income elasticity of housing was the same at the two sites. Yet if Pittsburgh recipients viewed the payments in differently from Phoenix recipients, the response to the payment would be different even though the income elasticity was not. Investigation of the way the Unconstrained households viewed allowance income when they made housing consumption choices showed that in Phoenix the allowance income was not viewed differently from nonallowance income while in Pittsburgh allowance income may have been discounted and was thus viewed as worth less than nonallowance income.[9] If the Minimum Standards households at each site treated the allowance income similarly to the way Unconstrained households did, this would, then, at least partially explain the site differences.

A third possible explanation for site differences is related to the fact that the allowance payments were typically much larger in Phoenix than in Pittsburgh. If allowance-induced rent changes were related to the size of the allowance, then the average response in Phoenix would be larger than the response in Pittsburgh. This larger payment may have been enough to induce some households in Phoenix to meet requirements by enabling those that had to spend more on the average to do so. Indeed, as indicated in Table 4-1, the effect of the allowance in inducing households to meet Minimum Standards was larger in Phoenix.

So far, this section has presented the estimated impact on expenditures of a constrained income transfer—a Housing Gap allowance payment conditional on meeting a housing requirement (the Minimum Standards). In contrast, the Unconstrained group received housing allowance payments without having to meet any housing requirements. The procedure used to estimate the impact of the housing allowance on the Unconstrained households was the same as that used to estimate the impact of the housing allowances on the Housing Gap households. These estimates were presented in Table 4-4. Unconstrained households increased their expenditures significantly more than normal only in Phoenix—the increase was 16.0% above normal there and only 2.6% above normal in Pittsburgh. The difference in response between the sites for Unconstrained households mirrors the differences for Minimum Standards households.

Since Unconstrained households receive a Housing Gap form of payment without having to meet any housing requirements, comparison of Housing Gap and Unconstrained responses can reveal the effect of imposing the requirements above and beyond that of the allowance payment. Table 4-5 presents this comparison for the Minimum Standards group (using the Minimum Standards requirement for determination of the hypothetical initial status of Unconstrained households). As was pointed out earlier, Housing Gap households that already met the Minimum Standards requirement at enrollment were essentially unconstrained in their behavior. Thus, they would be expected to show the same expenditure changes as similar Unconstrained households (after controlling for the size of the payments).

In fact, while Pittsburgh households that met requirements at enrollment showed no significant difference in response from Unconstrained

---

[9] See Friedman and Weinberg (1980*b*) for further details.

Table 4-5

Increase in Housing Expenditures for Minimum Standards Households above That for Unconstrained Households

Household group	Pittsburgh	Phoenix
All households	1.5	0.3
	(2.6)	(3.4)
Households that did not meet requirements at enrollment	3.1	6.2
	(5.1)	(7.7)
Households that met require- at enrollment	6.7[a]	-15.2*[a]
	(7.7)	(7.3)

Note: Standard errors in parentheses.

[a] Comparison based on 15 or fewer Unconstrained household observations.

* t-statistic of estimated effect significant at the 0.10 level.

households, those in Phoenix increased their housing expenditures significantly less, although the small sample sizes involved make inference precarious. This result might be explained if households in Phoenix already living in acceptable housing were reluctant to move and thus ended up spending less on housing than they would have with an unconstrained payment. Analysis of residential mobility, however, showed that households that met the requirement had the greatest increase in the probability of moving in Phoenix, followed by Unconstrained households, and then Minimum Standards households that did not meet requirements at enrollment (see MacMillan, 1980, pp. 57, A-111). Thus, it does not appear that, in comparison to a similar unconstrained income transfer, Minimum Standards requirements increased housing expenditures overall. As noted earlier, however, Minimum Standards did induce a significant increase in the proportion of households that met the Minimum Standards requirements, whereas the Unconstrained offer did not. Thus, the lack of any differences in housing expenditure changes may in part reflect the relatively weak link between dwelling unit rent and whether the unit met the Minimum Standards requirements.

Results for Movers

As is evident from the preceding discussion, a household's response to the allowance offer was largely determined by its housing requirement status at enrollment. Households that lived in units that met their housing requirements at enrollment had only normal increases in housing expenditures, while those that met requirements after enrollment had significantly above-normal increases in housing expenditures. The household's mobility status may also play an important role in determining changes in expenditures and services over the experimental period. Households that do not move typically do not make large changes either in their housing expenditures or in the characteristics of their unit. In contrast, movers are the households expected to be most responsive to any allowance payment and often make relatively large changes in their housing consumption. This section presents separate analyses for movers.

The normal behavior of Experimental movers was predicted using an equation derived from the sample of Control movers. By estimating the normal behavior for Housing Gap movers using solely Control movers, it is implicitly assumed that no households were induced to move by the allowance offer. However, MacMillan (1980) found that Housing Gap households that did not meet their requirements at enrollment were more likely to move than otherwise similar Control households. Since the offer did apparently induce some households to move and changes for movers are higher than those for nonmovers, the normal rent and housing services estimated for Housing Gap movers in this manner would be too high and thus the estimated experimental effects would be biased downward.

This analysis is nevertheless useful because it provides a better idea of the potential long-run response of households to an allowance program. MacMillan (1980, p. 26) found that most low-income households (70% in Pittsburgh and 88% in Phoenix) will have moved in a 5-year period. Thus, effects of the experiment due simply to induced moving might only be an acceleration of normal behavior. Consequently, direct comparison of the response of Housing Gap movers with that of Control movers, though an underestimate of short-run response, can be used to approximate the response of all households over a longer period of time.[10]

The estimates of the experimental effect for mover households follow the same pattern as the estimates for all households (see Table 4-6). The response of the movers was larger, even though the estimates may be downward biased. The effects for the movers that only met Minimum Standards after enrollment were 9.9% above normal in Pittsburgh and 27.1% in Phoenix, significant at the 0.10 level in Pittsburgh and at the 0.01 level in Phoenix. Unconstrained movers had above-normal increases in rent of 3.7% in Pittsburgh and 17.9% in Phoenix (the latter significant at the 0.05 level).

---

[10] See Friedman and Weinberg (1981*b*) for estimates that take induced moving into account.

Table 4-6

**Increase in Housing Expenditures above Normal for Minimum Standards
and Unconstrained Movers**

Household group	Pittsburgh		Phoenix	
	Median percentage change in expenditures	Sample size	Median percentage change in expenditures	Sample size
All Minimum Standards recipients	8.1 (5.3)	(31)	19.2*** (5.5)	(54)
Did not meet requirements at enrollment	9.9* (6.1)	(26)	27.1*** (7.3)	(43)
Met requirements at enrollment	[-6.4] (9.4)	(5)	[-4.0] (6.3)	(11)
Unconstrained recipients	3.7 (5.8)	(22)	17.9** (7.8)	(22)

Note: Standard errors in parentheses. Brackets indicate amounts based on 15 or
        fewer observations.
*   t-statistic significant at the 0.10 level.
**   t-statistic significant at the 0.05 level.
*** t-statistic significant at the 0.01 level.

Effects of the Size of the Payment

Thus far, the analysis has been focused on determining whether the housing allowances had any effect on housing expenditures. We now turn to analyze the relationship between the size of the payment and the experimental effect. As described earlier, the experimental effects are estimated under the specification

$$(r_A - r_N) = \mathbf{X}\mathbf{b} + e \tag{7}$$

where r_A is the actual log rent at 2 years after enrollment; r_N is the estimated log normal rent at 2 years; $(r_A - r_N)$ is the induced change in rent; $\mathbf{X}$ is a vector of experimental variables; $\mathbf{b}$ is a vector of experimental effects; and e is an error term. The first step in analyzing the payment effect was to

regress the induced change in expenditures on the amount of the payment
S using the simple specification

$$(r_A - r_N) = A + BS + e. \tag{8}$$

In this specification the parameter B measures the direct payment
effect—a one dollar increase in the payment S will result in a $B\%$ change in
rent. The estimates of B are shown in Table 4-7. None of the Pittsburgh
coefficients were significant, indicating that in that site there was no relationship between the size of the payment and the allowance-induced
change in rent. This may reflect the finding, previously noted, that households in Pittsburgh discounted the allowance payment. In contrast, the
payment had a significant effect in Phoenix. For all recipients, and for
those that met housing standards only after enrollment, a $10 increase in
payment (about 12% of an average payment of $81) resulted in about a 3%
increase in expenditures. For recipients that already met requirements at
enrollment, a $10 increase in payment resulted in about a 2% increase in
expenditures.

A second step in analyzing the payment effect is to utilize the experimental design. Recall that the Housing Gap payment formula was

$$S = aC^* - bY \tag{9}$$

Table 4-7

Estimated Effect of the Size of the Payment on Expenditures[a]

Household group	Pittsburgh	Phoenix
All households	0.0005	0.0032***
	(0.0007)	(0.0006)
Did not meet requirements at enrollment	0.0007	0.0032***
	(0.0012)	(0.0008)
Met requirements at enrollment	0.0003	0.0017*
	(0.0007)	(0.0010)

Note: Standard errors in parentheses.

[a] See Eq. (8).

*   t-statistic significant at the 0.10 level.

*** t-statistic significant at the 0.01 level.

where S is the amount of the allowance payment; aC^* is the basic payment level, where a was set at 1.2, 1.0, or 0.8, and C^* was the estimated cost of modest, existing, standard housing in each site; b is the benefit reduction rate, where b was set at 0.15, 0.25, or 0.35; and Y is household income. Variations in the basic payment level enabled estimation of the effect of a 40% change in the payment. Variations in the benefit reduction rate, b, enabled estimation of the effect of a 20 percentage point change in that rate. The Minimum Standards plans may be shown schematically as follows:

		b value	
C Level	0.15	0.25	0.35
$1.2C^*$		Plan 1	
C^*	Plan 10	Plan 2	Plan 11
$0.8C^*$		Plan 3	

Experimental response to the size of the payment may be due to two sources: variation in the size of the payment due to the experimental variables (the basic payment level and the benefit reduction rate), and variation in the size of the payment due to variations in household size and income. In fact, the two sources may operate in opposite directions. To determine the source of household response, further variables must be specified.

First, to control for variation in payment levels due to variation in income and household size, a reference payment level is defined for each household as the payment it would have received if it were a household in the central plan (with $a = 1.0$ and $b = 0.25$):

$$S_R = C^* - 0.25Y. \tag{10}$$

Therefore, in the specification

$$(r_A - r_N) = A + BS_R + C_1\, BLVL + C_2\, CLVL + e, \tag{11}$$

S_R controls for the effect of variation in payment due to income and household size, while $BLVL$ and $CLVL$ represent the effects of variations in payment parameters, as shown in Table 4-8.

As previously noted, households that already met Minimum Standards at enrollment would be expected to respond to the housing allowance in the same way they would to any additional income that the household expected to receive for 3 years. Thus, since a positive income response was expected, C_1, the coefficient of $BLVL$ in Eq. (11), was expected to be negative (for households with a given income and household size, larger b

Table 4-8

Definition of Experimental Variables Used to Characterize Variations in the Minimum Standards Plans

Variable	Definition	Interpretation of coefficient
S	$aC^* - bY$, where Y is income (actual payment level)	Overall effect of the payment
S_R	$C^* - 0.25Y$, the payment to a household in the central plan (reference payment level)	Effect of payment variations among households due to variations in household size and income
CLVL	1 if a = 1.2 0 if a = 1.0 -1 if a = 0.8	Effect of increasing the basic payment level by 20%
BLVL	1 if b = 0.35 0 if b = 0.25 -1 if b = 0.15	Effect of increasing the contribution rate by 0.1

Key: a = Experimental variation in basic payment level.
b = Experimental variation in contribution rate.
C^* = Estimated cost of standard housing (varied by household size and site).

means a smaller allowance payment), whereas C_2, the coefficient of *CLVL* in Eq. (11), was expected to be positive (for households with a given income and household size, larger *CLVL* means a larger allowance payment).

The expected response to larger allowance payments of households that only met Minimum Standards after enrollment is not simple to determine. As discussed earlier, this group of households includes both households that would normally have met the Minimum Standards after enrollment and those that were induced to meet them by the allowance offer. The former group is expected to respond to the allowance offer in much the same way as households that already met the requirements at enrollment, simply by treating the payment as additional income. Thus, these households would be expected to show a larger response at higher payment levels.

It is not clear what effect higher payments would have on the expenditure change of households that are induced to meet requirements. Higher payments would, however, be expected to induce additional households to meet the Minimum Standards after enrollment (since they would receive larger payments if they did so). Indeed, logit analysis of the probability of meeting Minimum Standards did reveal higher predicted probabilities for higher payment levels. (The logit equation included nonexperimental variables that affected the probability that a household would normally meet the Minimum Standards after enrollment as well as experimental variables that controlled for variations in the payment formula's parameters.) Table 4-9 presents the effect of these parameters on the probability of meeting the Minimum Standards requirement at 2 years for movers and nonmovers. (These probabilities were calculated holding the nonexperimental variables constant at their mean values.) Each effect was in the expected direction—both a higher basic payment level (C level) and a lower contribution rate (b level) led to a larger probability of meeting Minimum Standards for both movers and nonmovers. The effect was largest for movers in Phoenix.

Table 4-10 presents the estimated parameters of Eq. (11). Once again, none of the Pittsburgh coefficients is significant, confirming the result of the simpler specification (Eq. [8]). In Phoenix, S_R, which measured the

Table 4-9

Effects of Payment Parameters on the Probability of Meeting Minimum Standards Requirements after Two Years (Increase in Probability above Normal)

	Pittsburgh			Phoenix		
C level	b value			b value		
	0.15	0.25	0.35	0.15	0.25	0.35
	Stayed in enrollment unit					
$1.2c^*$	—	+0.06	—	—	+0.07	—
c^*	+0.10	+0.05	+0.01	+0.06	+0.04	+0.02
$0.8c^*$	—	+0.03	—	—	+0.02	—
	Moved from enrollment unit					
$1.2c^*$	—	+0.15	—	—	+0.21	—
c^*	+0.22	+0.08	0.00	+0.22	+0.15	+0.08
$0.8c^*$	—	+0.02	—	—	+0.09	—

Table 4-10

Coefficients of Payment Parameters in Equation (11)

Independent variables	Pittsburgh	Phoenix
All Minimum Standards households		
S_R	0.0008 (0.0007)	0.0026*** (0.0006)
CLVL	−0.0421 (0.0424)	0.0191 (0.0472)
BLVL	−0.0183 (0.0374)	−0.0938** (0.0471)
Households that did not meet requirements at enrollment		
S_R	0.0011 (0.0012)	0.0026*** (0.0009)
CLVL	−0.0226 (0.0670)	0.0088 (0.0665)
BLVL	−0.0088 (0.0599)	−0.0870 (0.0634)
Households that met requirements at enrollment		
S_R	0.0003 (0.0008)	0.0016 (0.0007)
CLVL	−0.0651 (0.0451)	−0.0105 (0.0531)
BLVL	−0.0197 (0.0392)	−0.0582 (0.0579)

Note: Standard errors in parentheses. See Table 4-8 for definitions of the independent variables.
** t-statistic significant at the 0.05 level.
*** t-statistic significant at the 0.01 level.

effect of larger payments due to larger household size or smaller income, has a significant coefficient. When household size and income are controlled for, there appears to be the expected negative relationship between the contribution rate and the housing response but not a significant relationship for variations in the basic payment level. It must be admitted that the lack of significance for some of the payment effects may result from the small sample sizes involved—of the five Housing Gap Minimum Standards plans, only one in each site had more than 15 households not meeting requirements at enrollment and none had more than 15 households meeting requirements at enrollment.

The site difference in expenditure response is thus partly explained by the difference in the size of the allowance. Since the size of the payment and the payment parameters were both unrelated to the rent changes in Pittsburgh but were strongly related to response in Phoenix, the larger Phoenix payment contributed to the larger response. Unresolved is the question of why there was so little response to the payment in Pittsburgh.

CONCLUSION

This chapter focused on the effect of housing allowances with a Minimum Standards requirement on the probability of meeting those standards and on housing consumption as measured by housing expenditures. Several major conclusions emerged from the analysis. The housing allowance offers *did* induce households to meet the housing standards more often than households normally would have in the absence of the experiment and more often than they would have under a general income transfer.

Table 4-11

Effect of the Allowance Offer on Measures of Housing Adequacy

Household group	Change in the probability[a] of:		
	Meeting Minimum Standards[b]	Living in minimally adequate housing	Living in clearly inadequate housing
Pittsburgh			
Minimum Standards households	+20***	+14	−2
Unconstrained households	+1	+8	−3
Phoenix			
Minimum Standards households	+28***	+11**	−14***
Unconstrained households	+8	+10	−22***

[a] Measured in percentage points at 2 years after enrollment relative to Control households, at the means of the other independent variables.

[b] For households that did not meet Minimum Standards at enrollment.

** t-statistic of logit coefficient significant at the 0.05 level.

*** t-statistic of logit coefficient significant at the 0.01 level.

Insofar as the experiment's minimum housing standards represent general public policy concerns about housing quality, this result is encouraging. Yet two alternative measures of housing adequacy/closely related to the Minimum Standards failed to indicate significant differences in housing improvement between Minimum Standards and Unconstrained households. This is summarized in Table 4-11. Housing allowances *can* be used to achieve specific housing improvements beyond those associated with a general income transfer, but it appears that any particular housing goals desired by policymakers must be explicitly required of participants.

This conclusion also holds when housing consumption is measured by housing expenditures. The changes in housing expenditures induced by the Minimum Standards plan were similar to those induced by the Unconstrained allowance offers. The changes in housing expenditures of recipients due to the allowance program were estimated to be

Treatment Group	Pittsburgh	Phoenix
Minimum Standards	4.3%	16.2%
Unconstrained	2.6%	16.0%

Chapter 5 extends the analyses of this chapter to the Minimum Rent plans in order to examine the feasibility of substituting an administratively simpler rent requirement for physical standards. Furthermore, since housing expenditures suffer the defect of not measuring exactly the housing quality provided by a dwelling unit, Chapter 6 examines the response of both Minimum Rent and Minimum Standards households with regard to the hedonic index of housing services described in Chapter 3.

Chapter 5

The Effect of Minimum Rent Housing Allowances on Housing Consumption

The Minimum Standards housing requirement discussed in Chapter 4 is the approach most often considered in discussions of housing allowances. However, administration of a program that imposes physical and occupancy requirements requires inspections of the dwelling units of applicant households to check whether they meet a variety of requirements for space, basic facilities, condition of structure and surfaces, light and ventilation, and the like. Such inspections are costly to the government and are likely to impose inconvenience on both tenants and landlords. Based on an assumption that housing quantity and quality increase with a unit's rent, an alternative requirement—setting a minimum rent level—was tested in the Demand Experiment. Such a requirement is easy to administer because rent payments can be verified by rent receipts.

Under the Minimum Rent alternatives that were tested in the experiment, households were required to live in units whose rent levels met or exceeded a certain minimum. Two levels of Minimum Rent were tested—70% and 90% of C^*, where C^* was the estimated cost of modest, existing, housing meeting the Minimum Standards requirement at each site. The two levels were referred to as Minimum Rent Low and Minimum Rent High. Setting the minimum rent level as a proportion of C^* was intended to ensure that recipient households spent enough on housing to enable them to rent modest but close to standard units. The main appeal of a minimum rent requirement is that it might enable participants to choose improvements that they desired. For example, a household might sacrifice number of rooms for location in a preferred neighborhood. Minimum Rent requirements are likely to have disadvantages also. It is possible, for instance, that a recipient household would pay high rents for substandard housing by choice. Furthermore, there is at least the potential for collusion between the landlord and the tenant to falsify rent receipts.

OVERVIEW OF HOUSING CHANGES

Figures 5-1 and 5-2 present the behavior of Minimum Rent and Control households with respect to each Minimum Rent requirement. As would be expected, noticeably more Minimum Rent Low households met their requirement at enrollment (62% in Pittsburgh and 54% in Phoenix) than did

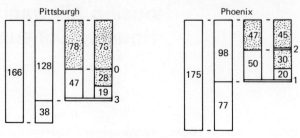

Minimum Rent Low households

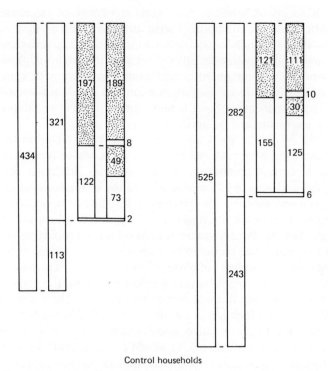

Control households

Figure 5-1. **Participation of Minimum Rent Low and Control households.**

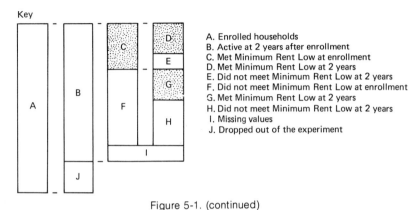

A. Enrolled households
B. Active at 2 years after enrollment
C. Met Minimum Rent Low at enrollment
D. Met Minimum Rent Low at 2 years
E. Did not meet Minimum Rent Low at 2 years
F. Did not meet Minimum Rent Low at enrollment
G. Met Minimum Rent Low at 2 years
H. Did not meet Minimum Rent Low at 2 years
I. Missing values
J. Dropped out of the experiment

Figure 5-1. (continued)

Minimum Rent High households (31% in Pittsburgh and 26% in Phoenix). The percentages of Minimum Rent High households that met their requirements at enrollment in each site were close to the percentage of Minimum Standards households that met the Minimum Standards at enrollment.

When only households that remained in the sample for the full 2-year experimental period are examined, the percentage of Minimum Rent Low households that met their requirements increased over the 2 years by a sizeable amount—from 62 to 85% in Pittsburgh (a change of 23 percentage points) and from 48 to 77% in Phoenix (a change of 29 percentage points). The change in the percentage of Minimum Rent High households that met the requirement was of the same magnitude—from 30 to 52% in Pittsburgh (22 percentage points) and from 20 to 50% in Phoenix (30 percentage points). The changes for Control households were smaller than those for Minimum Rent households, suggesting that some Minimum Rent households were induced to meet the Minimum Rent requirements by the offer of a housing allowance.

As was true for the Minimum Standards plans, nearly all households that met their Minimum Rent requirement at enrollment continued to meet it in their 2-year unit; the rates for Control households were almost as high. Thus, it appears that, as was the case for Minimum Standards, almost all Minimum Rent households that met the Minimum Rent requirement at enrollment would have continued to meet requirements normally, even without the allowance offer.

In contrast, in both sites, only 60% of Minimum Rent Low households that did not meet their requirement at enrollment had met the requirement by the end of 2 years. Comparable figures for Minimum Standards households were 32% in Pittsburgh and 49% in Phoenix, confirming that the

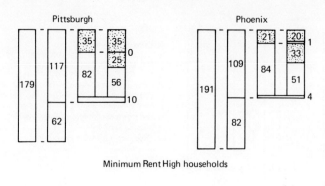

Minimum Rent High households

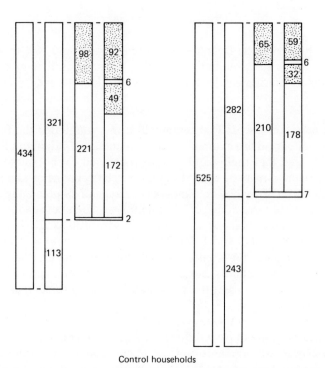

Control households

Figure 5-2. **Participation of Minimum Rent High and Control households.**

Minimum Rent Low requirement was easier to meet. Among Minimum Rent High households that did not meet their requirement in their enrollment units, only 32% in Pittsburgh and 39% in Phoenix met the requirements by the end of 2 years. These rates were below those for the Minimum Rent Low plans but about the same as the Minimum Standards rates.

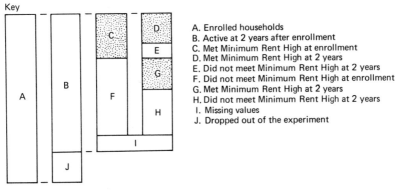

Key

A. Enrolled households
B. Active at 2 years after enrollment
C. Met Minimum Rent High at enrollment
D. Met Minimum Rent High at 2 years
E. Did not meet Minimum Rent High at 2 years
F. Did not meet Minimum Rent High at enrollment
G. Met Minimum Rent High at 2 years
H. Did not meet Minimum Rent High at 2 years
I. Missing values
J. Dropped out of the experiment

Figure 5-2. (continued)

The differences between figures for Experimental and Control households that did not meet Minimum Rent requirements at enrollment indicate that Experimental households were induced by the allowance offer to meet the Minimum Rent requirements. This finding was further confirmed by a logit analysis of households that did not meet their Minimum Rent requirement at enrollment. As shown in Table 5-1, the allowance offer did have a sizeable effect on the probability of meeting the requirements for households not meeting them at enrollment. The probability that a Minimum Rent Low household would meet the requirements after enrollment is 34 percentage points higher than that of a comparable Control household in Pittsburgh and 56 percentage points higher in Phoenix. These impacts are somewhat larger than the comparable changes for Minimum Standards households (20 percentage points in Pittsburgh and 28 percentage points in Phoenix). The probability that a Minimum Rent High household would meet the requirements after enrollment is 10 percentage points greater than that of a comparable Control household in Pittsburgh and 25 percentage points larger in Phoenix.

An important factor in deciding whether a Minimum Rent requirement can serve as an administrative proxy for a Minimum Standards requirement is the degree to which passing the two requirements is related. To receive an allowance payment, a Minimum Standards household had to rent a unit that passed the Minimum Standards. Minimum Rent households were neither required to meet the Minimum Standards, nor were they familiar with them. The fact that Minimum Rent households paid high enough rents to enable them to rent units that passed the Minimum Standards does not necessarily mean that they in fact chose to do so. For these reasons, the relationship between the two requirements is not predetermined. A strong empirical relationship between the two types of re-

Table 5-1
Probability of Meeting Minimum Rent Requirements for Households Who Did Not Meet Them at Enrollment

Household group	Pittsburgh	Phoenix
Requirement: Minimum Rent Low		
Control households	0.341	0.128
Unconstrained households	0.416[b]	0.394[c]
Minimum Rent Low households Computed using active sample only	0.681[d]	0.685[d]
Computed using active sample plus voluntary dropouts (lower bound estimate)[a]	0.560[d]	0.477[d]
Requirement: Minimum Rent High		
Control households	0.176	0.081
Unconstrained households	0.254[b]	0.202[c]
Minimum Rent High households Computed using active sample only	0.280[c]	0.335[d]
Computed using active sample plus voluntary dropouts (lower bound estimate)[a]	0.219[b]	0.211[d]

[a] This is a special sample that includes households that dropped out of the program for voluntary reasons. It is assumed that these households maintained their enrollment housing requirement status.

[b] Logit coefficient indicates probability not significantly different from that of Control households at the 0.10 level.

[c] Logit coefficient indicates probability significantly different from that of Control households at the 0.05 level.

[d] Logit coefficient indicates probability significantly different from that of Control households at the 0.01 level.

quirements must be demonstrated for a Minimum Rent requirement to be considered as a viable policy alternative. It should be remembered, though, that the Minimum Standards are highly specific. Since Minimum Rent households were unaware of the Minimum Standards requirements, they could have improved their housing materially and still failed to meet the Minimum Standards for some relatively minor reasons. Because of this possibility, alternative housing measures were also evaluated.

Figure 5-3, which shows the proportion of households that met the Minimum Standards requirement in the various experimental plans, indicates that neither Minimum Rent requirement serves as a good proxy for Minimum Standards. Furthermore, only about one-third to one-half of the

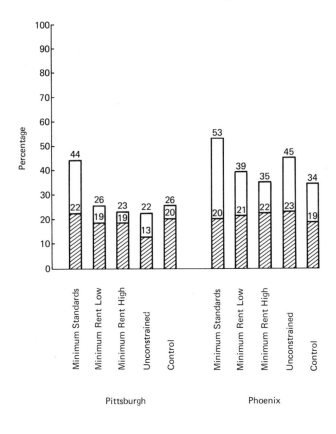

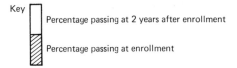

Figure 5-3. **Passing the Minimum Standards.**

households that met Minimum Rent Low or Minimum Rent High in either site passed Minimum Standards. That the Minimum Rent requirements were inadequate in this regard was confirmed by a logit analysis of the probability that Minimum Rent households met the Minimum Standards at 2 years. While the estimated effects of the Minimum Rent offers on the probability of passing Minimum Standards were generally positive, the estimates were always small and never significant. This was true both for households that did and that did not meet the Minimum Rent requirements at enrollment.

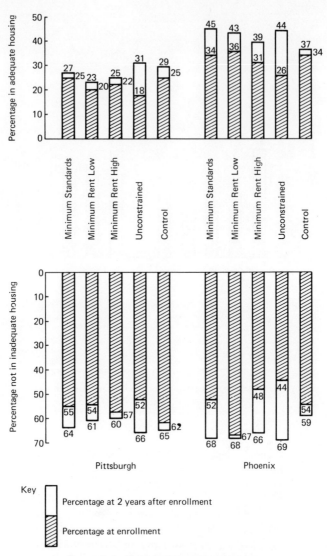

Figure 5-4. **Changes in housing adequacy.**

As was indicated in Chapter 4, the Minimum Standards categorization is somewhat arbitrary because it was designed for a specific program. Therefore, the effect of the Minimum Rent plans on Budding's measure of housing adequacy was also examined. Recall that this measure classifies housing as inadequate, ambiguous, or adequate. The inadequate category is intended to include only units with serious physical deficiencies, which would be unlikely to be acceptable under any reasonable policy standard. On the other hand, the adequate category represents units that seem likely to meet most public policy concerns for housing. Analysis of the impact of a Minimum Rent requirement on the proportion of households that were living in either inadequate or minimally adequate housing therefore can be used to examine the effectiveness of Minimum Rent requirements as proxies for a range of explicit physical standards, one less stringent than the Minimum Standards (not inadequate) and one more stringent (adequate).

Figure 5-4 summarizes the changes in housing adequacy. As for Minimum Standards households, there appears to be little or no effect for most Minimum Rent households. This further bolsters the finding that the Minimum Rent requirements alone do not focus households' housing changes on the particular physical standards usually called for by housing policymakers.

RENT CHANGES INDUCED BY THE MINIMUM RENT PLANS

Tables 5-2 and 5-3 present the changes in housing expenditures for Minimum Rent households that met their Minimum Rent requirements at 2 years after enrollment. Minimum Rent High households that met their requirement only after enrollment did increase their rent by more than similar Control households; however, Minimum Rent Low households that met their requirement only after enrollment did not. Recall, however, that Minimum Rent households that did not meet their requirements at enrollment may have been induced to meet the Minimum Rent requirements by the prospect of the housing allowance payment; so the relevant comparison is with normal rent, the amount they would have spent in the absence of the allowance offer (as computed in a manner similar to that for Minimum Standards households' normal rent; see Chapter 4).

A sizeable above-normal change in expenditures is indicated for each Minimum Rent group. Minimum Rent Low households meeting their requirement after enrollment had an increase in expenditures of 10% above normal in Pittsburgh and 42% above normal in Phoenix. The increases above normal for Minimum Rent High households meeting their requirement after enrollment were 18% in Pittsburgh and 36% in Phoenix. These increases were both larger than the increases for Minimum Standards households meeting housing standards after enrollment (9% in Pittsburgh and 17% in Phoenix).

The tabular comparisons presented above indicate that the housing allowance offers did induce increased housing expenditures. However,

Table 5-2
Mean Housing Expenditures for Minimum Rent Low and Control Households

Household group	Mean housing expenditures		Change in housing expenditures		Sample size
	At enrollment	At 2 years	Amount	Percentage[a]	
Pittsburgh					
All households that met Minimum Rent Low requirements at 2 years					
Minimum Rent Low households	$115	$138	$23	23	(104)
Control households	125	147	22	21	(228)
Households that did not meet requirements at enrollment					
Minimum Rent Low households	93	129	36	42	(27)
Control households	90	129	39	46	(48)
Households that met requirements at enrollment					
Minimum Rent Low households	123	141	18	16	(77)
Control households	134	152	18	15	(180)
Phoenix					
All households that met Minimum Rent Low requirements at 2 years					
Minimum Rent Low households	133	172	39	40	(69)
Control households	154	182	27	26	(134)
Households that did not meet requirements at enrollment					
Minimum Rent Low households	101	169	67	78	(27)
Control households	103	177	74	84	(28)
Households that met requirements at enrollment					
Minimum Rent Low households	154	174	20	15	(42)
Control households	168	183	15	10	(106)

a Mean of the ratio.

Table 5-3
Mean Housing Expenditures for Minimum Rent High and Control Households

Household group	Mean housing expenditures		Change in housing expenditures		Sample size
	At enrollment	At 2 years	Amount	Percentage[a]	
Pittsburgh					
All households that met Minimum Rent High requirements at 2 years					
Minimum Rent High households	$127	$165	$37	34	(59)
Control households	137	164	27	25	(136)
Households that did not meet requirements at enrollment					
Minimum Rent High households	105	166	67	60	(26)
Control households	106	154	48	50	(47)
Households that met requirements at enrollment					
Minimum Rent High households	145	164	19	13	(33)
Control households	153	169	16	12	(89)
Phoenix					
All households that met Minimum Rent High requirements at 2 years					
Minimum Rent High households	149	208	59	49	(46)
Control households	170	199	29	26	(85)
Households that did not meet requirements at enrollment					
Minimum Rent High households	128	213	84	73	(28)
Control households	132	201	69	66	(28)
Households that met requirements at enrollment					
Minimum Rent High households	183	202	19	11	(18)
Control households	189	199	10	6	(57)

[a] Mean of the ratio.

the comparisons are only suggestive because they lacked adequate adjustment for differences in initial condition, selection bias, and nonexperimental variables. To control for these differences we used the methodology described in Appendix III.

As with the Minimum Standards plans, the effect of the housing allowances on rent changes of recipients was defined as the median percentage change in rent relative to the normal rent level. Unlike the analysis of the effects of Minimum Standards plans on rental expenditures, the analysis of the effects of Minimum Rent plans had to utilize the method developed in Appendix III in order to correct for significant selection bias. This was not unexpected; while a Minimum Rent household's recipient status was directly related to the household's actual rent outlay, recipient status in the Minimum Standards plans was only indirectly related to rent (as the previous section indicated, the relationship between rent and the probability of passing the Minimum Standards is rather weak). The estimated effects corrected for selection bias are presented in Table 5-4.

In Pittsburgh, the Minimum Rent Low plans had only a small effect on expenditures. In contrast, in Phoenix these plans induced rather large and significant increases in rental expenditures above normal—the median increase was about 16%. Minimum Rent Low households that met the requirements only after enrollment had a median increase of 42% above normal while the change for similar Pittsburgh households was only 9% above normal (significant only at the 0.10 level).

Minimum Rent High plans had large and significant effects in both sites, with larger effects in Phoenix. In Pittsburgh Minimum Rent High plans clearly had much larger effects than the Minimum Rent Low plans (8% for all households and 16% for households meeting requirements after enrollment) than the Minimum Rent Low plans. In Phoenix, the effects of the two plan types were similar for households that met the requirements only after enrollment (42% above normal for Phoenix Minimum Rent Low households; 43% percent for Minimum Rent High households). Overall, however, the effect of the Minimum Rent High plans was larger in Phoenix than either the Minimum Rent Low or the Minimum Standards plans.

The site difference in response can be partially explained by the same reasons that led to site differences for Minimum Standards households: different initial housing conditions and different payment levels. An average Phoenix Minimum Rent household that met requirements after enrollment had to make larger changes in expenditures than did an average Pittsburgh household. As before, though, this difference in initial position can account for only part of the difference.

The response of Minimum Rent households can also be compared to that of a cash transfer as represented by the Unconstrained plan. Table 5-5

Table 5-4

Median Percentage Increase in Housing Expenditures above Normal for Minimum Rent Households

Household group	Pittsburgh		Phoenix	
	Change	Sample size	Change	Sample size
All Minimum Rent Low recipients	2.8 (2.5)	(101)	15.7*** (4.4)	(68)
Did not meet requirements at enrollment	8.7* (5.1)	(27)	42.0*** (9.3)	(26)
Met requirements at enrollment	2.4 (2.9)	(74)	-1.2 (3.3)	(42)
All Minimum Rent High recipients	8.5** (3.6)	(57)	28.4*** (6.3)	(45)
Did not meet requirements at enrollment	15.8*** (6.4)	(25)	42.6*** (9.7)	(28)
Met requirements at enrollment	4.6 (3.7)	(32)	7.4 (5.0)	(17)

Note: Standard errors in parentheses. Effects are corrected for selection bias using Control households that did not meet the requirements at 2 years after enrollment (see Appendix III for more
details).

*   t-statistic of estimated effect significant at the 0.10 level.
**   t-statistic of estimated effect significant at the 0.05 level.
*** t-statistic of estimated effect significant at the 0.01 level.

presents the comparison between the Unconstrained group and each Minimum Rent group (using the appropriate minimum rent requirement to determine the initial status of the Unconstrained households). Overall, Minimum Rent Low households increased their housing expenditures by about the same percentage as Unconstrained households. Minimum Rent High households in both sites increased their expenditures significantly more than Unconstrained households, although the difference is larger in Phoenix. There is no significant difference in the response of Minimum Rent households that met their requirement at enrollment from that of comparable Unconstrained households.

Minimum Rent households that only met requirements after enrollment would be expected to have to spend more on housing than similar Unconstrained households. While some of these households would probably

Table 5-5

Median Percentage Increase in Housing Expenditures for Minimum Rent Households above That for Unconstrained Households

	Pittsburgh		Phoenix	
Household Group	Minimum Rent Low	Minimum Rent High	Minimum Rent Low	Minimum Rent High
All households	0.1	5.8*	−0.2	10.7**
	(3.9)	(3.5)	(3.8)	(5.4)
Did not meet requirements at enrollment[a]	6.2	10.5	9.6	16.8*
	(7.2)	(7.4)	(10.9)	(10.4)
Met requirements at enrollment[a]	−1.0	6.1	−4.6	9.1[b]
	(4.6)	(5.9)	(5.7)	(8.8)

Note: Standard errors in parentheses.

[a] Comparison uses Unconstrained households that did or did not meet the appropriate Minimum Rent requirements at enrollment. There is no selection bias for households that met requirements at enrollment.

[b] Comparison based on 15 or fewer Unconstrained household observations.

* t-statistic based on estimated contrast significant at the 0.10 level.

** t-statistic based on estimated contrast significant at the 0.05 level.

spend enough to meet the requirements due solely to the income effect of the allowance payment, at least the Minimum Rent High requirements were large enough to induce additional expenditures. The difference between the groups was significant, however, only for Minimum Rent High households in Phoenix, apparently reflecting the relatively small number of Unconstrained households (and accordingly large standard errors of estimate).

An additional comparison is possible—between Minimum Rent and Minimum Standards households. Because of the direct link between additional expenditures and meeting the Minimum Rent requirements, Minimum Rent households that met their requirements after enrollment could be expected to increase their rent more than the Minimum Standards households. This is in general confirmed by the estimates in Table 5-6. Minimum Rent households that met their own requirements after enrollment show larger increases in expenditures than Minimum Standards households that met Minimum Standards requirements after enrollment. The difference is large and significant only in Phoenix. In contrast, there is no significant pattern for households that met requirements at enrollment.

Table 5-6

**Median Percentage Increase in Housing Expenditures for Minimum Rent Households
above That for Minimum Standards Households**

Household group	Pittsburgh		Phoenix	
	Minimum Rent Low	Minimum Rent High	Minimum Rent Low	Minimum Rent High
All households	-1.5	4.1**	-0.4	10.5**
	(3.5)	(3.4)	(3.8)	(5.4)
Did not meet requirements at enrollment	1.1	7.8	14.9	15.4**
	(4.8)	(5.9)	(7.5)	(7.9)
Met requirements at enrollment[a]	-1.3	3.6	-0.5	8.2
	(4.5)	(5.1)	(5.1)	(6.5)

Note: Standard error in parentheses.

[a] No selection bias for this group.

** t-statistic based on estimated contrast significant at the 0.05 level.

RESULTS FOR MOVERS

The separate analysis of Minimum Standards movers in Chapter 4 concluded that their experimentally induced change in housing expenditures followed the same pattern that was estimated for all households. Recall though that the response of the movers was larger than for all households despite the possible downward bias in the estimates of their change. The same downward bias is possible for Minimum Rent movers as well. The expenditures for these households are summarized in Table 5-7.

The effects for Minimum Rent movers that only met requirements after enrollment were significant at the 0.01 level, with one exception: for Minimum Rent Low movers, 5% (not significant) above normal in Pittsburgh but 33% above normal in Phoenix; for Minimum Rent High movers, 22% above normal in Pittsburgh and 36% in Phoenix. As was found for all Minimum Rent households, there were no significant above-normal increases in rent for the movers that already met requirements at enrollment. Unconstrained movers had above-normal increases in rent of 3.7% in Pittsburgh and 17.9% in Phoenix (the latter significant at the 0.05 level) (cf. Table 4-6). Only one experimental group of movers had a significantly larger increase than did similar Unconstrained households—Minimum Rent High households in Pittsburgh (but only at the 0.10 level).

Table 5-7

Median Percentage Increase in Housing Expenditures above Normal for Minimum Rent Movers

Household group	Pittsburgh		Phoenix	
	Change	Sample size	Change	Sample size
Minimum Rent Low movers	5.1	(41)	14.5***	(49)
	(4.6)		(5.5)	
Did not meet requirements at enrollment	[5.4]ᵃ	(15)	33.1***	(23)
	(7.4)		(9.8)	
Met requirements at enrollment	8.7	(26)	-2.8	(26)
	(6.1)		(4.8)	
Minimum Rent High movers	14.0***	(29)	26.4***	(39)
	(5.7)		(7.0)	
Did not meet requirements at enrollment	21.9***	(15)	36.1***	(28)
	(8.2)		(9.7)	
Met requirements at enrollment	[4.9]	(12)	[7.7]	(11)
	(7.3)		(7.1)	

Note: Standard error in parentheses. Effects are corrected for selection bias using Control households that did not meet the requirements at two years after enrollment (see Appendix III for more details). Brackets indicate amounts based on 15 or fewer observations.

ᵃ Correction for selection bias based on 15 or fewer Control observations.

*** t-statistic of estimated effect significant at the 0.01 level.

CONCLUSION

Table 5-8 summarizes the estimated effects of the various Housing Gap allowance plans on housing expenditures. The pattern of expenditure response was similar in the two sites, although response levels were generally higher in Phoenix. Overall, the allowance programs did lead to increased housing expenditures in both sites, although effects for all recipients in Pittsburgh are only significant for Minimum Rent High. The increase was concentrated among household that met their requirements only after enrollment. Effects for these households were substantial and significant in both sites ranging from 8 to 16% in Pittsburgh and from 24 to 43% in Phoenix. On the other hand, households that already met require-

Table 5-8

Summary of Experimental Effects on Expenditures (Percentage Increase above Normal)

Household group	Minimum Standards households	Minimum Rent Low households	Minimum Rent High households	Unconstrained households
		Pittsburgh		
All households	4.3 (2.7)	2.8 (2.5)	8.5** (3.6)	2.6 (3.1)
Did not meet requirements at enrollment	7.5** (3.9)	8.7* (5.1)	15.8*** (6.4)	NA
Met requirements at enrollment	1.1 (3.5)	2.4 (2.9)	4.6 (3.7)	NA
		Phoenix		
All households	16.2*** (3.9)	15.7*** (4.4)	28.4*** (6.3)	16.0*** (5.6)
Did not meet requirements at enrollment	23.6*** (5.4)	42.0*** (9.3)	42.6*** (9.7)	NA
Met requirements at enrollment	-0.7 (3.8)	-1.2 (3.3)	7.4 (5.5)	NA

Note: Standard errors in parentheses. NA means not applicable.

*   t-statistic based on estimated effect significant at the 0.01 level.

**   t-statistic based on estimated effect significant at the 0.05 level.

***   t-statistic based on estimated effect significant at the 0.10 level.

ments at enrollment showed generally modest and always insignificant increases in expenditures above normal levels. (Estimates for these households were, however, consistent with responses to changes in income estimated in Chapter 2.)

As summarized in Table 5-8, the different housing requirements did lead to different responses in terms of housing expenditures. In comparison to Minimum Standards, the Minimum Rent High requirement induced larger expenditure changes for recipients as a whole and for households that met requirements only after enrollment (both are significant only in Phoenix). Indeed, even increases among households that already met requirements at enrollment were larger for Minimum Rent High than for Minimum

Standards, although the difference was not significant. Expenditure effects for Minimum Rent Low households fell between those of Minimum Standards and Minimum Rent High. For all recipients, Minimum Rent Low induced overall increases comparable to (in Phoenix) or below (in Pittsburgh) those of Minimum Standards households. For households that only met requirements after enrollment, increases were similar to those of Minimum Standards households in Pittsburgh and similar to Minimum High Rent households in Phoenix.

On the other hand, the Minimum Standards requirement did lead to increases in the proportion of households that met it and other indicators of housing quality. Minimum Rent requirements did not. Thus, it appears that the response to the housing allowance payment was focused by the requirements on the measure dictated by the requirements (increased housing standards for Minimum Standards households or increased rent for Minimum Rent households).

Differences between the two sites may have been partly due to differences in the initial housing situation of participants. In particular, households in Phoenix that did not meet their requirements at enrollment generally had to increase their housing expenditures by much more than comparable households in Pittsburgh in order to meet requirements. Differences between the sites may have also reflected basic differences in the way in which households regarded the allowance. Expenditure changes by Unconstrained households showed the same pattern as Housing Gap households—markedly higher responses in Phoenix than in Pittsburgh. When the expenditure changes of Housing Gap recipients were compared to those of Unconstrained households, as summarized in Table 5-9, the differences between the sites, although still present, were much smaller.

Only Minimum Rent High plans led to significantly larger increases in housing expenditures for all recipients relative to the Unconstrained plan. Comparisons for households that did and did not meet the various requirements at enrollment were generally insignificant (due mainly to the small number of Unconstrained households). There is some indication that allowance recipients that only met requirements after enrollment tended to show larger differences when compared to Unconstrained households than recipients that already met requirements at enrollment. This is further evidence that the presence of the Minimum Rent requirements focused household response on increased expenditures relative to the response to an Unconstrained payment.

Overall, then, the analysis suggests that housing allowances affected recipients in two ways. First, the payment itself was sufficient to induce some increase in expenditures, as indicated in the response of the Unconstrained households (particularly in Phoenix). Second, the housing re-

Table 5-9

Median Percentage Increase in Housing Expenditures for Housing Gap Households above That for Unconstrained Households

Household group	Minimum Standards households	Minimum Rent Low households	Minimum Rent High households
	Pittsburgh		
All households	1.5	0.1	5.8*
	(2.6)	(3.9)	(3.5)
Did not meet requirements at enrollment	3.1 (5.1)	6.2 (7.2)	10.5 (7.4)
Met requirements at enrollment	6.7 (7.7)	-1.0 (4.6)	6.1 (5.9)
	Phoenix		
All households	0.3	-0.2	10.7**
	(3.4)	(3.8)	(5.4)
Did not meet requirements at enrollment	6.2 (7.7)	9.6 (10.9)	16.8* (10.4)
Met requirements at enrollment	-15.2* (7.3)	-4.6 (5.7)	9.1 (8.8)

* t-statistic based on estimated contrast significant at the 0.10 level.
** t-statistic based on estimated contrast significant at the 0.05 level.

quirements led to additional housing changes which varied according to the specific requirement used. Minimum Standards requirements resulted in additional households meeting the Minimum Standards but caused no increases in housing expenditures or in two housing adequacy measures above those of Unconstrained households. Minimum Rent requirements (when set at high enough levels) led to further increases in expenditures but no change in the proportion of households meeting Minimum Standards. This last finding indicates the undesirability of using minimum rent requirements as administrative proxies for physical housing standards.

Chapter 6

The Effect of Housing Gap Allowances on the Consumption of Housing Services

The previous two chapters analyzed the effect of Housing Gap allowances on housing consumption in terms of changes in the physical housing standards and the housing expenditures of recipients. However, as discussed in Chapter 3, in certain situations changes in housing expenditures may differ from changes in housing services. Therefore, this chapter examines housing consumption in terms of housing services, as measured by the hedonic indices described in Chapter 3. In addition, the chapter examines the effect of the allowance payments on the way households look for rental units, that is, their shopping behavior in the housing market.

Like the rent rebates given to Percent of Rent households, Housing Gap allowance offers could potentially alter households' shopping behavior in a way that would result in recipients paying above market-average rents (overpaying) for their units. If this indeed happened, then in terms of the model developed in Chapter 3, allowance recipients would be expected to have, on average, bad deals (a positive hedonic residual w). That is, they would be getting a less than average amount of housing services per dollar of rent.

In general, there is no particular reason to expect a randomly selected group of households, such as the Control households, to have rented housing that provides below- or above-average amounts of housing services per dollar of housing expenditure. Similarly, households in the Unconstrained plan would be expected to have purchased an average amount of housing services per dollar of expenditure. Unconstrained households were free to treat the allowance income just as they would income from any other source, so there is no reason why their shopping behavior would have been altered.

This reasoning would also apply to changes in housing expenditures by

Housing Gap households that already met their housing requirements at enrollment, since, as the analyses of Chapters 4 and 5 indicated, these households were effectively unconstrained also. Note, however, that the initial housing expenditures of these households may well have resulted from unusual shopping behavior. In particular, households that were paying rents high enough to meet the Minimum Rent requirement may well have included those that were paying more than the market average rent for their housing (in other words, this group may include a disproportionate number of households whose housing may be considered a bad deal). Likewise, households that met Minimum Standards at enrollment may to some extent have been households that had purchased exceptionally good housing as well as being households that spent more, or happened by chance to buy standard housing.

In contrast, the allowance offers *were* likely to have altered the shopping behavior of households that did not meet the housing requirements at enrollment. Consider first a household in a Minimum Rent plan. At enrollment, the household did not spend enough money on rent to pass the requirement. Therefore, to qualify for the allowance payments, it had to find a more expensive unit. This could have led the household to prefer a unit that would normally be considered a bad deal, but which passed the Minimum Rent requirement, over a unit that would be considered a good deal, but which did not pass the requirement.

This can be seen with the aid of Figure 6-1. In this figure, the vertical axis measures housing services (H) and the horizontal axis measures housing expenditures (R). The diagonal line represents the average relationship between housing expenditures and housing services, that is, $R = p_H H$, or $w = 0$. Units to the left of the diagonal would be considered good deals ($w < 0$); units to the right of the diagonal would be considered bad deals ($w > 0$). In the absence of a housing allowance offer, a utility-maximizing household would normally prefer unit A which provides H_A units of housing services and rents for R_A dollars over unit B which provides H_B units of housing services and rents for R_B dollars, because unit A both provides more housing services and leaves more income for other purchases. Thus,

$$U(H_A, Y - R_A) > U(H_B, Y - R_B) \tag{1}$$

where U is the household's utility function, and Y is the household's income.

However, the allowance offers may change this inequality. Since unit B passes the Minimum Rent requirement and unit A does not, it is possible to find an allowance payment, S, high enough such that

$$U(H_A, Y - R_A) < U(H_B, Y + S - R_B). \tag{2}$$

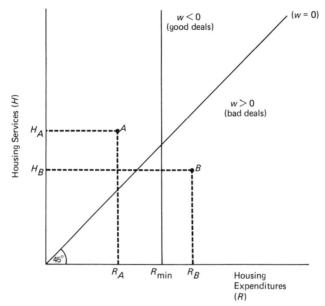

Figure 6-1. **The relationship between housing expenditures and housing services.**

Of course, some units may both meet the Minimum Rent requirement and be good deals. However, finding these units may require additional search effort, during which the household may both spend part of its preallowance income on search costs and get no allowance payment. Thus, under these circumstances, the mean value of the hedonic residual at 2 years after enrollment for recipient households that met the Minimum Rent requirements only after enrollment might easily be positive; their units might be classified as bad deals.

For Minimum Standards households the argument is similar, although for them the incentive to choose overpriced units ($w > 0$) was less direct. These households were looking for units that passed the Minimum Standards, not for more expensive units. However, if in their search for units that passed the Minimum Standards, they found a unit that passed the standards but was overpriced ($w > 0$), they could have chosen to occupy it even if they would normally have continued searching. To the extent that continued search for units that met Minimum Standards required additional effort, it is reasonable that, on average, this group of households could also have positive hedonic residual. For example, if any household has difficulty finding a dwelling unit with attributes it likes, it may overpay simply to avoid further search costs.

There are two serious consequences of overpayment, should it occur.

First is the potential for housing price inflation. If there is a reduced incentive on the part of tenants to hold down the rent levels they are willing to pay, landlords will have more freedom to raise rents. This would have particularly unfortunate consequences on those low-income households not participating in the housing allowance program who would suffer rent inflation without receiving a housing subsidy. The second consequence is the presence of wasted dollars. That is, housing allowance dollars would not purchase as many housing services as they should, leaving the program somewhat inefficient.

ALLOWANCE EFFECTS ON OVERPAYMENT

In this section, the allowance effects on overpayment are analyzed separately for each of the three types of housing requirement. As in Chapter 3, the logarithm of the overpayment, $\hat{w}$, was computed as the difference between the logarithms of the unit's actual and predicted rent (as explained there, the predictions were based on hedonic regressions which predict a unit's average rent based on its characteristics and tenure conditions):

$$\hat{w} = \ln(R) - [\ln(Q) + \ln(Z)]. \tag{3}$$

The median percentage overpayment was therefore computed as $\exp(\hat{w}) - 1$.

The effect of the Minimum Standards requirement on overpayment is shown in Table 6-1, which presents the median percentage overpayment for the Minimum Standards, Control, and Unconstrained households according to their status relative to the Minimum Standards requirements at 2 years after enrollment. Recall that of these three groups, only the Minimum Standards households were told about these standards, and only they were required to meet them. *No* significant overpayment relative to the market average was found in either site for any of the three groups. Nor does it appear that the Minimum Standards allowance offer induced households to overpay for their units—there is no significant difference between overpayment by Minimum Standards and Control households or between that by Minimum Standards and Unconstrained households.

The effects of the Minimum Rent requirements on overpayment are shown in Tables 6-2 and 6-3, which present the median percentage overpayment for Minimum Rent, Control, and Unconstrained households relative to the two Minimum Rent requirements, respectively, at 2 years after enrollment. The tables indicate that significant overpayment did occur in both sites for both Control and Experimental households that met the

Table 6-1
Estimated Overpayment Relative to the Market Average—The Minimum Standards Requirement

Household group	Pittsburgh		Phoenix	
	Percentage overpayment	Sample size	Percentage overpayment	Sample size
All households that met Minimum Standards requirements at two years after enrollment				
Control households	2.8 (1.8)	(81)	-1.7 (2.0)	(87)
Minimum Standards households	0.3 (2.3)	(83)	1.8 (3.0)	(84)
Unconstrained households	[-3.0] (4.9)	(14)	5.4 (6.2)	(17)
Households that did not meet Minimum Standards requirements at enrollment				
Control households	1.5 (0.9)	(29)	-5.7 (6.5)	(49)
Minimum Standards households	0.2 (3.0)	(45)	1.1 (3.5)	(59)
Unconstrained households	[-10.2] (6.9)	(6)	[3.4] (8.3)	(9)
Households that met Minimum Standards requirements at enrollment				
Control households	3.6 (2.3)	(52)	3.7 (4.6)	(38)
Minimum Standards households	0.5 (3.3)	(38)	3.4 (5.3)	(25)
Unconstrained households	[2.8] (7.0)	(8)	[7.8] (9.5)	(8)

Note: Brackets indicate amounts based on 15 or fewer observations. Standard errors in parentheses. Estimated overpayment of Control and Unconstrained households not significantly different from that of Minimum Standards households at the 0.10 level.

Minimum Rent requirements (either Low or High). This effect is to be expected because, as mentioned earlier, these groups by definition included households with above-average housing expenditures and were likely to include households that paid more than market average rent for the housing they obtained.

There was however no significant difference between the Minimum

Table 6-2

Estimated Overpayment Relative to the Market Average—The Minimum Rent Low Requirement

Household group	Pittsburgh		Phoenix	
	Percentage overpayment	Sample size	Percentage overpayment	Sample size
All households that met Minimum Rent Low requiremetns at two years after enrollment				
Control households	4.9*** (0.6)	(214)	7.9*** (1.5)	(125)
Minimum Rent Low households	6.8** (2.3)	(95)	9.0** (3.7)	(84)
Unconstrained households	2.7 (3.2)	(39)	5.5 (5.5)	(23)
Households that did not meet Minimum Rent Low requirements at enrollment				
Control households	-2.1*** (0.3)	(43)	7.5*** (1.5)	(28)
Minimum Rent Low households	3.7 (4.2)	(24)	13.5** (5.9)	(25)
Unconstrained households	[-8.0] (5.7)	(10)	[1.9] (9.7)	(7)
Households that met Minimum Rent Low requirements at enrollment				
Control households	6.8*** (0.8)	(171)	8.0*** (1.5)	(97)
Minimum Rent Low households	7.9*** (2.6)	(71)	6.1 (4.4)	(38)
Unconstrained households	6.7* (3.7)	(29)	7.0 (6.6)	(16)

Note: Brackets indicate amounts based on 15 or fewer observations. Standard errors in
parentheses. Estimated overpayment of Control and Unconstrained households not
significantly different from that of Minimum Rent Low households at the 0.10
level.

* t-statistic of residual significant at the 0.10 level.
** t-statistic of residual significant at the 0.05 level.
*** t-statistic of residual significant at the 0.01 level.

Table 6-3

Estimated Overpayment Relative to the Market Average—The Minimum Rent High Requirement

Household group	Pittsburgh		Phoenix	
	Percentage overpayment	Sample size	Percentage overpayment	Sample size
All Households that met Minimum Rent High requirements at two years after enrollment				
Control households	10.9***a (1.2)	(129)	10.4*** (2.3)	(80)
Minimum Rent High households	17.7*** (3.1)	(58)	14.1*** (4.4)	(44)
Unconstrained households	4.4b (3.2)	(25)	[14.1]* (5.5)	(15)
Households that did not meet Minimum Rent High requirements at enrollment				
Control households	7.6*** (0.8)	(41)	9.1*** (2.0)	(26)
Minimum Rent High households	20.3*** (4.7)	(25)	14.9*** (5.7)	(26)
Unconstrained households	[-1.2]b (5.5)	(12)	[11.9] (9.7)	(8)
Households that met Minimum Rent High requirements at enrollment				
Control households	12.5*** (1.3)	(88)	11.1*** (2.5)	(54)
Minimum Rent High households	15.7*** (3.9)	(33)	13.1* (6.7)	(18)
Unconstrained households	[9.8]* (5.7)	(13)	[16.6] (10.9)	(7)

Note: Brackets indicate amounts based on 15 or fewer observations. Standard errors in parentheses.

a Estimated overpayment significantly different from that of Minimum Rent High households at the 0.05 level.

b Estimated overpayment significantly different from that of Minimum Rent High households at the 0.01 level.

* t-statistic of residual significant at the 0.10 level.

*** t-statistic of residual significant at the 0.01 level.

Rent Low and the Control groups or between Minimum Rent Low and the Unconstrained households. This suggests that the Minimum Rent Low requirements did not induce very substantial overpayment. In contrast, significant effects on overpayment were found for Minimum Rent High households in Pittsburgh. The difference between all Minimum Rent High and all Control households that met the Minimum Rent High requirement at 2 years after enrollment (and between those two groups that only met them after enrollment) was significant at the 0.05 level. Furthermore, Minimum Rent High households overpaid by significantly more than similar Unconstrained households in Pittsburgh. The fact that this did not occur in Phoenix (which had a relatively high vacancy rate during the experiment) suggests that the Minimum Rent High requirements themselves may induce significant overpayment only in a relatively tight housing market, where the vacancy rates are low (as was true of Pittsburgh during the experimental period). Figure 6-2 summarizes the findings.

The demographic differences in the pattern of expenditures and housing services changes in response to rent rebates indicated in Chapter 3 suggest that there may have been demographic differences in overpayment in response to the Housing Gap offers as well. Furthermore, when faced with the need to meet housing requirements, certain groups of households may have found it particularly difficult to shop for housing. For example, minority households may face discrimination; elderly households may find housing searches difficult; and very poor households may not be able to afford extensive searches. Disadvantages of these kinds may result in such households ending up in overpriced units.

Table 6-4 indicates that, relative to similar Control households, poverty households were overpaying significantly more than nonpoverty households in both sites (mainly for units meeting the Minimum Standards). This suggests that poorer households found it difficult to locate housing that met the Minimum Standards without overpaying (relative to nonpoverty households). Poverty households that met the Minimum Rent Low requirement in Pittsburgh were also overpaying relative to nonpoverty households, although this was not true in Phoenix or for the Minimum Rent High households in either site.

Finally, it should be noted that minority households paid significantly more than nonminority households for units that met the Minimum Standards in Pittsburgh but not in Phoenix. Together with the other findings, this suggests that, in a tight housing market, disadvantaged households may find it difficult to locate housing that meets the Minimum Standards requirement without overpaying for those units. From findings presented earlier in the chapter, it does not appear that it was the Minimum Stan-

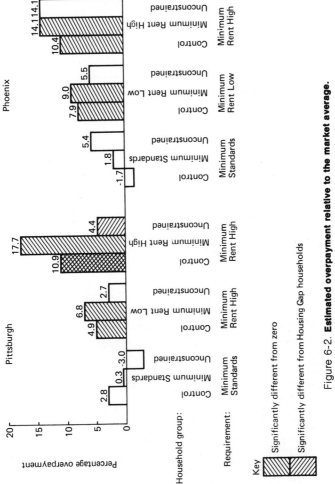

Figure 6-2. **Estimated overpayment relative to the market average.**

123

Table 6-4

Median Percentage Overpayment above That of Similar Control Households by Demographic Characteristics

Household group	Minimum Standards	Minimum Rent Low	Minimum Rent High
	Pittsburgh		
All households	-2.4	1.8	6.1*
	(2.8)	(2.1)	(2.8)
Nonminority	-3.9	2.1	6.2*
	(2.9)	(2.3)	(2.7)
Minority[a]	18.0*c	2.8	5.5
	(9.9)	(6.1)	(11.5)
Nonelderly	-2.3	1.8	6.9**
	(3.4)	(2.4)	(3.2)
Elderly	-2.8	1.4	2.7
	(5.3)	(4.4)	(5.4)
Nonpoverty	-6.0c	-1.7b	7.6**
	(3.6)	(3.0)	(3.3)
Poverty	8.0	6.5**	4.7
	(5.6)	(3.4)	(5.0)
	Phoenix		
All households	3.5	1.1	3.4
	(3.7)	(3.6)	(4.4)
Nonminority	0.3	0.3	4.0
	(4.1)	(4.3)	(5.0)
Minority[a]	4.0	1.8	-2.7
	(9.9)	(6.1)	(11.5)
Nonelderly	0.1	2.7	3.1
	(4.0)	(4.1)	(4.5)
Elderly	13.2	-3.2	3.3
	(8.6)	(7.9)	(13.0)
Nonpoverty	-6.0c	-1.7b	7.6**
	(3.6)	(3.0)	(3.3)
Poverty	31.9***	4.6	3.3
	(10.7)	(8.0)	(12.4)

Note: Standard errors in parentheses.
[a] Minority is black households in Pittsburgh and Hispanic Households in Phoenix.
[b] Overpayment by the two groups of households in this stratification is significantly different at the 0.10 level.
[c] Overpayment by the two groups of households in this stratification is significantly different at the 0.05 level.
[d] Overpayment by the two groups of households in this stratification is significantly different at the 0.01 level.
* Overpayment by Housing Gap households in this group is significantly above that for similar Control households at the 0.10 level.
** Overpayment by Housing Gap households in this group is significantly above that for similar Control households at the 0.05 level.
*** Overpayment by Housing Gap households in this group is significantly above that for similar Control households at the 0.01 level.

dards allowance offer itself that induced these households to overpay, since there was no significant difference between overpayment by Minimum Standards and Control households or between that by Minimum Standards and Unconstrained households.

ALLOWANCE EFFECTS ON THE CONSUMPTION
OF HOUSING SERVICES

The same methodology that was used to determine the experimental impact on the expenditures of Housing Gap households was used to determine the experimental impact on the consumption of housing services as measured by the hedonic index. As discussed in Chapter 3, because of omitted quality measures in Pittsburgh, changes in housing services estimated using the hedonic indices can only be considered lower bounds on the actual changes in real housing. In addition, selection bias was indicated for each group of Housing Gap households. The estimates presented in the following paragraphs for the median increase in housing services above normal have therefore been corrected for this bias by the methods described in Appendix III (used earlier in the analysis of the allowance effects on the expenditures of Minimum Rent households).

The overall effects of the allowance payment on housing services are much the same for the four groups analyzed—Minimum Standards, Minimum Rent Low, Minimum Rent High, and Unconstrained households. As was true for housing expenditures, the overall increase in housing services above normal for households in Pittsburgh was not significant (see Table 6-5). Unlike housing expenditures, there was also no significant effect on housing services even for households that met requirements only after enrollment in Pittsburgh. The estimated changes in housing expenditures for each group of recipients in Pittsburgh were all about 40% higher than the estimated changes in housing services. As suggested in Chapter 3, because there is evidence that the hedonic index in Pittsburgh omitted some quality items, an upward adjustment (of about 50%) is reasonable there. This would make the estimated change in housing services match the change in expenditures for Minimum Standards households almost exactly. The expenditure estimates and the adjusted housing services estimates were then:

Household group	Increase above normal in	
	Expenditures	Adjusted housing services
All Minimum Standards recipients	4.3%	4.6%
Minimum Standards recipients that met requirements after enrollment	7.5	8.4
Minimum Standards recipients that met requirements at enrollment	1.1	1.2

The changes in housing services in Phoenix are significant at at least the 0.05 level both for all households and for households that only met re-

Table 6-5

Increase in Housing Services above Normal (Percentage of Change)

Household group	Minimum Standards Percentage	Sample size	Minimum Rent Low Percentage	Sample size	Minimum Rent High Percentage	Sample size
			Pittsburgh			
All recipients	3.1 (2.5)	(79)	0.0 (2.0)	(85)	0.9 (2.6)	(53)
Did not meet requirements at enrollment	5.6 (4.1)	(43)	-0.9 (4.4)	(20)	3.1 (4.8)	(23)
Met requirements at enrollment	0.8 (2.6)	(36)	0.5 (2.2)	(65)	-0.7 (2.7)	(30)
			Phoenix			
All recipients	10.2*** (3.7)	(71)	11.0*** (3.8)	(55)	18.0*** (4.9)	(41)
Did not meet requirements at enrollment	10.5** (4.7)	(50)	20.2*** (7.2)	(20)	26.0*** (7.3)	(25)
Met requirements at enrollment	8.1* (4.9)	(21)	2.5 (4.0)	(35)	4.2 (5.2)	(16)

*   t-statistic of the estimated effect significant at the 0.10 level.
** t-statistic of the estimated effect significant at the 0.05 level.
*** t-statistic of the estimated effect significant at the 0.01 level.

quirements after enrollment. As with expenditures, these increases were larger than those estimated for Pittsburgh (even after the Pittsburgh estimates are inflated by a factor of 1.5, as suggested earlier). The increases in housing services in Phoenix were, however, much lower than increases in expenditures. This suggests, contrary to Table 6-1, that Phoenix Minimum Standards households did overpay, at least in terms of the changes in expenditures associated with the allowance. This overpayment is concentrated among Phoenix households that did not meet the Minimum Standards requirements at enrollment. Indeed, households that already met requirements at enrollment show a significant (at the 0.10 level) increase in housing services even though they showed no significant increase in expenditures. Why this should be the case is not clear, and the result must be treated with some caution.

Table 6-5 also presents the estimates of housing services changes for Minimum Rent households. Minimum Rent Low households in Pittsburgh showed no significant increase in housing services (recall that they also did not show any significant increase in expenditures). Even Pittsburgh Minimum Rent Low and Minimum Rent High households that only met requirements after enrollment showed no increase in housing services. This is in contrast to significant housing expenditures increases for this group (almost 9% expenditure increase for Minimum Rent Low households, and almost 16% increase for Minimum Rent High households). Thus, it appears that the allowance had little or no effect on the housing services obtained by Minimum Rent households in Pittsburgh. Such additional housing expenditures as there were by households in that site went largely for increased rents without any material change in real housing.

In Phoenix, the median allowance-induced increases in housing services above normal were significant for both Minimum Rent groups (about 11% for households in the Minimum Rent Low plans and about 18% for households in the Minimum Rent High plans). Households that met the housing requirements only after enrollment had the largest increases (20% in Minimum Rent Low plans and 26% in the Minimum Rent High plans), while those that already met requirements at enrollment showed no significant increases. Nevertheless, the change in housing services above normal was still substantially less than the change in expenditures.[1]

Unconstrained households had an increase in housing services above normal of 3% in Pittsburgh and 13% in Phoenix, the latter being significant at the 0.01 level.[2] These increases are not significantly different from those of the Housing Gap groups. Unconstrained households did not overpay for their units, and this increase in housing services reflects the change for expenditures: 3% above normal in Pittsburgh and 16% above normal in Phoenix.

CONCLUSION

In summary, the three housing allowance plans with housing requirements had about the same overall effect on the housing services of participants as the Unconstrained payments. In no case is the estimated overall

---

[1] The percentage change in expenditures from Chapter 5 was:

	Pittsburgh	Phoenix
All households		
Minimum Rent Low	2.8	15.7
Minimum Rent High	8.5	28.4
Households that did not meet requirements at enrollment		
Minimum Rent Low	8.7	42.0
Minimum Rent High	15.8	42.6

[2] The percentage increase in housing services above normal for Unconstrained households was 3.4% in Pittsburgh (with a standard error of 2.5 percentage points) and 12.6% in Phoenix (with a standard error of 4.7 percentage points).

increase in housing services significantly different from that found for Unconstrained households. For Minimum Rent High plans in Pittsburgh and for Minimum Standards plans in Phoenix, this partly reflects induced abnormal shopping behavior. Households in these groups increased their expenditures by more than Unconstrained households. However, they were apparently induced by the allowance to shop less carefully that Unconstrained households, so that their overall increase in housing services was effectively the same.

It must be emphasized that both the evidence on overpayment and the changes in housing services depend on the acceptance of the hedonic indices as a reliable measure. As was already noted, there is evidence that the Pittsburgh index tends to understate the value of housing services provided by a unit because of some omitted quality items. Even if the hedonic index does understate the absolute level of housing change, however, there is little reason to believe that the relative magnitude of error between the index for Housing Gap and for Unconstrained households is misstated.

Chapter 7 _____

Policy Implications

Any examination of the information on the housing situation of low-income households clearly reveals a housing problem in the United States. The proportion of poor households whose housing is substandard, overcrowded, or too expensive is large. More than 40 years of local, state, and federal housing programs indicates that the housing problem has been perceived as one that should be ameliorated by public intervention. There is no consensus, however, on the type or mix of programs that should be used or even the level of government that should be providing the programs.

The traditional approach was to try and solve the U.S. housing problem by a variety of construction-oriented programs. The programs varied in detail, but their goal was simple. Supply-oriented programs provided low-income households with newly constructed standard housing at below-market rents. Public subsidy payments were used for both construction and operating costs. These programs had only a limited impact, however, because the programs required large subsidies per program unit. The Congressional Budget Office estimated that in 1980 the cost ranged from $2200 to $2530 per dwelling unit per year (Congressional Budget Office, 1979).

Because the cost per unit was so very high, only a limited number of housing units could be built with the available housing funds each year. Consequently, only a small number of income-eligible households could be helped each year. Indeed, in recent years, less than 10% of income-eligible households were receiving housing assistance by occupying subsidized housing. The remaining, often equally deserving, 90% received nothing. National housing policy has thus created inequities within the low-income population. It has provided large and costly subsidies for relatively few and nothing for the rest.

A related problem is the high cost of construction programs. Mayo *et al.* (1980b) estimated that the total annual program cost (including administration costs) required to provide a minimum standard unit by a new construction program was from 35 to 91% higher than the cost required to rent such a unit in the housing market. This much higher cost associated with new construction programs probably reflects construction, operation, and implementation inefficiencies.

Another problem with the programs is that they restrict the participants' choices of location and tend to create high concentrations of the poor in racially segregated neighborhoods. The problems of such a concentration were graphically illustrated by the colossal failure of the Pruitt-Igoe Public Housing project in St. Louis.[1] Although that project should be considered an atypical extreme, the demolition of the project in 1970 convinced many housing experts that a new approach to solving the housing problem was needed.

The alternative housing program of housing vouchers should be evaluated against this background of inequity, inefficiency, and failure. In addition, the more general question of whether a special housing program is indeed needed has to be answered. If housing deprivation in the U.S. occurs mainly among poor households, advocates of general antipoverty programs such as an unrestricted income maintenance program might suggest that the best way to eliminate housing deprivation is by eliminating poverty itself. The research presented in this book as well as the work of our colleagues provides guideposts in addressing these issues.[2]

CASH TRANSFERS VERSUS HOUSING ASSISTANCE

Basic direct cash assistance to poor families has the advantage of permitting the recipients to spend the money on the goods and services *they* deem most important. Only if the donor (the public) believes that the families in question will not make the "right" choices (according to the donor's values) should it intervene in this process. The motivation for

---

[1] The Pruitt-Igoe project, completed in 1956, consisted of 43 buildings on 57 acres near St. Louis' city center. By 1970, the project was so riddled with crime and vandalism and was so deteriorated as a result of the inability of the St. Louis Housing Authority to keep up proper maintenance and repair that it became impossible to find tenants for the many vacant units in the project. At first, the Housing Authority responded by closing down more than half of the buildings. Eventually the entire project was vacated and demolished (Heilbrun, 1981, p. 369).

[2] Our colleagues' work is summarized in three books—Bradbury and Downs (1981), Friedman and Weinberg (1983), and Struyk and Bendick (1981).

intervention need not be patronizing, however. A poverty household's "incorrect" choices could result from lack of information or even misinformation.

Assuming for the sake of argument that the government just provided additional income to poverty households, what then would their housing response be? Evidence from both our analyses in this book and analysis of DIME—the Denver Income Maintenance Experiment (Ohls and Thomas, 1979)—suggests that the answer to this question is "not very much." That is, if the program merely augments the income of its beneficiaries, as in the case of the Unconstrained households in the Demand Experiment and all experimental households in DIME, relatively little of the additional income is spent on housing. Using the income elasticity estimate reported in Chapter 2 and an income subsidy of the same magnitude as that used in the Demand Experiment (an increase in income of about 20%), one would expect an increase in housing expenditures of only about 5–10% and a similar increase in the consumption of housing services. Averaging the estimated changes in the two Demand Experiment sites, this was indeed the range of actual response for Unconstrained households. (Their experimental response was a 9% increase in housing expenditures and an 8% increase in services.)[3] If, instead of expenditures, specific physical housing standards are the basis of comparison, the answer is similar. Households receiving a general income transfer without housing requirements to meet did *not* achieve any significant physical housing improvements beyond those of similar unsubsidized (Control) households. The low income elasticity of demand for housing by poor renter households implies that they would use the bulk of any cash transfer they might receive for nonhousing expenditures. Thus, while a general income transfer program might mitigate the problem of excessive housing cost (since rental expenditures would increase at a slower rate than income), the problems of substandard and overcrowded housing would be likely to remain.

The alternative to a direct income transfer program to help improve poor families' housing is a program that includes some tie to housing. Two methods of focusing the subsidy on housing were tested in the Demand Experiment—one, Percent of Rent, was tied directly to rent levels; the other, Housing Gap, imposed housing requirements. We have shown in Chapter 2 that the Percent of Rent program is a housing price subsidy program. From a theoretical point of view, a housing price subsidy will always induce greater changes in housing consumption than an equivalent

---

[3] This response is somewhat larger than the 6% change in housing expenditures found by Kaluzny (1979) for Gary Income Maintenance Experiment households. (The finding for Gary is, however, identical to the result found in Pittsburgh, a similar heavy industry-oriented metropolitan area.)

(in dollar terms) income subsidy. With an equivalent income subsidy, the household can purchase the same amounts of housing and other goods as it purchases under the price subsidy. However, under the income subsidy it still faces the original, higher price for housing and so may be expected to buy less housing than under the price subsidy, which offers the incentive of lower housing prices.[4]

For example, for an initial rent-income ratio of 0.30, the payment needed to induce a given housing change under a price discount plan would range from less than one-half (with a 20% rebate) to less than one-third (with a 60% rebate) of the payment needed under an unrestricted income transfer. For a household spending 30% of its monthly income of $500 on rent ($148), a price subsidy of 40% would lead to an $18 increase in rent to $166 and result in a subsidy payment of $66. To induce the same $18 change in rent, an income subsidy would have to be $183. This relative efficiency in converting subsidy payments into housing changes is obtained at the cost of a reduced value of the payment to the recipient. Just as rent rebates are always more efficient than direct income transfers in achieving a given change in rent, an income transfer is theoretically more efficient than rent rebates at making people "better off" (in their own terms). More of the income subsidy is spent on nonhousing

[4] The extent of the difference in housing expenditures under the two types of subsidies depends on the income and price elasticities (b_1 and b_2), the initial rent-income ratio (R_0/Y), and the percentage of rent rebated, a. The relative efficiency of price subsidies (the ratio of the subsidy needed under a price subsidy, S_p, to that needed under an income subsidy, S_Y, for the same change in housing, in translating an allowance payment into a given additional expenditure on housing is, as based on the log-linear formulation,

$$E = \frac{S_p}{S_Y} = a \left(\frac{R_0}{Y}\right) \left[(1-a)^{-b_2[1-(1/b_1)]} - (1-a)^{-b_2}\right]^{-1}. \tag{1}$$

The efficiency is generally larger (for a given initial rent-income ratio), as the price elasticity is larger in absolute value, and is larger as the income elasticity is smaller. The following table presents the efficiency of a price subsidy relative to an income subsidy for various rent-income ratios and price discounts based on a log-linear demand function with a price elasticity of -0.22 and an income elasticity of 0.36, assuming households are initially consuming an amount of housing determined by the demand function using initial prices as can be seen in the table below.

Efficiency of Price and Income Subsidy

Price discount (Percentage rebate)	Initial rent–income ratio		
	0.20	0.30	0.40
20	0.29	0.43	0.57
40	0.24	0.37	0.49
60	0.20	0.29	0.39

goods, a result of allowing households unrestricted consumption opportunities.

While rent rebates induce increased housing expenditures, they do not necessarily reduce the incidence of substandard or overcrowded housing. The proportion of Percent of Rent households in adequate housing did not change materially over the course of the first 2 experimental years. (There was an increase of 3% in Phoenix and a decrease of the same magnitude in Pittsburgh.) Thus, rent rebates are just as ineffective as general cash transfers in reducing the incidence of substandard or overcrowded housing. Our analysis indicated that such a reduction can be achieved only if the payment is conditional on recipients occupying standard housing. A price reduction program with housing requirements was not tested in the Demand Experiment, but the Housing Gap programs that were tested imposed housing requirements and can shed light on the role of the requirements in housing change.

Some allocation of housing allowance payments to nonhousing expenditures may be desirable. Indeed, to the extent that the allowance program's housing requirements adequately reflect public policy objectives with respect to adequate housing, there may be little interest in inducing households that already meet these requirements to spend more on housing. In fact, the response to the allowance offer was concentrated among households that met their housing requirements only after enrollment. Households that already met their housing requirements at enrollment automatically qualified for allowance payments and used only a small portion of the allowance payment for increased housing expenditures and services. Similarly, unconstrained households allocated only an average of 12% of their payments toward increased housing expenditures. In contrast, households that only met their requirements after enrollment increased their housing expenditures and housing services substantially and devoted a much larger portion of the payment to increased expenditure (see Table 7-1).

Households receiving a rent rebate also devoted about one-quarter to one-third of the allowance payment to increased housing expenditures. (While the proportion of a rent rebate allowance payment used for increased housing expenditures tends to increase with the rebate level, the estimated responses to changes in housing prices indicate that even a rebate of 90% of rent would result in increases in housing expenditures amounting to less than half the total payment.)

As a result of the use of much of the payments for non-housing purposes, all plans, including the general income transfer plan, led to sharp reductions in rent burden (the fraction of income spent on rent). At enrollment, recipients in each site were spending well over 30% and often over 40% of

Table 7-1

Percentage of Allowance Payment Used for Increased Expenditures above Normal

Household group	Pittsburgh			Phoenix		
	All	Met requirements at enrollment	Did not meet requirements at enrollment	All	Met requirements at enrollment	Did not meet requirements at enrollment
Minimum Standards households	9	2	14	27	−2	33
Minimum Rent Low households	6	6	15	25	−3	42
Minimum Rent High households	23	14	39	41	15	50
Unconstrained households	6	−	−	19	−	−

their disposable income on rent. At the end of the second year, net median rent burdens of allowance recipients were reduced by approximately 15 percentage points to about 25% of income or less.[5]

The effect of the housing allowance on housing consumption beyond that of a similar general income transfer was closely tied to the housing requirement used. Thus, for example, increases in the probability that a household would meet the minimum dwelling unit standards occurred only when the minimum standards were explicitly required by the allowance offer and not under a similar general income transfer program (or a program of rent rebates). However, in comparison to a general income transfer, even the Minimum Standards allowance plan showed no substantial additional effect on the proportion of households that met two alternative physical standards (see Table 7-2). Nor did the rent rebate plans show any improvement in these measures. In terms of changes in a general index of housing services, the effect of each allowance program on recipients' housing was about the same as that of the Unconstrained plan. These results indicate that housing allowances can be used to achieve specific housing improvements beyond those associated with a general income transfer but that any particular housing goals desired by policymakers must be explicitly required of participants.

The changes in housing expenditures induced by the Housing Gap plans were different from those obtained under a general income transfer

[5] Historically, low-income households that spend more than 25% of their income on housing are often considered to be "housing-deprived" in the sense that their residual income is insufficient for them to buy enough nonhousing goods and services to achieve a modest standard of living. As discussed in Chapter 1, the 25% level is essentially arbitrary.

Table 7-2

Effect of the Allowance Offer on Measures of Housing Adequacy

	Pittsburgh			Phoenix		
	Change in the probability[a] of:			Change in the probability[a] of:		
Household group	Meeting Minimum Standards[b]	Living in minimally adequate housing	Living in clearly inadequate housing	Meeting Minimum Standards[b]	Living in minimally adequate housing	Living in clearly inadequate housing
Minimum Standards households	+20***	+4	-2	+28***	+11**	-14***
Minimum Rent Low households	+4	-2	+1	+4	+5	-12***
Minimum Rent High households	-1	-4	+6	+4	+6	-11***
Unconstrained households	+1	+8	-3	+8	+10	-22***

[a] Measured at 2 years after enrollment in percentage points relative to Control households, at the means of the other independent variables.

[b] For households that did not meet the Minimum Standards at enrollment.

** t-statistic of logit coefficient significant at the 0.05 level.

*** t-statistic of logit coefficient significant at the 0.01 level.

only for allowance programs that imposed specific requirements on rent, and only for households that met their requirements after enrollment. Housing expenditure response for household that met their requirements at enrollment was generally consistent with the estimated relationship between the housing expenditures of low-income households and changes in housing prices and income as estimated using Control and Percent of Rent households (Chapter 2). These estimates indicate only small changes in gross housing expenditures in response to change in price or income (see Table 7-3).

Real changes in the housing of Percent of Rent households were smaller than expenditure changes. It appears that from one-fifth to one-half or more of the expenditure changes induced by the rent rebates represented increasing spending without concomitant increases in housing services obtained.[6] Minimum Standards, Minimum Rent Low, and Unconstrained

[6] Whether this gap is "waste" is open to question. From the point of view of the landlords, it clearly is not—they receive above normal returns on their housing investment, and it is at least conceivable that this could lead to increased housing production for low–income households. From the point of view of the tenant, there may also be attenuating circumstances. For example, there is some evidence that the time spent searching for housing is reduced in the presence of rent rebates with the implication that some of the household's benefits accrue in the form of reduced search effort and cost.

Table 7-3

Median Percentage Increase in Housing Expenditures and Housing Services above Normal by Initial Housing Status

Household group	Pittsburgh		Phoenix	
	Percentage change in expenditures	Percentage change in services	Percentage change in expenditures	Percentage change in services
All households that met requirements at two years after enrollment				
Minimum Standards households	4.3	3.1	16.2***	10.2***
	(2.7)	(2.5)	(3.9)	(3.7)
Minimum Rent Low households	2.8	0.0	15.7***	11.0***
	(2.5)	(2.0)	(4.4)	(3.8)
Minimum Rent High households	8.5**	0.9	28.4***	18.0***
	(3.6)	(2.6)	(6.3)	(4.9)
Households that did not meet requirements at enrollment				
Minimum Standards households	7.5**	5.6	23.6***	10.5***
	(3.9)	(4.1)	(5.4)	(4.7)
Minimum Rent Low households	8.7*	-0.9	42.0***	20.2***
	(5.1)	(4.4)	(9.3)	(7.2)
Minimum Rent High households	15.8**	3.1	42.6***	26.0***
	(6.4)	(4.8)	(9.7)	(7.3)
Households that met requirements at enrollment				
Minimum Standards households	1.1	0.8	-0.7	8.2*
	(3.5)	(2.6)	(3.8)	(4.9)
Minimum Rent Low households	2.4	0.5	-1.2	2.5
	(2.9)	(2.2)	(3.3)	(4.0)
Minimum Rent High households	4.6	-0.7	7.4	4.2
	(3.7)	(2.7)	(5.0)	(5.2)
All Unconstrained households	2.6	3.4	-16.0***	12.6***
	(3.1)	(2.5)	(5.6)	(4.7)

Note: Standard errors in parentheses. Expenditures amounts are changes above median normal expenditures; services amounts are changes above median normal services.
*   t-statistic of estimated effect significant at the 0.10 level.
** t-statistic of estimated effect significant at the 0.05 level.
*** t-statistic of estimated effect significant at the 0.01 level.

households all obtained increases in housing services in roughly the same proportion to their increases in housing expenditures. The Minimum Rent High plans, however, like the Percent of Rent plans, apparently induced households to overpay for their units. Thus, the larger increases in expenditures obtained under a Minimum Rent High requirement were not matched by larger increases in services (see Table 7-4).

The effect of the housing requirements in focusing housing change among households that were in the worst housing at enrollment (as defined by the housing requirements) was apparent in demographic differences in response. Although small sample sizes preclude strong conclusions, participants from demographic groups in the worst housing at enrollment (minority, nonelderly, and poverty households) made larger increases in

Table 7-4

Median Percentage Overpayment at Two Years after Enrollment Relative to the Market Average by Initial Housing Status

Household group	Pittsburgh		Phoenix	
	Control	Housing Gap	Control	Housing Gap
All households that met requirements at two years				
Minimum Standards households	2.8 (1.8)	0.3 (2.3)	-1.7 (2.0)	1.8 (3.0)
Minimum Rent Low households	4.9*** (0.6)	6.8*** (2.3)	7.9*** (1.5)	9.0** (3.7)
Minimum Rent High households	10.9*** (1.2)	17.7***a (3.1)	10.4*** (2.3)	14.1*** (4.4)
Households that did not meet requirements at enrollment				
Minimum Standards households	1.5 (0.9)	0.2 (3.0)	-5.7 (6.5)	1.1 (3.5)
Minimum Rent Low households	-2.1*** (0.3)	3.7 (4.2)	7.5*** (1.5)	13.5** (5.9)
Minimum Rent High households	7.6*** (0.8)	20.3***a (4.7)	9.1*** (2.0)	14.9*** (5.7)
Households that met requirements at enrollment				
Minimum Standards households	3.6 (2.3)	0.5 (3.3)	3.7 (4.6)	3.4 (5.3)
Minimum Rent Low households	6.8*** (0.8)	7.9*** (2.6)	8.0*** (1.5)	6.1 (4.4)
Minimum Rent High households	12.5*** (1.3)	15.7*** (3.9)	11.1*** (2.5)	13.1* (6.7)

Note: Standard errors in parentheses.

a Estimated overpayment significantly different from that of Control households at the 0.05 level.

* t-statistic of residual significant at the 0.10 level.

** t-statistic of residual significant at the 0.05 level.

*** t-statistic of residual significant at the 0.01 level.

their housing expenditures under all three types of Housing Gap allowance plans than nonminority, elderly, and nonpoverty households, respectively. It does appear, though, that minority household ordinarily make smaller changes in housing expenditures in response to changes in the price of housing (or in unrestricted income) than nonminorities.

OTHER HOUSING OUTCOMES

Upgrading

An important way of meeting Minimum Standards requirements and thus qualifying for allowance payments was upgrading of existing dwellings (see Merrill and Joseph, 1980). Almost 36% of the households that met the Minimum Standards after enrollment did so by upgrading their enrollment dwelling unit. Overall, the upgrading process involved only a modest extension of normal maintenance and repair activities. Nevertheless, the housing allowance offer does appear to have induced some additional upgrading of units that were in moderately worse condition than those normally upgraded. This additional upgrading occurred early in the experiment and was generally concentrated in better quality units and usually involved only small changes to the unit, with no above-normal increase in rent.

Substantial and frequent maintenance and repair of the rental housing stock was undertaken by both landlords and tenants. As might be expected, while the mean number of repairs was the same for landlords and tenants, the types of repairs undertaken were different. Tenants more often made fairly easy and lower-cost improvements such as interior painting, wall-papering, repairs to floors, or installation of carpets. Landlords more often made more major repairs—they installed or repaired plumbing, heating, or air conditioning equipment and added landscaping more often than did tenants. The various allowance offers had no apparent effect on the overall level of maintenance and repair activity by either landlords or tenants.

Residential Mobility

A substantial fraction of enrolled households did not move during the 2 years of the experiment and others either already met the requirements at enrollment or were able to meet their requirements with only small changes in their units. Since recipients that did not move showed only small changes in either expenditures or services, the housing change induced by an allowance program might be expected to grow over time. Estimated changes for nonmover households were not significantly above normal, even for those households that met their requirements only after enrollment. The responses of the recipient movers were much larger. At the same time, estimates for recipient movers were not substantially different from the estimates for all recipients, suggesting that the response to a long-term housing allowance program will not be appreciably larger than that observed during the 2 years of the experiment. This in part reflects the fact that the 2-year estimates include the effects of additional moving induced by the experiment (which would disappear as the remaining households move). The lack of any substantial increase in recipients' housing consumption responses over time is further confirmed by comparison of estimated responses for the first and second years of the experiment and by other evidence that indicates there is no apparent effect of experimental duration on response, though this conclusion is open to debate (see Burtless and Greenberg, 1980; see also Appendix V).

Rent Inflation

The possibility that a housing allowance program will cause rent inflation was a major drawback mentioned in preexperimental discussions. Such fear was expressed because it was assumed that the allowances would unleash strong demand for standard housing, and the response of landlords and other housing suppliers was unknown. Our analysis indicates that this fear was unfounded. The allowance program could not release a tidal wave of unsatisfied housing demand for several reasons. First, large changes in housing take place only when households move, and mobility occurs only gradually over time. Second, because of the low income elasticity of housing expenditures, only a small fraction of the allowance payment is used for housing. Finally, because of the fairly stringent housing requirements, participation is not universal.

Results from the Housing Assistance Supply Experiment (HASE) support this conclusion and provide additional information. With an open enrollment program as tested in HASE, the participation rate increased slowly over time and reached a plateau at a rate of slightly over 40% of all income-eligible renters after 4 years of program operation (Rydell *et al.*, 1978). As participation was increasing, the housing market showed remarkable flexibility in its ability to absorb the new demand. Both landlords and tenants were willing to repair small defects in their units in order

to convert them from substandard to standard.[7] Another way by which
the housing market accommodated the added demand for standard housing was by a reduction in the vacancy rate (see Rydell, 1979, for further
details).

EXISTING HOUSING PROGRAMS

An important part of the Demand Experiment analysis was a comparison of the Housing Gap Minimum Standards plan with several existing
federal rental housing programs—Public Housing owned by local housing
authorities, Section 23 leased (existing) housing, and Section 236 housing
with and without Rent Supplements. We will first summarize the results
of this analysis[8] and then draw some implications of this and the analysis
in earlier chapters for the major current federal housing program—Section 8, the successor to Section 23. Finally, we offer an outline of an
alternative proposal for a housing allowance program.

The major differences among the comparison programs studied were
the extent to which they relied on the private market to supply housing
and the extent to which they placed the responsibility for obtaining decent
housing on recipients, as opposed to federal and local governmental agencies. In Public Housing and Section 236, units are newly built or rehabili-
tated, either under direct contract to local Public Housing Agencies (in the
case of Public Housing) or under regulations administered by the Federal
Housing Administration (in the case of Section 236). These units are then
offered to eligible households at rents below costs. The extent of the
subsidy is usually, but not always, conditioned by income and household
size.

The Section 23 leased (existing) housing program and housing allowances, on the other hand, use the existing rental housing stock. Under the
original Section 23 program, acceptable units were generally leased from
private landlords by a local Public Housing Agency (PHA) and in turn
sublet to eligible households at below market rents. Under housing allowances, the responsibility for finding and renting acceptable units in the
private market rested entirely with recipients. Payments were then made
directly to households. The revised Section 23 program (and its successor,

---

[7] The major repairs were installation of a handrail (29% of all improvements, $10 average
cost) and window repairs (25% of all improvements, $9 average cost). These types of im-
provements, while not costly, are clearly important from a health and safety viewpoint.

[8] Descriptions of the comparison programs and their relative benefits and costs are from
Mayo *et al.* (1980*a* and 1980*b*). Our shortened summary, focusing on housing consumption,
cannot do justice to the extensive analyses of other issues presented therein.

the Section 8 Existing Housing program) fall between housing allowances and the original Section 23 program. Under these programs responsibility for finding acceptable units is generally placed with recipients, but the actual leasing of the unit involves all three parties—the landlord, the tenant, and the PHA—with a restriction on the total rent that may be paid.

In both Pittsburgh and Phoenix, housing provided by housing allowances and the comparison programs was, on average, close in rental value to the median rent of all private unsubsidized housing, but the range of housing provided in housing programs was more limited than that of the unsubsidized stock. Section 236 consistently provided housing with the highest average estimated market value. Other programs varied in their rankings between the sites. There was, however, a considerable degree of overlap in the market values of units provided in each program. Housing allowances, in particular, provided units with a wide range of market values which, in each site, almost completely spanned the range of values encompassed by all three comparison programs combined. Housing allowances thus appear to present a wide range of choice relative to that available in the subsidized housing stock.

Housing allowances provided economic benefits to tenants that were generally comparable to those provided by most comparison programs and significantly greater than those provided by Section 236. Public housing and housing allowances provided roughly comparable benefits at each site; followed by Section 23, which provided a lower level; and Section 236, which provided the lowest level. Benefits were higher in Phoenix than in Pittsburgh, a result of generally higher market rental values of units in Phoenix and roughly comparable tenant rents in the two sites.

Participants in subsidized housing programs obtained housing that is only modestly different in rental value than that occupied by similar unsubsidized households. Only Section 236 appears likely to provide similar participants with a consistently greater change in housing than does a housing allowance. The greatest apparent source of economic benefits to tenants provided by both housing allowances and comparison programs (with the single exception of Section 236) was increases in disposable income (reductions in rent) relative to similar unsubsidized households. For housing allowances, Public Housing, and Section 23, from roughly two-thirds to three-fourths of the economic benefits from the programs appeared to be in the form of increased income rather than increased housing. Section 236, which both provides higher market value housing than other programs and charges tenants higher rents, appeared to provide benefits entirely in the form of better housing in Pittsburgh and to provide about 40% of its economic benefits in the form of increased income in Phoenix.

In general, participants in housing allowances and comparison programs occupied housing which passed the Minimum Standards housing requirements at high rates (but less than 100%), well in excess of rates observed for similar unsubsidized households. Furthermore, median rent burdens in housing allowances, Public Housing, Section 23, and Section 236 with rent supplements were all below the most commonly expressed threshold of policy concern, 25%, although some households in each of those programs paid more than 25% of their disposable incomes for rent. In each of these programs, moreover, both median rent burdens and the fraction of households paying more than 25% of income for rent were well below those of similar unsubsidized households. Section 236 without rent supplements, by contrast, had median rent burdens not only above 25% but also above the level of similar unsubsidized households.

Program outcomes relating to the type and market value of housing, the ability to pass standards, and the level and distribution of tenant benefits are subject to varying degrees of influence by program rules and administrative practices. In many cases, it appears that comparative outcomes in these areas could be changed by straightforward program changes which would, nevertheless, leave basic program structures intact. Some differences among programs will remain, particularly with regard to *program costs*. The comparative analysis unequivocally showed that housing allowances can provide decent housing at a fraction of the cost of construction-oriented programs, are capable of serving from two to three times as many households per dollar of subsidy, and can provide more housing value in relation to cost than either owned Public Housing or Section 236. Such comparative outcomes are the result not only of program features of housing allowances and other programs, but also of pervasive economic trends that have affected the relative costs of new construction and rehabilitation vis-à-vis leased existing housing. Thus cost differences are firmly rooted in the institutional structure and the economic environment of the housing programs. As such, they are much less subject to influence and control than are the other comparative outcomes.

The Section 8 Lower Income Housing Assistance Program was begun as the successor program to the Section 23 revised program. Its goal was the same—enabling low-income families to live in decent housing at affordable cost. Two major modifications to the Section 23 program were undertaken. The first was extension of benefits to a slightly higher income class, moderate-income families—those up to approximately 80% of an area's median income (the proportion varying by family size). The second was the addition of two components to the program: the New Construction and the Substantial Rehabilitation programs. In the Section 8 Existing Housing Program, as in Section 23 revised, eligible households are to find acceptable dwelling units in the private market, and then a public housing authority makes payments to the landlords on behalf of those households. Under the New Construction and the Substantial Rehabilitation Programs, HUD guarantees private developers that it will provide subsidies for income-eligible households who apply for rental housing directly to the project's owner.

Some of the findings of our analysis of the Demand Experiment reinforce the findings of a recent evaluation of the Section 8 New Construction and Existing Housing programs (for details, see Wallace et al., 1981). In particular, it seems clear that many of the participants moved from units that did not meet the Section 8 acceptability criteria (which were not very different from the Demand Experiment Minimum Standards) to units that were supposed to meet them. This type of change emphasizes the importance of designing the standards—the evidence from the Demand Experiment shows that Section 8 households will search carefully enough to get the specifics required of them but no more. Furthermore, detailed standards are likely to reduce participation as households find it cumbersome to find units that are acceptable to the program. Indeed, under limited resources, reducing participation to the funded level may be bureaucratically necessary, and the standards could conceivably be manipulated as a rationing device to balance supply and demand. Such an approach, though, would be inequitable, as it is the lowest income households, often in the poorest housing, that tend to drop out first. Furthermore, even if the program's funding level can theoretically be tempered to equalize supply of and demand for acceptable units in each housing market, there is no evidence that the federal government is capable of implementing or is willing to implement such housing market manipulations.

In addition to more care in setting standards requirements, removal of the Fair Market Rent (FMR) ceiling on rents that can be paid for existing housing would likely have beneficial effects on Section 8, as long as the payment computation method (subsidizing rent only up to FMR) does not change. We agree with the arguments advanced by Zais et al. (1979) that such an action would not result in wasteful expenditures by recipients. Minimum Standards households did not overpay for their units under such circumstances (subsidized rents were limited to C^*, the estimated cost of standard housing, but households could rent any standard unit). Furthermore, removing the FMR restriction would be likely to mitigate the unfortunate apparent tendency of landlords to increase their rents up to the FMR ceiling (Drury et al., 1978, p. 71).

Both of these changes—reevaluating the standards and eliminating the FMR ceiling—would help increase the effectiveness of the Section 8 program, though in the end its effectiveness in reducing housing deprivation depends on the level of congressional funding. Each of these changes, coupled with direct payment of the subsidy to the household, would bring the Section 8 Existing Housing Program very close to a Minimum Standards housing allowance program.[9]

There is one major problem in giving unqualified endorsement to a housing allowance program. Even though it appears that a program can be designed that performs the dual purpose of improving recipients' housing and reducing the proportion of income that they spend on housing, these benefits are limited to participants. To the extent that the poor families fail to participate, such a plan would be a failure. It is indeed unfortunate, therefore, that it appears to be those most in need who are the least likely to participate in a housing allowance scheme. Kennedy and MacMillan (1980, p. 53) estimated that the Housing Gap programs tested in the Demand Experiment were able to reach less than one-fourth of the eligible households that would normally live in program-defined substandard housing. Furthermore, "because households in housing that did not meet program requirements were unlikely to participate, participation rates in the Housing Gap programs were significantly lower for those in the worst housing, including the very poor, minorities, and very large households" (Kennedy and MacMillan, 1980, p. S-5). Such households might be better served by supply-oriented programs. For example, the study by Mayo *et al.* (1980a) previously summarized found that minority households participated at a higher rate than nonminority households in some of the supply-oriented housing programs (Public Housing and Section 236). While this greater participation appears to have resulted in part from the peculiar location of this housing (i.e., a tendency to be concentrated in minority areas), it appears that minority households, at least, can be served to a greater extent than nonminority households by such programs.[10]

---

[9] One additional change we advocate is permitting wider locational choice. Currently Section 8 recipients are usually restricted to one jurisdiction, and eliminating this constraint can only improve their welfare and satisfaction, although though there may be opposition to this change at the local level. Zais *et al.* (1979) also advocate extending the program to homeowners and providing subsidy payments directly to households. We agree that these changes are also warranted, particularly if some provision is made to consider home equity in determining eligibility and payment level.

[10] On the other hand, Wallace *et al.* (1981) found that the Section 8 New Construction program reaches a smaller fraction of minority households than are in the eligible population. This may be due to the fact that most new projects were located in suburban, low-minority areas.

SUMMARY

The major findings of our analysis are as follows. First, housing allowances should be preferred over new construction programs—allowances can provide similar housing at roughly one-half to three-fourths the cost, with greater recipient satisfaction and equal or lower levels of racial and economic segregation.[11] Second, the advantages of an allowance program over a similar expansion of cash transfer payments are not as clear cut— housing allowance recipients can achieve substantially greater improvements in housing than those obtained by participants in a similar program of unrestricted cash transfers only when the allowance program imposes stringent housing requirements. However, the additional housing change is focused on the specific requirements imposed and sharply reduces participation by households in substandard housing.

The best housing program may not be one program at all, but rather it may be a combination of programs, each taking a different approach. A program of housing allowances appears to be viable for many of the households that Frieden and Solomon (1977) termed as housing-deprived by reducing substandardness, overcrowding, and excessive housing costs for recipients while providing them with freedom of choice among neighborhoods. For households choosing not to participate in a housing allowance scheme, an alternative supply-oriented program may be worthwhile. It is worth pointing out, though, that such supply-oriented programs appear to be extremely inefficient, with costs greatly outweighing benefits (Mayo et al., 1980b; Weinberg, 1982).

One possible solution to the problem of reduced participation due to enforced housing standards is a program that couples graduated standards with graduated incentives. Investigation of the decision of enrolled Minimum Standards households to participate resulted in two major findings: participation increased as the subsidy level increased and the imposition of the Minimum Standards requirement significantly reduced participation (Kennedy and MacMillan, 1980). Unfortunately, the program design did not include variations in the physical requirements themselves, so that conjectures about the impact of alternate standards must remain speculative. Nevertheless, it seems clear that less stringent physical standards are easier to meet and would result in a higher participation rate than the standards required in the Demand Experiment.

It is clear from the analysis of alternate housing standards in Chapter 4 that specific housing requirements should be imposed *only* if the policymakers have very strong preferences about the particular require-

---

[11] See Mayo et al. (1980a) for a comparative discussion of geographic impacts.

ments, because housing allowance recipients apparently try to obtain
housing that satisfies just those requirements while otherwise obtaining a
normal level of "quality" per dollar of expenditure. Once a basic level of
standards is established as an irreducible minimum level of dwelling unit
quality the government is willing to subsidize, a corresponding basic level
of payment can be established which trades off increased participation
against increased program cost. A second, higher level of standards could
then be established that includes additional requirements by associating
this higher level of requirements with a higher housing allowance payment.

_____

Design of the Demand Experiment

This appendix presents a brief overview of the Demand Experiment's data collection procedures, experimental design, and sample allocation.

DATA COLLECTION

The Demand Experiment was conducted in two Standard Metropolitan Statistical Areas (SMSAs)—Allegheny County, Pennsylvania (Pittsburgh), and Maricopa County, Arizona (Phoenix). HUD selected these two sites from among large SMSAs on the basis of their growth rates, rental vacancy rates, degree of racial concentration, and level of housing costs. Pittsburgh and Phoenix were chosen to provide a contrast between an older, more slowly growing eastern metropolitan area and a newer, relatively rapidly growing western metropolitan area. In addition, Pittsburgh has a substantial black and Phoenix a substantial Hispanic minority population.

Information on participating households was collected using several methods:

1. *Baseline Interviews,* conducted before households were offered enrollment;
2. *Initial Household Report Forms* and monthly *Household Report Forms* (which provided data on household size and income and on housing expenditures), completed by participating households during and after enrollment, respectively;
3. *Supplements* to the Household Report Forms (which provided data on assets, income from assets, actual taxes paid, income from self-

employment, and extraordinary medical expenses), completed annually by participating households;

4. Payments and status data on each household;
5. *Housing Evaluation Forms* (which provided information on housing quality), completed by evaluators at least once each year for every dwelling unit occupied by participants;
6. *Periodic Interviews,* conducted approximately 6, 12, and 24 months after enrollment; and
7. *Exit Interviews,* conducted for a sample of households who declined the enrollment offer or dropped out of the program.

Since households were enrolled throughout the first 10 months of program operation, the operational phase of the experiment extended over nearly 4 years in total. Analysis was based on data collected from households during their first 2 years after enrollment in the experiment. The experimental programs were continued for a third year in order to reduce confusion between participants' reactions to the experimental offers and their adjustment to the phaseout of the experiment. During their last year in the experiment, eligible and interested households were aided in entering other housing programs, such as Section 8.

ALLOWANCE PLANS USED IN THE DEMAND EXPERIMENT

The Demand Experiment tested a number of combinations of payment formulas and housing requirements and several variations within each of these combinations. These variations allowed estimation of key responses such as participation rates and changes in participant housing in terms of basic program parameters such as the level of allowances and the level and type of housing requirements. These response estimates can be used to address the policy questions for a larger set of potential program plans, beyond the plans directly tested.

Two payment formulas were used in the Demand Experiment—Housing Gap and Percent of Rent. Under the Housing Gap formula, payments to households were determined by the difference between a basic payment level C and some reasonable fraction of income. The payment formula was $S = zC - bY$, where S was the payment amount; C was the basic payment level; z was a parameter that experimentally varied the payment level; b was the rate at which the allowance was reduced as income increased; and Y was net family income. Payments could not exceed actual rent. The basic payment level, C, varied with household size and was proportional to C^*, the estimated cost of "modest, existing, standard housing" of each size at each site, as determined by a panel of housing experts. Thus, payment under the Housing Gap formula can be interpreted as making up the difference between the cost of decent housing and the amount of a household's own income that it should be expected to pay for housing.

Under the Percent of Rent formula, the payment was a percentage of the household's rent. The payment formula was $S = aR$, where R was rent, and a was the fraction of rent paid by the allowance; to aid analysis, this fraction remained constant once the household had been enrolled.

The Percent of Rent formula was tied directly to rent: A household's allowance payment was proportional to total rent. Under the Housing Gap formula, however, specific housing requirements were needed to tie the allowance to housing. Two types of housing requirements were used— Minimum Standards and Minimum Rent.

Under the Minimum Standards requirement, participants received the allowance payment only if they occupied dwellings that met certain physical and occupancy standards. Participants occupying units that did not meet those standards either had to move or arrange to improve their current units to meet the standards. Participants already living in housing that met standards could use the allowance to pay for better housing or to reduce their rent burden (the fraction of income spent on rent) in their present units. These requirements are presented in Table I-1.

If housing quality is broadly defined to include all residential services and if rent levels are highly correlated with the level of services, then a

Table I-1
Components of Minimum Standards (Program Definition)

1. Complete plumbing:
   Private toilet facilities, a shower or tube with hot and cold running water, and a washbasin with hot and cold running water will be present and in working condition.

2. Complete kitchen facilities:
   A cooking stove or range, refrigerator, and kitchen sink with hot and cold running water will be present and in working condition.

3. Living room, bathroom, kitchen presence:
   A living room, bathroom, and kitchen will be present. (This represents the dwelling unit "core," which corresponds to an efficiency unit.)

4. Light fixtures:
   A ceiling or wall-type fixture will be present and working in the bathroom and kitchen.

5. Electrical:
   At least one electric outlet will be present and operable in both the living room and kitchen. A working wall switch, pull-chain light switch, or additional electrical outlet will be present in the living room.[a]

Table I-1 (continued)

---

6. Heating equipment:
   Units with no heating equipment; with unvented room heaters which burn gas, oil, or kerosene; or which are heated mainly with portable electric room heaters will be unacceptable.

7. Adequate exits:
   There will be at least two exits from the dwelling unit leading to safe and open space at ground level (for multifamily buildings only). Effective November 1973 (retroactive to program inception), this requirement was modified to permit override on case-by-case basis where it appears that fire safety is met despite lack of a second exit.

8. Room structure:
   Ceiling structure or wall structure for all rooms must not be in a condition (such as severe buckling or leaning) requiring replacement.

9. Room surface:
   Ceiling surface or wall surface for all rooms must not be in a condition (such as surface material that is loose, containing large holes, or severely damaged) requiring replacement.

10. Ceiling height:
    Living room, bathroom, and kitchen ceilings must be 7 feet (or higher) in at least one-half of the living room area.[a]

11. Floor structure:
    Floor structure for all rooms must not be in a condition (such as large holes or missing parts) requiring replacement.

12. Floor surface:
    Floor surface for all rooms must not be in a condition (such as large holes or missing parts) requiring replacement.

13. Roof structure:
    The roof structure must be firm.

14. Exterior walls:
    The exterior wall structure/exterior wall surface must not need replacement. (For structure, this could include such conditions as severe leaning, buckling, or sagging, and for surface conditions such as excessive cracks or holes.)

15. Light/ventilation:
    The unit will have a 10% ratio of window area to floor area and at least one openable window in the living room, bathroom, and kitchen or the equivalent in the case of properly vented kitchen and/or bathrooms.[a]

16. Occupancy:
    No more than two persons per adequate room.

---

[a] This housing standard is applied to bedrooms in determining the number of adequate bedrooms for the program occupancy standard (number 16).

straightforward housing requirement that is relatively inexpensive to administer would be the stipulation that recipients spend some minimum amount on rent. Such a Minimum Rent requirement was considered in the Demand Experiment to observe differences in response and cost, allowing assessment of the relative merits of the two types of requirements. Although the design of the experiment used a fixed minimum rent for each household size, an assistance program could employ more flexible formulas. For example, some features of the Percent of Rent formula could be combined with the Minimum Rent requirement—instead of receiving a zero allowance if their rent is less than the Minimum Rent, households might be paid a fraction of their allowance depending on the fraction of Minimum Rent paid.

The three combinations of payment formulas and housing requirements used in the Demand Experiment were Housing Gap Minimum Standards, Housing Gap Minimum Rent, and Percent of Rent. A total of 17 allowance plans were tested. The 12 Housing Gap alowance plans are shown in Figure I-1. The first 9 plans included three variations in the basic payment level, C ($1.2C^*$, C^*, and $0.8C^*$), interacted with three variations in housing requirements [Minimum Standards, Minimum Low Rent ($0.7C^*$), and Minimum Rent High ($0.9C^*$)]. The value of b (the rate at which the allowance was reduced as income increased) was 0.25 for each of these plans. The next 2 plans had the same level of C (C^*) and used the Minimum Standards housing requirement, but used different values of b, (0.15 and 0.35). Finally, the twelfth plan was unconstrained, that is, it had no housing requirement for the households to meet. This Unconstrained plan allowed a direct comparison with general income-transfer programs. Eligible households that did not meet the housing requirements were still able to enroll. They received full payments as soon as they met the requirements during the 3 years of the experiment. Even before meeting the housing requirements, such households received a cooperation payment of $10 per month as long as they completed all reporting and interview requirements.

In addition to the various allowance plans, a control group was necessary in order to establish a reference level for responses, since a number of uncontrolled factors could also induce changes in family behavior during the course of the experiment. Control households received a cooperation payment of $10 per month and reported the same information as did families that received allowance payments. Two control groups were used in the Demand Experiment. Members of one group (Plan 24) were offered a Housing Information Program when they joined the experiment and were paid $10 for each of five sessions attended. (This program was also offered to households enrolled in the experimental allowance plans, but they were not paid for their attendance.) The other control group (Plan 25) was not offered the Housing Information Program.

All the households in the various allowance plans had to meet a basic income eligibility requirement. This limit was approximately the income

Housing Gap: (Payment = $C - bY$)

b value	C level	HOUSING REQUIREMENTS			
		Minimum Standards	Minimum Rent Low ($0.7C^*$)	Minimum Rent High ($0.9C^*$)	No requirement (Unconstrained)
$b = 0.15$	C^*	Plan 10			
	$1.2C^*$	Plan 1	Plan 4	Plan 7	
$b = 0.25$	C^*	Plan 2	Plan 5	Plan 8	Plan 12
	$0.8C^*$	Plan 3	Plan 6	Plan 9	
$b = 0.35$	C^*	Plan 11			

Percent of Rent (Payment = aR):

$a = 0.6$	$a = 0.5$	$a = 0.4$	$a = 0.3$	$a = 0.2$
Plan 13	Plans 14-16	Plans 17-19	Plans 20-22	Plan 23

Control:

With housing information	Without housing information
Plan 24	Plan 25

Symbols: C^* = Basic payment level varied by household size and site
$\quad\quad\quad Y$ = Net income
$\quad\quad\quad R$ = Rent
$\quad\quad\quad a$ = Percentage of rent subsidized
$\quad\quad\quad b$ = Rate at which the Housing Gap allowance was reduced
$\quad\quad\quad\quad$ as income increased

Figure I-1. **Allowance plans tested.**

level at which the household would receive no payment under the Housing Gap formula ($C^*/0.25$). In addition, households in plans with lower payment levels (Plans 3, 6, 9 and 11) had to have incomes low enough at enrollment to receive payment under these plans. Finally, only households with incomes in the lower third of the eligible population were eligible for enrollment in Plan 13, and only those in the upper two-thirds were eligible for Plan 23.

Final analysis of the impact of the housing allowance was based on the first 2 years of experimental data. Thus, the key sample sizes for this book are the number of households in the experiment at the end of the first 2 years, shown in Figure I-2, and constitutes households that were still

Housing Gap

b value	C level	HOUSING REQUIREMENTS			
		Minimum Standards	Minimum Rent Low (0.7C*)	Minimum Rent High (0.9C*)	No requirement (Unconstrained)
b = 0.15	C*	PGH = 45 PHX = 36			
b = 0.25	1.2C*	PGH = 33 PHX = 30	PGH = 34 PHX = 24	PGH = 30 PHX = 30	
	C*	PGH = 42 PHX = 35	PGH = 50 PHX = 39	PGH = 44 PHX = 44	PGH = 63 PHX = 40
	0.8C*	PGH = 43 PHX = 39	PGH = 44 PHX = 35	PGH = 43 PHX = 35	
b = 0.35	C*	PGH = 41 PHX = 34			

Total Housing Gap: 512 households in PGH, 421 households in PHX.

Percent of Rent

a = 0.6	a = 0.5	a = 0.4	a = 0.3	a = 0.2
PGH = 28 PHX = 21	PGH = 109 PHX = 81	PGH = 113 PHX = 66	PGH = 92 PHX = 84	PGH = 65 PHX = 46

Total Percent of Rent: 407 households in PGH, 298 households in PHX.

Control:

With housing information	Without housing information
PGH = 159 PHX = 137	PGH = 162 PHX = 145

Total Control: 321 households in PGH, 282 households in PHX.

NOTE: This sample included households that were active although not necessarily receiving payments after 2 years of enrollment; households whose enrollment income was above the eligibility limits or that moved into subsidized housing or their own homes were excluded. PGH = Pittsburgh; PHX = Phoenix.

Figure I-2. **Sample size after two years.**

active in the sense that they were continuing to fulfill reporting requirements. (The sample size for a particular analysis may be smaller due to missing data.)[1]

Table I-2 sets out the preexperimental (baseline) demographic characteristics for the eligible, enrolled and 2-year active population. Comparison of the baseline characteristics of experimental and control households at enrollment and at 2 years after enrollment shows that the mean preexperimental sample characteristics change by only small amounts due to the acceptance of the enrollment offer and attrition from the experiment. This suggests that no substantial selection on demographic characteristics

---

[1] Households with an annual income of less than $1000 were excluded from the analysis.

was introduced by analyzing the 2-year active sample. More sophisticated analysis of such issues is presented in Appendices II and III.

KEY VARIABLES

Key variables used in this book include income, rent, and housing standards. Definitions of the variables used in this book are discussed in the following subsections. The hedonic index of housing services, described briefly in Chapter 3, is discussed at length in Merrill (1980).

Income

A major variable used in the analysis in this report is "Net Income for Analysis," a measure of household disposable income. Net Income for Analysis was an estimate of the annual income received by all household members aged 18 or over; it was the sum of earned and other income after

Table I-2
Selected Household Characteristics at Baseline for the Eligible, Enrolled, and Two-year Active Samples

Sample	Mean rent	Mean monthly income	Mean household size	Elderly-headed	Minority-headed	Female-headed	Sample size
			Pittsburgh				
Eligible households	$107	$335	2.8	37%	20%	54%	(2948)
Enrolled households							
Percent of Rent	111	377	3.0	28	25	49	(480)
Housing Gap	108	350	3.2	25	26	60	(575)
Minimum Standards	104	344	3.2	29	26	58	(258)
Minimum Low Rent	109	357	3.2	24	24	61	(155)
Minimum Rent High	114	354	3.3	22	27	62	(162)
Unconstrained	110	355	2.9	28	28	56	(71)
Control	114	389	3.2	23	20	50	(403)
Households active at two years							
Percent of Rent	112	384	3.0	28	21	50	(382)
Housing Gap	110	351	3.2	25	25	62	(414)
Minimum Standards	107	344	3.2	28	26	59	(188)
Minimum Rent Low	109	359	3.3	24	26	65	(119)
Minimum Rent High	114	354	3.1	21	23	65	(107)
Unconstrained	112	342	2.9	32	27	55	(60)
Control	115	399	3.3	21	19	51	(297)

Table I-2 (continued)

				Phoenix				
Eligible households	128	417	3.2	22	34	34	(2956)
Enrolled households							
Percent of Rent	134	442	3.2	2.0	31	37	(454)
Housing Gap	127	424	3.4	21	34	37	(632)
Minimum Standards	126	434	3.6	19	35	35	(303)
Minimum Low Rent	126	427	3.3	25	36	36	(151)
Minimum Rent High	129	407	3.2	22	33	43	(178)
Unconstrained	133	508	3.2	14	27	37	(63)
Control	131	434	3.4	18	31	35	(477)
Households active at two years							
Percent of Rent	130	429	3.3	23	36	43	(274)
Housing Gap	120	395	3.3	27	38	43	(342)
Minimum Standards	121	401	3.3	26	36	38	(157)
Minimum Rent Low	117	391	3.2	35	41	47	(86)
Minimum Rent High	122	389	3.3	21	40	49	(99)
Unconstrained	131	438					(35)
Control	124	420	3.4	22	36	44	(258)

Samples: Eligible households—all experimental and control households that completed the Baseline Interview that were determined to be eligible for the experiment on the basis of their baseline income and household size.
Enrolled households—all experimental and control households, excluding those with enrollment incomes over the eligibility limits.
Two-year active households—all experimental and control households active at 2 years after enrollment, excluding those with enrollment incomes over the eligibility limits and those living in their own homes or in subsidized housing.

taxes and alimony were paid. A complete list of all components that are included in this definition of net income and its relationship to two other income measures (the income definition used to determine eligibility for the experimental program and that used by the Bureau of the Census) are given in Table I-3. (Census gross income was used to determine household status with respect to the official poverty line.)

Rent

Analysis of participant expenditures on housing can take two basically different approaches: (a) how much households spend on rent; (b) how much it costs to rent a dwelling unit with particular characteristics. These differences in approach require different analytical definitions of rent. For

Table I-3

Components Included in the Definition of Net Income for Analysis and Comparison with Census and Program Eligibility Definitions

Components	Net Income for Eligibility	Net Income for Analysis	Census (Gross income)
Gross income			
Earned Income			
Wages and salaries	X	X	X
Net business income	X	X	X
Income–conditioned transfers			
Aid to Families with Dependent			
Children	X	X	X
General Assistance	X	X	X
Other welfare	X	X	X
Food Stamps subsidy	–	X*	X
Other transfers			
Supplemental Security Income	X	X	X
Social Security	X	X	X
Unemployment compensation	X	X	X
Workman's compensation	X	X	X
Government pensions	X	X	X
Private pensions	X	X	X
Veteran's pensions	X	X	X
Other income			
Education grants	X	X	X
Regular cash payments	X	X	X
Other Regular Income	X	X	X
Alimony received	X	X	X
Asset income	X*	X*	X*
Income from roomers and boarders	–	–	X
Gross Expenses			
Taxes			
Federal tax withheld	X*	X*	–
State tax withheld	X*	X*	–
FICA tax withheld	X*	X*	–
Work–conditioned expenses			
Child care expenses	X	–	–
Care of sick at home	X	–	–
Work-related expenses	X*	–	–
Other expenses			
Alimony paid out	X	X	–
Major medical expenses	X	–	–

* The amounts of these income and expense items were derived using data reported by the household. All other amounts are included in the income variables exactly as reported by the household.

example, reduction in rent for contributions from roomers and boarders is appropriate for the first approach but not the second.

Analytical adjusted contract rent was defined as the monthly payment for an unfurnished dwelling unit including basic utilities. The formula is

adjusted contract rent = contract rent + utilities − furnishings
                     + work-in-lieu-of-rent adjustment.

The components are

1. *Contract rent.* Contract rent was adjusted to a monthly amount to provide a common rental period.
2. *Utilities adjustment.* If the costs of utilities were not included in the household's contract rent, utilities adjustments were added to contract rent. Adjustments were made via site-specific tables for electricity, gas, heat, water, and garbage and trash collection. The amount of the adjustments depended on the numbers of rooms reported in the Housing Evaluation Form. No adjustment was made for any other utilities or services, such as parking. Allowance was made for increased utility costs over the 2-year experimental period.
3. *Furnishings adjustment.* For furnished units, a deduction of 11.5% of gross rent was made for the rent equivalent of furnishings.
4. *Work-in-lieu-of-rent adjustment.* If the contract rent paid by the household was reduced because a household member worked for the landlord, the amount of the reduction was added to contract rent. (The adjustment was not added to income.)

The analytical adjusted contract rent used in this book for the analysis of housing expenditures refers to shelter costs borne by the household, so contributions from roomers and boarders were subtracted from contract rent.

Rent Burden

Rent burden was calculated as the ratio of analytical rent to net income for analysis, adjusted for the allowance payments. Rent burden was thus defined as net rent over net income:

$$\text{Rent burden} = \frac{\text{contract rent-allowance payment}}{\text{monthly net income for analysis}}.$$

Rent burden statistics are highly sensitive to the definition of income used. Statistics calculated from different sources using different definitions of income may have to be recalculated or adjusted before comparisons may be made. The Housing Allowance Demand Experiment data appear to be unique both in attempting to use an analytic definition of net disposable income and in having the data to do so.

Program Housing and Occupancy Standards

The main housing and occupancy measures used in the analysis were based on the Minimum Standards housing requirements used in one part of the experiment. They were developed from elements of a model housing ordinance developed by the American Public Health Association with the Public Health Service in 1971. Table I-1 lists the Minimum Standards housing requirements as they applied to the dwelling unit itself. The requirements were grouped into 15 components of related items.

The occupancy requirement, Component 16, set a maximum of two persons for every adequate bedroom, regardless of age. An adequate bedroom was a room that could be completely closed off from other rooms and that met the following program housing standards: ceiling height, light/ventilation, and electrical service. (A studio or efficiency apartment was counted as a bedroom for the occupancy standards.) In addition, for a unit to meet Minimum Standards, all rooms had to meet the housing standards for the condition of room structure, room surface, floor structure, and floor surface.

_____

Selection Bias in Price Elasticity Estimates[1]

The sample of households offered rent rebates was carefully designed to be a random sample of the low-income population in each site. The equilibrium demand functions were, however, estimated on a different sample of households—households that accepted the enrollment offer, were verified to be within the income eligibility limit, remained in the experiment, and moved sometime between enrollment and 2 years after enrollment. Each of these selection criteria may have introduced bias in the estimated coefficients, so that they may differ from the population coefficients, as follows:

1. *Acceptance bias.* Households offered higher payments may have been more likely to accept the enrollment offer than households offered lower payments. Since, for each rebate level, payments increased with housing expenditures, households that accepted the rent rebate offers may have tended to spend more for housing than Controls. In this case, cross-sectional comparison of Experimental and Control households might overestimate the effect of the rebate.

2. *Attrition bias.* Likewise, households may be more likely to remain in the program if they received higher payments. Again, Experimental households that tend to spend more on housing regardless of the experiment may have been more likely to remain in the experiment.

3. *Mobility bias.* In theory, households move to change their housing and the larger their desired change, other things equal, the more likely the move. Households may move in order to spend less or to spend more on housing. The rent rebates offered to Experimental households would be expected to encourage moving by households

---

[1] This appendix was written with Stephen D. Kennedy and is based on Kennedy (1978).

that would have moved to increase their spending. Thus the sample of Experimental movers may not be comparable to the sample of Control movers.

This appendix evaluates the actual extent of such selection bias.

As suggested by Kennedy (1978), the selection bias problem may be formally characterized in terms of the stochastic error term in the estimated demand function. Specify, for example, the log-linear expenditure function as

$$\ln(R_t) = b_0 + b_1 \ln(Y_t) + b_2 \ln(1 - a) + e_t. \tag{1}$$

Under Eq. (1), if households had not received the rent rebates, the value of $\ln(1 - a)$ would have been zero ($a = 0$), and their rental expenditures would have been determined by

$$\ln(R_t^N) = b_0 + b_1 \ln(Y_t) + e_t \tag{2}$$

where R_t^N is, therefore, the normal level of expenditures that would have occurred in the absence of the experiment.

All the sample selection biases described above suggest that, at various periods, Experimental households with higher levels of $\ln(R_t^N)$—that is, with higher values of e_t—were more likely to accept enrollment, stay in the experiment, or move than households with lower levels of $\ln(R_t^N)$. Furthermore, this effect is likely to be larger at higher rebate levels. Thus, even if households were randomly assigned so that e_t was, for the entire assigned population, independent of $\ln(1 - a)$, among selected households e_t and $\ln(1 - a)$ may be correlated. In this case, the OLS estimate of b_2 will be biased.

The expenditure functions estimated in this paper were based on cross-sectional observations at the end of the second year of the experiment ($t = 2$). Thus the concern for estimation is sample selection that directly or indirectly affects e_2. The problem is that observations at 2 years after enrollment cannot distinguish between genuine experimental effects and the artifacts of sample selection. Some indirect way must be found to identify sample selection.

The basic method used here for testing for selection bias is based on serial correlation between e_0 (i.e., at enrollment) and e_2. To the extent that the stochastic term, e_t, reflects underlying differences in tastes or other slowly changing factors, it is reasonable to assume that the value of e_t for any individual household will change only gradually over time. Thus e_t and e_{t+1} or e_{t-1} are expected to be correlated. More exactly, the usual assumption is that e_t and e_{t-1} have a bivariate normal distribution with means u_t and u_{t-1}, variances s_t^2 and s_{t-1}^2, and correlation coefficient, p. But this means that e_2 and e_0 (the values of e at 2 years and at enrollment, respectively) are linked by the relationships

$$e_2 = u_2 + p \, \frac{S_2}{S_0} \, (e_0 - u_0) + n_2$$

$$e_0 = u_0 + p \, \frac{S_0}{S_2} \, (e_2 - u_2) + w_0 \tag{3}$$

where p is the correlation between e_2 and e_0, and n_2 and w_0 are stochastic terms distributed independently of e_0 and e_2, respectively with mean zero. (The estimated 2-year serial correlation for movers is 0.478 in Pittsburg and 0.461 in Phoenix.)

Now assume that there is some selection, S, of households between t_0 and t_2. Observations are available at t_0 for both selected and nonselected households and at t_2 for selected households. Given the serial correlation of Eq. (3), if the selection S affects the distribution of e_2 for the selected sample, so that

$$e_2^S = u_2 + f_0 + f_1 \ln(1 - a) + g_2 \tag{4}$$

where e_2^S is e_2 for the selected sample, and $E(g_2) = 0$, then e_2^S will also be related to $(1 - a)$, using Eq. (3) by

$$e_0^S = u_0 + p \, \frac{S_0}{S_2} \, (e_2^S - u_2) + w_0, \tag{5}$$

or

$$e_0^S = u_0 + p \, \frac{S_0}{S_2} \, [f_0 + f_1 \ln(1 - a) + g_2] + w_0. \tag{6}$$

Since households were randomly selected, the effect of the subsequent selection, S, can be identified by

$$e_0 = u_0 + \left(p \, \frac{S_0}{S_2} f_0 \right) d + \left(p \, \frac{S_0}{S_2} f_1 \right) d \ln(1 - a) + x_0$$

$$= u_0 + f_0^* + f_1^* d \ln(1 - a) + x_0 \tag{7}$$

where

$$d = \begin{cases} 1 & \text{if the household is subsequently selected,} \\ 0 & \text{if the household is not subsequently selected,} \end{cases}$$

$$f_0^* = p \, \frac{S_0}{S_2} f_0,$$

$$f_1^* = p \, \frac{S_0}{S_2} f_1,$$

and

$$E(x_0) = 0.$$

Equation (7) can be used to test for the effects of selection by testing the hypothesis that the coefficients of d and $d \ln(1 - a)$ are zero. If they are significantly different from zero, the bias introduced into e_2^S by the selection can be inferred by dividing the estimated coefficient of $d \ln(1 - a)$ by the term (ps_0/s_2).

Fortunately, neither f_0^* nor f_1^* is significantly different from zero at the 0.05 level, indicating that sample selection processes if they occurred were not severe enough to materially alter the conclusions of Chapter 2. These estimates are

	Pittsburgh	Phoenix
f_0^*	0.053	−0.009
	(0.028)	(0.029)
f_1^*	0.053	−0.056
	(0.064)	(0.063)

(Standard errors in parentheses.)

_____

The Methodology for Estimating the Experimental Effects on Housing Gap Households

Experimental effects for Housing Gap households were measured under the assumption that the actual housing consumption of households at 2 years after enrollment, R_A, could be separated into two parts—the normal housing consumption that would have been made in the absence of the experiment, R_N, and an additional amount that is induced by the experiment, R_X.[1] Thus,

$$R_A = R_N + R_X \qquad (1)$$

where R_A is actual expenditures 2 years after enrollment; R_N is normal expenditures 2 years after enrollment; and R_X is the experimental effect on expenditures. The experimental effect can be measured either as the difference between actual and normal expenditures or as their ratio:

$$\frac{R_A}{R_N} = \frac{R_N + R_X}{R_N} = 1 + \frac{R_X}{R_N}. \qquad (2)$$

Because log-linear functions proved useful in analyzing housing demand in response to experimental rent rebates for households enrolled in the Percent of Rent plans of the Demand Experiment (see Chapter 2), throughout this book the experimental effect is measured in terms of the ratio.

Experimental effects are estimated under the assumption that the ratio of actual to normal housing expenditures is functionally related to ex-

_____

[1] In this appendix, housing consumption is measured in terms of housing expenditures, although the same methodology was used to estimate the experimental effects in terms of housing services, as measured by hedonic indices.

perimental variables and a random error, specifically

$$\frac{R_A}{R_N} = \exp(\mathbf{Xb} + w) \qquad (3)$$

or

$$\ln(R_A/R_N) = \ln(R_A) - \ln(R_N) = \mathbf{Xb} + w \qquad (4)$$

where $\mathbf{X}$ is a vector of experimental variables; $\mathbf{b}$ is a vector of experimental effects; and w is a random error term distributed $N(0, s_w^2)$. The coefficients $\mathbf{b}$ of Eq. (4) measure the proportional change in (R_A/R_N) in response to a unit change in the variables in $\mathbf{X}$.

Since the log of normal rent, $\ln(R_N)$, was not observed for allowance recipients, it had to be estimated. The procedure used in estimation is described next.

PREDICTING NORMAL HOUSING CONSUMPTION

Assume that the log of normal housing expenditures for Control households at time t is given by

$$r_t = \ln(R_t) = a_t + b_t \ln(Y_t) + \mathbf{c}_t \mathbf{D}_t + e_t \qquad (5)$$

where Y is household income; $\mathbf{D}$ is a vector of household demographic characteristics; and e is a stochastic residual. Given the specification of Eq. (5) and the fact that observations on each household i are available for two time periods, $t = 0$ (enrollment) and $t = 2$ (2 years), a critical issue in estimating the parameters of the equation is the assumptions about the nature of the stochastic residual, e_t^i. If e_0^i and e_2^i are serially correlated, as is likely, then the Ordinary Least Squares (OLS) estimation of this equation, which ignores this possibility, would be inefficient. An asymptotically more efficient estimation technique, seemingly unrelated regression (SUR), developed by Zellner (1962), was used.

Using the SUR procedure, Eq. (5) was estimated separately for the two time periods using OLS; then $\hat{p}$, the correlation between the estimated errors, $\hat{e}_0^i$ and $\hat{e}_2^i$ is computed, which is an unbiased estimate of the serial correlation coefficient. Finally, the estimated $\hat{p}$ is used to transform the independent and dependent variables in Eq. (5) to provide more efficient estimates for the parameters.

A prerequisite of efficiency gains in estimation using SUR is that the values of the explanatory variables in the two equations vary from one period to the next. If there is no temporal variation, then the OLS and SUR coefficient estimates will be identical. In fact, there was only small temporal variation in the independent variables used here. Many of the household demographic characteristics did not change between enrollment and 2 years. Furthermore, there was a high correlation between enrollment and 2-year income. Yet, the goal is to obtain good predictive equations, and if there is any temporal variation in the demographic variables, relationships estimated using SUR will have superior predictive power since they use the estimated serial correlation for prediction. Additional independent variables describing initial housing conditions were valuable in further improving the predictive power of the regression beyond that provided by serial correlation alone.

Once the parameters of Eq. (5) and the serial correlation and coefficient, p, are estimated, the asymptotically best linear unbiased predictor (see, for example, Pindyck and Rubinfeld, 1976) of r_2^i (the natural logarithm of the rental expenditures at 2 years) for a household i, given rental expenditures (at enrollment) and income (at enrollment and at 2 years) is provided by the following equation, which takes account of serial correlation:

$$\hat{r}_2^i = \hat{a}_2 + \hat{b}_2 \ln(Y_2^i) + \hat{c}_2 D_2^i + \hat{p}\hat{e}_0^i. \tag{6}$$

Since e_0^i is the difference between the predicted and actual values at enrollment ($t = 0$), Eq. (6) may be rewritten as

$$\hat{r}_2^i = \hat{a}_2 - \hat{p}\hat{a}_0 + \hat{b}_2 \ln(Y_2^i) - \hat{p}\hat{b}_0 \ln(Y_0^i) + \hat{c}_2 D_2^i - \hat{p}\hat{c}_0 D_0^i + \hat{p}r_0^i. \tag{7}$$

The demographic variables **D** used were minority status and household composition. Minority status indicated whether the head of the household was a member of a minority group (black in Pittsburgh, black or Hispanic in Phoenix). Household composition indicated whether the household was a single person (restricted by program rules almost exclusively to elderly persons), was a single head of household (with children or other family members present), or was a couple (with or without children). Also included in the model were dummy variables that indicated whether the household met each of the three housing requirements (Minimum Standards, Minimum Rent Low, and Minimum Rent High) at enrollment. These dummy variables effectively ensure, for Control households, that the expected value of the difference between actual and predicted log rent will be zero for subsamples selected on the basis of enrollment housing requirement status. Finally, separate equations were estimated for each site.

The estimated equations are presented in Tables III-1 through III-4. Three statistics can be used to evaluate the predictive ability of the models. The first statistic was the correlation coefficient between actual and predicted log rent (or housing services). The second statistic was the

Table III-1

Predicting Equations for Normal Log Housing Expenditures: All Households

Independent variables	Pittsburgh Coefficients		Phoenix Coefficients	
	At two years	At enrollment	At two years	At enrollment
Constant	3.838 (0.235)	3.673 (0.184)	3.303 (0.264)	3.556 (0.191)
Log (monthly income)	0.132 (0.037)	0.127 (0.030)	0.244 (0.043)	0.174 (0.031)
Nonminority single-person household[a]	−0.152 (0.051)	−0.184 (0.038)	−0.210 (0.062)	−0.183 (0.049)
Nonminority single head of household with others present[a]	0.026 (0.036)	0.009 (0.027)	−0.045 (0.049)	−0.025 (0.037)
Minority single-person household[a]	−0.222 (0.109)	−0.035 (0.094)	−0.308 (0.118)	−0.414 (0.124)
Minority single head of household with others present[a]	0.055 (0.047)	0.119 (0.035)	0.067 (0.063)	−0.022 (0.043)
Minority household headed by a couple[a]	0.036 (0.057)	0.037 (0.046)	−0.087 (0.057)	−0.041 (0.040)
Enrollment unit passed Minimum Standards requirement[b]	0.043 (0.036)	0.051 (0.028)	0.045 (0.053)	−0.031 (0.039)
Enrollment unit passed Minimum Rent Low requirement[b]	0.205 (0.034)	0.284 (0.266)	0.311 (0.049)	0.395 (0.037)
Enrollment unit passed Minimum Rent High requirement[b]	0.247 (0.036)	0.326 (0.028)	0.142 (0.059)	0.252 (0.043)
Serial correlation	0.417		0.431	
Correlation of actual and predicted rent	0.77		0.77	
Standard error of estimate	0.20		0.26	
Sample size	(289)		(256)	

Note: Standard errors in parentheses.

[a] Dummy variables; omitted category is nonminority household headed by a couple.
[b] Dummy variables.

Percentage Root-Mean-Square error (PRMS) and is defined as (see Pindyck and Rubinfeld, 1976):

$$\text{PRMS} = \frac{1}{N}\sqrt{\sum_{i=1}^{N}\left[\frac{(r_i - \hat{r}_i)}{r_i}\right]^2} \tag{8}$$

Table III-2
Predicting Equations for Normal Log Housing Expenditures: All Movers

Independent variables	Pittsburgh Coefficients		Phoenix Coefficients	
	At two years	At enrollment	At two years	At enrollment
Constant	3.244 (0.516)	3.037 (0.363)	3.241 (0.401)	3.427 (0.317)
Log (monthly income)	0.247 (0.083)	0.228 (0.060)	0.280 (0.065)	0.198 (0.051)
Nonminority single-person household[a]	0.111 (0.124)	0.186 (0.103)	-0.225 (0.102)	-0.156 (0.096)
Nonminority single head of household with others present[a]	0.116 (0.069)	0.854 (0.049)	-0.089 (0.072)	0.0025 (0.056)
Minority single-person household[a]	0.000 (0.000)	0.000 (0.000)	-0.273 (0.177)	-0.496 (0.226)
Minority single head of household with others present[a]	0.069 (0.084)	0.174 (0.060)	0.132 (0.094)	0.0032 (0.065)
Minority household headed by a couple[a]	0.041 (0.129)	0.012 (0.100)	-0.172 (0.092)	-0.004 (0.060)
Enrollment unit passed Minimum Standards requirement[b]	0.048 (0.079)	0.037 (0.059)	0.108 (0.085)	-0.016 (0.062)
Enrollment unit passed Minimum Rent Low requirement[b]	0.073 (0.070)	0.295 (0.050)	0.212 (0.072)	0.375 (0.052)
Enrollment unit passed Minimum Rent High requirement[b]	0.226 (0.072)	0.391 (0.053)	0.059 (0.087)	0.215 (0.062)
Serial correlation	0.107		0.247	
Correlation of actual and predicted rent	0.63		0.66	
Standard error of estimate	0.24		0.28	
Sample size	(94)		(126)	

Note: Standard errors in parentheses.

[a] Dummy variables; omitted category is nonminority household headed by a couple.

[b] Dummy variables.

where $\hat{r}_i$ is the predicted log rent at 2 years; r_i is the actual log rent at 2 years; and N is the number of households. This statistic measured the deviation of predicted log rent from actual log rent in terms of percentages. The third statistic was the standard error of estimate. Tables III-5 and III-6 present the three statistics computed both for the normal rent

Table III-3

Predicting Equations for Normal Log Housing Services: All Households

Independent variables	Pittsburgh Coefficients		Phoenix Coefficients	
	At two years	At enrollment	At two years	At enrollment
Constant	3.739 (0.196)	3.665 (0.174)	3.737 (0.223)	3.955 (0.180)
Log (monthly income)	0.141 (0.031)	0.148 (0.029)	0.181 (0.036)	0.120 (0.030)
Nonminority single-person household[a]	-0.041 (0.043)	-0.047 (0.035)	-0.124 (0.053)	-0.113 (0.045)
Nonminority single head of household with others present[a]	0.025 (0.032)	0.018 (0.025)	-0.003 (0.042)	-0.020 (0.035)
Minority single-person household[a]	-0.046 (0.089)	-0.012 (0.075)	-0.346 (0.120)	-0.487 (0.111)
Minority single head of household with others present[a]	0.129 (0.042)	0.069 (0.034)	0.003 (0.051)	-0.103 (0.039)
Minority household headed by a couple[a]	-0.043 (0.052)	0.021 (0.043)	-0.066 (0.047)	-0.088 (0.038)
Enrollment unit passed Minimum Standards requirement[b]	0.072 (0.032)	0.108 (0.027)	0.030 (0.045)	0.114 (0.036)
Enrollment unit passed Minimum Rent Low requirement[b]	0.101 (0.031)	0.107 (0.026)	0.193 (0.043)	0.275 (0.352)
Enrollment unit passed Minimum Rent High requirement[b]	0.164 (0.033)	0.187 (0.027)	0.153 (0.051)	0.152 (0.040)
Serial correlation	0.539		0.388	
Correlation of actual and predicted housing services	0.77		0.75	
Standard error of estimate	0.16		0.21	
Sample size	(254)		(230)	

Note: Standard errors in parentheses.

[a] Dummy variables; omitted category is nonminority household headed by a couple.

[b] Dummy variables.

equations and the normal housing services equations. All three statistics indicate reasonably good fit.

Even though the equations predict normal rent and housing services well, a potential problem may arise because the focus of the analysis is recipient households who are selected based on their housing consumption status at 2 years after enrollment. This issue is addressed next.

Table III-4

Predicting Equations for Normal Log Housing Services: All Movers

Independent variables	Pittsburgh Coefficients		Phoenix Coefficients	
	At two years	At enrollment	At two years	At enrollment
Constant	3.084 (0.459)	3.381 (0.340)	3.392 (0.326)	3.626 (0.283)
Log (monthly income)	0.258 (0.740)	0.187 (0.057)	0.261 (0.053)	0.166 (0.046)
Nonminority single-person household[a]	0.155 (0.109)	−0.138 (0.092)	−0.119 (0.093)	−0.063 (0.087)
Nonminority single head of household with others present[a]	0.080 (0.064)	0.076 (0.046)	−0.065 (0.061)	0.024 (0.052)
Minority single-person household[a]	0.000 (0.000)	0.000 (0.000)	−0.505 (0.242)	−0.605 (0.194)
Minority single head of household with others present[a]	0.333 (0.083)	0.102 (0.060)	0.048 (0.075)	0.014 (0.059)
Minority household headed by a couple[a]	−0.235 (0.113)	−0.004 (0.090)	−0.093 (0.075)	−0.086 (0.057)
Enrollment unit passed Minimum Standards requirement[b]	0.038 (0.075)	0.100 (0.058)	−0.050 (0.077)	0.100 (0.061)
Enrollment unit passed Minimum Rent Low requirement[b]	0.003 (0.065)	0.112 (0.049)	0.127 (0.067)	0.295 (0.052)
Enrollment unit passed Minimum Rent High requirement[b]	0.144 (0.067)	0.232 (0.051)	0.170 (0.076)	0.161 (0.060)
Serial correlation	0.282		0.108	
Correlation of actual and predicted housing services	0.68		0.67	
Standard error of estimate	0.20		0.22	
Sample size	(83)		(108)	

Note: Standard errors in parentheses.

[a] Dummy variables; omitted category is nonminority household headed by a couple.

[b] Dummy variables.

SPECIFICATION OF SELECTION BIAS

As previously discussed, the overall experimental effect r_X is estimated as the mean of

$$\hat{r}_X = r_A - \hat{r}_N \qquad (9)$$

Table III-5
Statistics for the Evaluation of the Housing Expenditures Predicting Equations

Household group	Pittsburgh				Phoenix			
	Correlation[a]	PRMS[b]	Standard error of estimate	Sample size	Correlation[a]	PRMS[b]	Standard error of estimate	Sample size
All households	0.77	0.25	0.20	(289)	0.77	0.35	0.26	(256)
Households that did not meet requirements at enrollment	0.75	0.35	0.22	(190)	0.70	0.46	0.29	(182)
Households that met requirements at enrollment	0.75	0.37	0.18	(99)	0.82	0.42	0.18	(74)
All movers	0.63	0.52	0.24	(94)	0.66	0.53	0.28	(126)
Households that did not meet requirements at enrollment	0.62	0.65	0.25	(62)	0.57	0.72	0.32	(88)
Households that met requirements at enrollment	0.64	0.83	0.23	(32)	0.69	0.61	0.20	(38)

[a] Correlation between actual and predicted log rent.
[b] Percentage root-mean-square error.

170

Table III-6

Statistics for the Evaluation of the Housing Services Predicting Equations

Household group	Pittsburgh				Phoenix			
	Correlation[a]	PRMS[b]	Standard error of estimate	Sample size	Correlation[a]	PRMS[b]	Standard error of estimate	Sample size
All households	0.77	0.21	0.16	(254)	0.75	0.28	0.21	(230)
Households that did not meet requirements at enrollment	0.72	0.29	0.17	(166)	0.69	0.35	0.23	(171)
Households that met requirements at enrollment	0.82	0.29	0.13	(88)	0.79	0.37	0.15	(59)
All movers	0.68	0.45	0.20	(83)	0.67	0.43	0.22	(108)
Households that did not meet requirements at enrollment	0.63	0.62	0.22	(54)	0.63	0.53	0.23	(82)
Households that met requirements at enrollment	0.77	0.61	0.16	(29)	0.62	0.68	0.19	(26)

a Correlation between actual and predicted log rent.
b Percentage root-mean-square error.

where r_A is the actual log rent at 2 years, and $\hat{r}_N$ is the estimated normal log rent at 2 years (using the Control sample). The analysis focuses on recipient households whose housing requirement was met at 2 years after enrollment. Therefore, because of the correlation between the housing requirements and housing expenditures, bias in the estimate of r_X may have been introduced when households were selected for analysis based on whether they met their housing requirement at 2 years after enrollment.

Figure III-1 illustrates one way in which bias may have been introduced in analyzing recipients. The figure shows a hypothetical scatter diagram and regression of actual on predicted rent. In the population, the regression line has no intercept and a 45° slope. The relationship has an error with mean zero and some variance, hence, the scatter of the points around the regression line.

In the Minimum Rent plans, recipient status depended on the actual rent level of the household—the recipient group consisted therefore of households with rents above the Minimum Rent line. Thus, the selection of households into the group of recipients may have selected households that were more likely to have had positive differences between actual and predicted rent and omitted households that were more likely to have had negative differences. The observed mean differences for the group of recipients was therefore likely to be positive even if there were no true effect. In Minimum Standards plans the connection between recipient status and rent was less direct, but it undoubtedly existed.

An alternate way of looking at the effect of selection is presented in Figure III-2. The normal curve represents the distribution of residuals (actual minus predicted rent) and has a mean of zero. If households that did not meet the Minimum Rent requirements had residuals less than X and

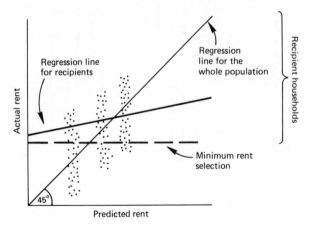

Figure III-1. **The effect of selection on regression parameters.**

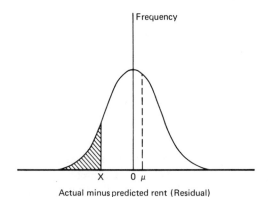

Figure III-2. **The effect of selection on the distribution of residuals.**

are therefore removed from the sample, the mean of the remaining households would have increased to μ. Interpreting the mean μ as an effect of
the allowance payment would be misleading.

The estimated experimental effect $\hat{r}_X$ is thus related to the true experimental effect r_X as

$$\hat{r}_x = r_x + d, \tag{10}$$

where d is the expected value of normal residuals for selected households
(the selection bias). Estimation of the bias rests on the tautology that for
the entire population (that is, when no subsample of households is selected), the expected value of the prediction error in normal rent, e, is
zero.

When the entire sample of enrolled households, for which $E(e) = 0$, is
divided into three groups—recipient households (status R), households
remaining in the sample but not participating (status $\bar{R}$), and households
that dropped out of the experiment before the end of 2 years (status D)—
the relationship between the expected value of e for each of the three
groups and the expected value of e for the entire sample is given by

$$E(e) = \frac{N_R}{N} E(e \mid R) + \frac{N_{\bar{R}}}{N} E(e \mid \bar{R}) + \frac{N_D}{N} E(e \mid D) = 0, \tag{11}$$

or

$$E(e \mid R) = - \frac{N_{\bar{R}}}{N_R} E(e \mid \bar{R}) - \frac{N_D}{N_R} E(e \mid D) \tag{12}$$

where N is the total number of enrolled households, N_R is the total number of recipient households, $N_{\bar{R}}$ is the total number of nonparticipating

households, N_D is the total number of households that dropped out of the experiment, and $E(e \mid i)$ is the expected value of e for households of status i. Under the assumption that $E(e \mid D) = 0$, the bias d [equal to $E(e \mid R)$] can be determined from

$$d = - \frac{N_{\bar{R}}}{N_R} E(e \mid \bar{R}). \tag{13}$$

The assumption that $E(e \mid D) = 0$ was supported by the data. To the extent that households that dropped out of the experiment because their incomes rose too high to leave them eligible for payment were balanced by those whose housing consumption was too low for them to attempt to meet the requirements, there is no clear expectation about the sign of $E(e \mid D)$. Unfortunately, since these households did drop out of the experiment, there was no information available to compare their actual rent with their normal rent at 2 years. Inference had to rely on an approximation to this comparison—the difference between actual rent and normal rent at enrollment. Since rents at enrollment and at 2 years after enrollment were so highly correlated, this comparison provided a reasonable approximation.

Table III-7 presents the means of the difference between actual and predicted log rent at enrollment for various groups of households that dropped out of the experiment. All the means are statistically insignificantly different from zero indicating that for each group attrition bias was negligible. These findings on the absence of attrition bias are reinforced by findings on the role of attrition in other social experiments. For example, Hausman and Wise (1979) found that their estimate of experimental effects in the New Jersey Graduated Work Incentive Experiment was unaffected by attrition, when demographic covariates were included in their model.

The value of $E(e \mid \bar{R})$ was estimated as the mean of the prediction error for the group of Control households whose units did not meet the housing requirements at 2 years after enrollment. Tables III-8 and III-9 summarize the findings on the significance of the bias, for housing expenditures and services, respectively.

The implicit assumption made in using Control households not meeting the requirements at 2 years to estimate $E(e \mid \bar{R})$ is equivalent to an assumption that the Experimental households that were induced to meet the requirements were drawn at random from among households that would normally not meet them (that is, drawn without regard to their normal expenditure levels). An objection against this method may be raised if the Housing Gap households that became recipients after enrollment were

Table III-7

Residual of Predicted Rent at Enrollment for Households Who Dropped Out of the Program within Two Years after Enrollment

Household group	Pittsburgh		Phoenix	
	Mean	t-statistic	Mean	t-statistic
Minimum Standards households	−0.029	1.12	0.016	0.95
Did not meet requirements at enrollment	−0.026	0.93	0.011	0.56
Met requirements at enrollment	−0.067	0.92	0.042	1.05
Minimum Rent Low households	−0.012	0.37	0.017	0.78
Did not meet requirements at enrollment	−0.054	0.69	0.035	0.78
Met requirements at enrollment	−0.011	0.41	0.005	1.24
Minimum Rent High households	−0.021	0.74	0.006	0.30
Did not meet requirements at enrollment	−0.037	1.03	0.014	0.54
Met requirements at enrollment	−0.014	0.33	0.011	0.41

Note: No t-statistic is significant at the 0.10 level.

precisely those that were closest to meeting the requirements at enrollment. Comparison of $E(e \mid \bar{R})$ for Experimental and Control households suggested that this assumption was reasonable, though.

An alternative method assumed that the experiment had no effect on the housing consumption of nonrecipient households in sample $\bar{R}$ (households enrolled in Housing Gap plans that did not receive allowance payments because their units did not meet the housing requirements of their particular plans). If the mean experimental effect for the group of nonrecipient households is assumed to be zero, any estimated experimental effect for this group must be due to bias alone. An objection can be raised to the assumption that the experiment did not affect the housing consumption of nonrecipient households. Some households in this group may have attempted to receive allowance payments but were somehow unsuccessful in that attempt, and if true, then the true experimental effect for this group would be greater than zero, and therefore the mean of the estimated experimental effect for this group would overestimate the bias.

Table III-8
Summary Table Indicating Significance of Bias on Housing Expenditures

Household group	Pittsburgh				Phoenix		
	Minimum Standards households	Minimum Rent Low households	Minimum Rent High households		Minimum Standards households	Minimum Rent Low households	Minimum Rent High households
All households	NS	0.01	0.01		NS	0.01	0.01
Did not meet requirements at enrollment	NS	0.01	0.01		NS	0.01	0.05
All movers	NS	[0.01]	0.01		NS	0.01	0.01
Did not meet requirements at enrollment	NS	[0.01]	0.01		NS	0.01	0.05

Note: Brackets indicate estimates based on 15 or fewer observations. Significance level is of mean residual of normal rent.

NS means not significant at the 0.10 level.

Table III-9

Summary Table Indicating Significance of Bias on Housing Services

Household group	Pittsburgh			Phoenix		
	Minimum Standards households	Minimum Rent Low households	Minimum Rent High households	Minimum Standards households	Minimum Rent Low households	Minimum Rent High households
All households	NS	0.01	0.05	0.01	0.01	NS
Did not meet requirements at enrollment	NS	0.01	0.05	0.01	0.01	NS
All movers	NS	[0.10]	NS	0.05	0.05	NS
Did not meet requirements at enrollment	NS	[NS]	NS	0.05	0.05	NS

Note: Brackets indicate amounts based on 15 or fewer observation. Significance level is of mean residual of housing services index.

NS means not significant at the 0.10 level.

Both methods of estimating the bias clearly had drawbacks. The method of using comparable Control households was used in the text to estimate the bias. Estimates based on the assumption of no effect for nonparticipating households indicated qualitatively similar results (see Friedman and Weinberg, 1980*b*, for more details).

APPENDIX IV _____

Additional Tables

Table IV-1

Overall Characteristics of Variables Used in Regression Analyses

Equations	Pittsburgh			Phoenix		
	Mean	Standard deviation	Sample size	Mean	Standard deviation	Sample size
			All households			
Log-linear expenditures			(674)			(532)
Log (rent)	4.869	0.313		4.966	0.385	
Log (average monthly income)	5.958	0.395		5.982	0.442	
Log (current monthly income)	6.040	0.452		5.999	0.491	
Log (1 - %age rebate)	-0.292	0.294		-0.265	0.291	
Linear expenditures			(674)			(532)
Rent	136.72	44.43		153.89	56.02	
Average monthly income/ (1 - %age rebate)	573.69	266.91		588.07	303.01	
Current monthly income/ (1 - %age rebate)	638.84	334.19		612.90	362.26	
1/(1 - %age rebate)	1.400	0.435		1.362	0.429	
Log-linear housing services			(635)			(486)
Log (hedonic index of housing services)	4.739	0.235		4.931	0.325	
Log (average monthly income)	5.954	0.393		5.986	0.438	
Log (1 - %age rebate)	-0.291	0.293		-0.264	0.289	

Table IV-1 (continued)

			Movers			
Log-linear expenditures			(236)			(292)
Log (rent)	4.977	0.308		5.085	0.347	
Log (average monthly income)	5.968	0.356		5.998	0.426	
Log (current monthly income)	5.968	0.416		6.006	0.478	
Log (1 - %age rebate)	-0.311	0.294		-0.305	0.306	
Linear expenditures			(236)			(292)
Rent	152.08	48.76		171.13	56.62	
Average monthly income/ (1 - %age rebate)	579.81	243.50		617.93	305.59	
Current monthly income/ (1 - %age rebate)	652.54	312.48		640.70	377.73	
1/(1 - %age rebate)	1.426	0.435		1.423	0.459	
Log-linear housing services			(214)			(257)
Log (hedonic index of housing services)	4.783	0.251		5.005	0.329	
Log (average monthly income)	5.954	0.354		6.001	0.422	
Log (1 - %age rebate)	-0.313	0.292		-0.304	0.302	

Table IV-2
Log-Linear Expenditure Functions

Household group	Constant	Income elasticity	Price elasticity	R^2	SEE	Sample Size
			Pittsburgh			
All households						
Current income	3.065 (0.149)	0.291 (0.024)	−0.164 (0.037)	0.08	0.28	(674)
Average income	2.835 (0.169)	0.333 (0.028)	−0.178 (0.038)	0.18	0.28	(674)
Mover households						
Current income	2.955 (0.271)	0.324 (0.044)	−0.195 (0.062)	0.20	0.28	(236)
Average income	2.744 (0.317)	0.363 (0.052)	−0.211 (0.063)	0.18	0.28	(236)
			Phoenix			
All households						
Current income	2.678 (0.179)	0.371 (0.030)	−0.239 (0.050)	0.25	0.33	(532)
Average income	2.303 (0.195)	0.435 (0.032)	−0.234 (0.049)	0.27	0.33	(532)
Mover households						
Current income	3.065 (0.229)	0.325 (0.038)	−0.219 (0.059)	0.23	0.31	(292)
Average income	2.834 (0.256)	0.364 (0.042)	−0.219 (0.059)	0.23	0.31	(292)

Note: Standard errors in parentheses. All t-statistics are significant at the
0.01 level. The model used here is

$$\ln(\text{rent}) = b_0 + b_1 \ln(\text{income}) + b_2 \ln(1-a)$$

where a is the percentage rebate for Percent of Rent households.
SEE is the standard error of estimate.

Table IV-3
Log-Linear Expenditure Functions (Sites Pooled)

Household group	Constant	Income elasticity	Price elasticity	Phoenix dummy	R^2	SEE	Sample size
			Pooled site intercept				
All households							
Current income	2.907 (0.117)	0.324 (0.019)	−0.189 (0.031)		0.20	0.31	(1206)
Average income	2.544 (0.129)	0.387 (0.021)	−0.200 (0.030)		0.23	0.31	(1206)
Mover households							
Current income	3.068 (0.177)	0.316 (0.029)	−0.205 (0.044)		0.20	0.30	(528)
Average income	2.765 (0.200)	0.369 (0.033)	−0.205 (0.044)		0.21	0.30	(528)
			Different site intercepts				
All households							
Current income	2.817 (0.116)	0.330 (0.019)	−0.199 (0.030)	0.117 (0.018)	0.23	0.31	(1206)
Average income	2.517 (0.128)	0.385 (0.021)	−0.207 (0.030)	0.094 (0.018)	0.24	0.30	(1206)
Mover households							
Current income	2.942 (0.175)	0.325 (0.028)	−0.209 (0.043)	0.128 (0.026)	0.24	0.29	(528)
Average income	2.738 (0.197)	0.364 (0.033)	−0.216 (0.043)	0.098 (0.026)	0.23	0.29	(528)

Note: Standard errors in parentheses. All t-statistics are significant at the
        0.01 level. The model used here is

$$\ln(\text{rent}) = b_0 + b_1 \ln(\text{income}) + b_2 \ln(1-a) + b_3 D$$

where a is the percentage rebate for Percent of Rent households, and
   D is a dummy variable for Phoenix (different intercepts equation only).
F-tests of overall homogeneity indicate rejection at the 0.01 level. F-tests
of the elasticities (allowing for different site intercepts) indicate rejection only for all households (at the 0.05 level). See table below.

	Overall Homogeneity		Different Elasticities	
	F-statistic	d.o.f.	F-statistic	d.o.f.
All households—current income	16.111	(3,1200)	2.804	(2,1201)
All households—average income	11.535	(3,1200)	3.161	(2,1201)
Movers—current income	8.203	(3, 522)	0.035	(2, 523)
Movers—average income	4.825	(3, 522)	0.001	(2, 523)

SEE is the standard error of estimate.

Table IV-4
Linear Expenditure Functions

Household group	Constant	Income coefficient	Price coefficient	R^2	SEE	Sample size
			Pittsburgh			
All Households						
Current income	115.47 (5.36)	0.0577 (0.0053)	−11.15 (4.10)	0.16	40.9	(674)
Average income	113.98 (5.43)	0.0714 (0.0069)	−13.00 (4.26)	0.14	41.2	(674)
Mover households						
Current income	120.79 (9.83)	0.0804 (0.0102)	−14.86** (7.34)	0.22	43.3	(236)
Average income	117.41 (10.03)	0.1027 (0.0136)	−17.43 (7.63)	0.21	43.7	(236)
			Phoenix			
All Households						
Current income	122.80 (7.25)	0.0745 (0.0069)	−10.69 (5.80)	0.20	50.2	(532)
Average income	120.11 (7.09)	0.1021 (0.0083)	−19.28 (5.89)	0.24	49.0	(532)
Mover households						
Current income	138.60 (9.69)	0.0733 (0.0090)	−10.14[a] (7.42)	0.21	50.6	(292)
Average income	133.25 (9.55)	0.1018 (0.0114)	−17.57** (7.58)	0.24	49.7	(292)

Note: Standard errors in parentheses. All t-statistics are significant at the 0.01 level except where noted. The model used here is

$$\text{Rent} = A\,[1/(1-a)] + B\,[\text{Income}/(1-a)] + C$$

where a is the percentage rebate for Percent of Rent households.
[a] t-statistic not significant at the 0.10 level.
** t-statistic significant at the 0.05 level.
SEE is the standard error of estimate.

Table IV-5

Stratified Log-Linear Expenditure Functions (Movers Sample)

Household group	Constant	Income elasticity	Price elasticity	R^2	SEE	Sample size
		Pittsburgh				
All Households	2.768*** (0.322)	0.359*** (0.053)	-0.213*** (0.064)	0.18	0.28	(234)
Single-person households	3.272*** (1.048)	0.274 (0.184)	-0.077 (0.189)	0.07	0.28	(33)
Single heads of household with others	3.958*** (0.605)	0.165 (0.102)	-0.156* (0.092)	0.05	0.27	(98)
Households headed by a couple	1.131** (0.566)	0.613*** (0.090)	-0.364*** (0.096)	0.33	0.27	(103)
Nonminority households	2.606*** (0.346)	0.386*** (0.057)	-0.210*** (0.069)	0.20	0.28	(196)
Nonminority single-person households	3.352*** (1.196)	0.258 (0.210)	-0.072 (0.202)	0.05	0.30	(30)
Nonminority single heads of household with others	3.881*** (0.629)	0.182* (0.107)	-0.121 (0.096)	0.06	0.25	(77)
Nonminority households headed by a couple	0.792 (0.622)	0.668*** (0.100)	-0.377*** (0.104)	0.37	0.27	(89)
Minority households	3.643*** (0.899)	0.212 (0.148)	-0.204 (0.179)	0.07	0.30	(38)
Minority single-person households	[not estimated]					(3)
Minority single heads of household with others	4.121* (1.845)	0.133 (0.307)	-0.303 (0.296)	0.06	0.35	(21)
Minority households headed by a couple	3.059* (1.506)	0.301 (0.237)	-0.193 (0.279)	0.13	0.27	(14)

Table IV-5 (continued)

Household group	Constant	Income elasticity	Price elasticity	R^2	SEE	Sample size
		Phoenix				
All Households	2.796*** (0.260)	0.370*** (0.043)	-0.219*** (0.060)	0.23	0.31	(285)
Single-person households	2.179*** (0.457)	0.480*** (0.080)	-0.245* (0.138)	0.57	0.20	(32)
Single heads of household with others	2.995*** (0.429)	0.342*** (0.072)	-0.128 (0.087)	0.16	0.31	(121)
Households headed by a couple	2.669*** (0.518)	0.383*** (0.083)	-0.327*** (0.100)	0.19	0.33	(132)
White households	2.463*** (0.286)	0.431*** (0.047)	-0.287*** (0.068)	0.35	0.27	(185)
Nonminority single-person households	2.407*** (0.570)	0.444*** (0.099)	-0.147 (0.157)	0.46	0.21	(27)
Nonminority single heads of household with others	2.563*** (0.555)	0.410*** (0.091)	-0.297** (0.115)	0.26	0.29	(71)
Nonminority households headed by a couple	2.739*** (0.503)	0.390*** (0.080)	-0.290*** (0.104)	0.26	0.27	(87)
Minority households	3.643*** (0.493)	0.177** (0.083)	-0.179* (0.105)	0.07	0.34	(100)
Minority single-person households	[not estimated]					(5)
Minority single heads of household with others	3.771*** (0.757)	0.213 (0.132)	0.029 (0.132)	0.05	0.32	(50)
Minority households headed by a couple	3.415*** (1.092)	0.227 (0.178)	-0.415** (0.177)	0.15	0.34	(45)
Hispanic households	4.148*** (0.606)	0.133 (0.101)	-0.137 (0.122)	0.04	0.33	(72)
Black households	3.524*** (0.965)	0.224 (0.188)	-0.255 (0.217)	0.12	0.37	(28)

Note: Standard errors in parentheses. Dependent variable is ln(rent).
*   t-statistic significant at the 0.10 level.
**   t-statistic significant at the 0.05 level.
*** t-statistic significant at the 0.01 level.
SEE is the standard error of estimate.

Table IV-6

Stratified Log-Linear Expenditure functions (Sites Pooled)

Household group	Constant	Income elasticity	Price elasticity	Phoenix dummy	R^2	SEE	Sample size
All households	2.723*** (0.201)	0.366*** (0.033)	−0.217*** (0.044)	0.096*** (0.026)	0.23	0.30	(519)
Nonminority households	2.433*** (0.219)	0.413*** (0.036)	−0.249*** (0.048)	0.145*** (0.028)	0.32	0.27	(381)
Minority households	3.818*** (0.431)	0.184*** (0.071)	−0.183** (0.089)	−0.006 (0.063)	0.07	0.33	(138)
Single-person households	2.389*** (0.473)	0.426*** (0.083)	−0.175 (0.116)	0.111* (0.064)	0.34	0.25	(65)
Single heads of household with others	3.210*** (0.345)	0.294*** (0.058)	−0.137** (0.063)	0.066* (0.040)	0.12	0.29	(219)
Households headed by a couple	2.032*** (0.382)	0.468*** (0.061)	−0.327*** (0.070)	0.111*** (0.040)	0.26	0.30	(235)

Note: Standard errors in parentheses. Dependent variable is ln(rent).
*   t-statistic significant at the 0.10 level.
**   t-statistic significant at the 0.05 level.
*** t-statistic significant at the 0.01 level.
SEE is the standard error of estimate.

Table IV-7

Stratified Log-Linear Housing Services Functions (Movers Sample)

Household group	Constant	Income elasticity	Price elasticity	R^2	SEE	Sample size
		Pittsburgh				
All Households	3.402*** (0.287)	0.226*** (0.047)	–0.113* (0.057)	0.10	0.24	(214)
Single-person households	3.338*** (0.929)	0.241 (0.163)	–0.118 (0.168)	0.07	0.25	(32)
Single heads of household with others	3.745*** (0.562)	0.181* (0.095)	–0.038 (0.085)	0.04	0.23	(87)
Households headed by a couple	1.681*** (0.473)	0.489*** (0.076)	–0.246*** (0.080)	0.32	0.21	(95)
Nonminority households	3.126*** (0.291)	0.269*** (0.048)	–0.143** (0.057)	0.16	0.22	(180)
Nonminority single-person households	3.135*** (1.025)	0.275 (0.180)	–0.112 (0.174)	0.08	0.25	(29)
Nonminority single heads of household with others	3.316*** (0.627)	0.245** (0.107)	–0.121 (0.091)	0.10	0.22	(69)
Nonminority households headed by a couple	1.742*** (0.471)	0.484*** (0.075)	–0.202*** (0.077)	0.35	0.19	(82)
Minority households	4.922*** (0.923)	–0.012 (0.151)	0.067 (0.201)	0.004	0.30	(34)
Minority single-person households	[not estimated]					(3)
Minority single heads of household with others	6.639*** (0.993)	–0.273 (0.165)	0.275 (0.166)	0.23	0.18	(18)
Minority households headed by a couple	0.941 (1.738)	0.575* (0.274)	–0.611 (0.353)	0.34	0.31	(13)

Table IV-7 (continued)

	Phoenix					
All Households	2.739** (0.259)	0.375*** (0.043)	-0.045 (0.050)	0.23	0.29	(257)
Single-person households	2.201*** (0.578)	0.464*** (0.101)	-0.366* (0.197)	0.48	0.25	(29)
Single heads of household with others	2.549*** (0.401)	0.416*** (0.067)	0.045 (0.081)	0.27	0.27	(111)
Households headed by a couple	2.753*** (0.510)	0.365*** (0.082)	-0.121 (0.098)	0.15	0.31	(117)
Nonminority households	2.379*** (0.272)	0.440*** (0.045)	-0.129** (0.065)	0.38	0.24	(168)
Nonminority single-person households	2.309*** (0.711)	0.454*** (0.123)	-0.249 (0.225)	0.40	0.25	(24)
Nonminority single heads of household with others	2.042*** (0.497)	0.497*** (0.082)	-0.145 (0.101)	0.38	0.24	(64)
Nonminority households headed by a couple	2.315*** (0.464)	0.448*** (0.074)	-0.123 (0.097)	0.32	0.25	(80)
Minority households	3.962*** (0.501)	0.154* (0.085)	0.023 (0.106)	0.04	0.32	(89)
Minority single-person households	[not estimated]					(5)
Minority single heads of household with others	3.752*** (0.704)	0.205* (0.122)	0.185 (0.125)	0.10	0.29	(47)
Minority households headed by a couple	4.906*** (1.229)	-0.012 (0.199)	-0.120 (0.193)	0.01	0.35	(37)
Hispanic households	4.345*** (0.611)	0.100 (0.102)	0.116 (0.121)	0.03	0.31	(62)
Black households	3.818*** (0.949)	0.159 (0.165)	-0.138 (0.218)	0.06	0.35	(27)

Note: Standard errors in parentheses. Dependent variable is ln(rent).
* t-statistic significant at the 0.10 level.
** t-statistic significant at the 0.05 level.
*** t-statistic significant at the 0.01 level.
SEE is the standard error of estimate.

able IV-8

▮milog Hedonic Equation: Pittsburgh

riable description		Coefficient	t-statistic[a]
▮nure char- acteristics	Related to landlord (0,1)	-0.102	5.813
	Length of residence (exponential function)	-0.141	11.570
	Landlord lives in building (0,1)	-0.067	4.376
	Number of persons per room	0.082	5.946
	Number of landlord contacts for maintenance	0.012	3.491
▮elling unit features	Area per room (natural log)	0.170	6.449
	Total number of rooms (natural log)	0.565	29.073
	Building age (years)	-0.002	4.168
	Stove and refrigerator provided (0,1)	0.111	6.382
	Inferior or no heat (0,1)	-0.077	6.403
	Garage provided (0,1)	0.091	4.912
	Off-street parking provided (0,1)	0.022	1.352
	Overall evaluator rating (4 point scale)	0.053	5.846
	Dishwasher and/or garbage disposal provided (0,1)	0.054	2.692
	Recent interior painting or papering (0,1)	0.052	3.497
	Many high quality features (0,1)	0.038	1.576
	Poor wall and ceiling surface (factor score)	-0.019	4.020
	Poor window condition (factor score)	-0.018	3.697
	Poor bathroom wall and ceiling surface (factor score)	-0.013	2.992
	High quality kitchen (0,1)	0.034	1.982
	Presence of adequate exits (0,1)	0.046	2.709
	Air-conditioning present (0,1)	0.025	1.698
	Presence of adequate ceiling height (0,1)	0.034	2.170
	Adequate kitchen facilities present (0,1)	0.117	2.267
	Large multifamily structure (0,1)	0.038	2.527
	Working condition of plumbing (5 point scale)	0.008	1.539
	Presence of private yard (0,1)	0.015	1.468
▮eighborhood features	Good recreational facilities and access (factor score)	0.024	4.964
	Traffic and litter problems (factor scores)	-0.009	1.607
	Problems with crime and public services (factor score)	-0.015	2.926
	Census tracts with higher priced units and higher socioeconomic status	0.032	5.626
	Nonminority census tracts with higher socioeconomic status	0.032	5.542
	Blue collar workers and nonminority residents in census tracts	-0.026	5.694
	High quality block face (0,1)	0.043	4.160
▮nstant		2.629	

$R^2 = 0.662$ $\qquad$ F = 89.140 $\qquad$ Sample size = 1,583

▮urce: Merrill, 1980, Table 3-2.
t-statistic > 1.0 indicates significance at the 0.25 level of significance for a two-tailed
test and 0.125 level of significance for a one-tailed test.

Table IV-9

Semilog Hedonic Equation: Phoenix

Variable description		Coefficient	t-statistic[a]
Tenure characteristics	Related to landlord (0,1)	-0.129	7.037
	Length of residence (exponential function)	-0.195	13.508
	Number of persons per room	0.064	6.287
	Number of landlord contacts for maintenance	0.014	4.463
Dwelling unit features	Area per room (natural log)	0.310	13.146
	Total number of rooms (natural log)	0.679	34.543
	Building age (years)	-0.002	5.330
	Stove and refrigerator provided (0,1)	0.032	2.549
	Central heat present (0,1)	0.039	2.744
	Garage or carport provided (0,1)	0.031	3.128
	Dishwasher and/or garbage disposal provided (0,1)	0.036	2.486
	Recent interior painting or papering (0,1)	0.015	1.391
	Average surface and structural quality (4 point scale)	0.125	9.571
	Adequate light and ventilation (0,1)	0.035	3.665
	Central air-conditioning present (0,1)	0.050	3.132
	Large multifamily structure (0,1)	0.023	1.674
	Plumbing present (0,1)	0.046	2.507
	Inferior or no heat (0,1)	-0.026	2.049
	Presence of adequate ceiling height (0,1)	0.020	1.279
Neighborhood features	Overall neighborhood quality (factor score)	0.019	3.284
	Recreational facilities (factor score)	0.024	3.144
	Access to shopping and parking (factor score)	0.013	2.265
	Census tracts with higher priced units and higher socioeconomic status	0.025	3.266
	Owner-occupied, single-family dwelling units in census tract	0.006	1.025
	Poor quality housing in census tract	-0.029	5.559
	Distance from Central Business District (miles)	-0.004	3.611
	Quality of block face landscaping (4 point scale)	0.021	3.867
Constant		1.902	

$R^2 = 0.804$ F= 238.060   Sample size= 1,593

Source: Merrill, 1980, Table 3-4.
[a] t-statistic > 1.0 indicates significance at the 0.25 level of significance for a two-tailed test and 0.125 level of significance for a one-tailed test.

Table IV-10

Sample Sizes at Enrollment and at Two Years

Treatment group	Pittsburgh		Phoenix	
	Sample size at enrollment	Sample size at two years	Sample size at enrollment	Sample size at two years
All Housing Gap households	626	449	695	381
Minimum Standards households	281	204	329	174
Plan 1	43	33	48	30
Plan 2	59	42	74	35
Plan 3	62	43	66	39
Plan 10	57	45	64	36
Plan 11	60	44	77	34
Minimum Rent Low households	166	128	175	98
Plan 4	43	34	42	24
Plan 5	62	50	70	39
Plan 6	61	44	63	35
Minimum Rent High households	179	117	191	109
Plan 7	45	30	43	30
Plan 8	67	44	78	44
Plan 9	67	43	70	35
Unconstrained households	75	63	70	40
Percent of Rent households	510	407	490	298
Plan 13	34	28	32	21
Plans 14–16	121	109	110	81
Plans 17–19	145	113	118	66
Plans 20–22	118	92	140	84
Plan 23	92	65	84	46
Control households	434	321	525	282

Sample at enrollment: All enrolled households, excluding those with enrollment incomes over the eligibiltiy limits.

Sample at two years: All households active at 2 years after enrollment, excluding those with enrollment incomes over the eligibility limits and those living in their own homes or in subsidized housing.

Note: The sample size for a particular analysis may be smaller due to sample selection, missing values, or both.

Intraurban Residential Mobility: The Role of Transactions Costs, Market Imperfections, and Household Disequilibrium[1]

DANIEL H. WEINBERG, JOSEPH FRIEDMAN, AND STEPHEN K. MAYO

A clear understanding of intraurban residential mobility is vital to understanding the housing market behavior of urban consumers. Yet, recent analyses have produced inconsistent evidence and ambiguous findings on the major determinants of moving (see [9] for a recent review of residential mobility studies). This paper uses the theoretical framework of microeconomics to formulate and quantify a model of household residential search and mobility that is both theoretically plausible and empirically tractable. Previous models of mobility were based on a loose theoretical perspective of the decision-making process, emphasizing the somewhat vague concepts "dissatisfaction" and "stress." (Two representative models are [1] and [10]). In contrast, the model presented here is cast explicitly in terms of a rigorous microeconomic model of housing demand. This model permits changes in household and housing market characteristics to influence a household's decision to search for and move to a different

[1]An earlier version of this paper was presented at a conference on the Housing Choices of Low Income Families, Washington, D. C., March 8–9, 1979. Financial support for this research was provided by the U.S. Department of Housing and Urban Development under Contract H-2040R to Abt Associates Inc. The authors wish to thank Stephen Kennedy and a referee whose comments and suggestions were helpful. Responsibility for the results reported here remains with the authors. Reprinted from the *Journal of Urban Economics*, Vol. 9, pp. 332–348, 1981.

[2,3] [Omitted.]

residence. The basic motivating factor is the benefit from moving; the basic deterring factor is costs.

A MICROECONOMIC MODEL OF SEARCH AND MOBILITY

Households typically adjust housing consumption to desired (equilibrium) levels by moving. Households search for housing and move when the expected gains from changing their housing outweigh the costs of finding and moving to a new unit. If there were no costs, a household would adjust its housing immediately when desired consumption changed. For renters, the typical method of changing housing consumption is by moving.

Instantaneous adjustments are, however, implausible because the costs of searching and moving are often substantial (see Muth [8], for example). Having once chosen a satisfactory unit, the existence of transaction costs (both monetary and psychological) suggests that households do not necessarily move when small changes render their current unit nonoptimal. This immobility leads to utility losses, in the sense that utility attainable in the optimal unit exceeds utility actually attained in the current unit. The household moves only when the utility loss of staying in the current unit outweighs the costs of moving.

In principle, the utility gain foregone when a household does not move to its equilibrium may be measured in monetary terms using the concept of the compensating income variation—the maximum amount of money that the household could spend on transactions costs (given the prevailing prices and income) and be as well off after the move as before. If the compensating income variation is larger then the *actual* costs of moving, the household would, in theory, move.

In any given period the household is assumed to maximize its utility $U(H, Z)$, where H represents housing services and Z represents other goods, subject to a budget constraint. This maximization implies an equilibrium housing demand function

$$H^* = H(p_H, Y),\tag{1}$$

where

p_H = the relative price of housing

Y = household income.

Assume that the household is consuming a nonoptimal level of housing H_0 and is spending R_0 on rent. The income compensation is simply the amount of money IC that if subtracted from a household's income, would leave the household as well off with its nonoptimal housing H_0 as it would if it were to consume the optimal amount H^* at a rent of R^*. The value of IC is obtained by solving the equation

$$U(H_0, Y - R_0) = U(H^*, Y - R^* - IC).$$ (2)

If there are transactions costs, TC, the household moves only if $TC < IC$. The optimal amount of housing after moving under a regime of transactions costs therefore lies between H_0 and H^*.

If the utility function is known, the exact (Hicksian) measure of the compensating income of any disequilibrium can be derived directly from (2). Alternatively, if the household demand function (but not utility function) is known, the Marshallian income compensation, a close approximation to the exact Hicksian income compensation, can be computed.[4] It is simply the difference in consumer's surplus between consuming the equilibrium level of housing services H^* at a rent of R^* and the initial position of consuming H_0 housing services at a rent of R_0:

$$IC = \left[\int_0^{H^*} [D(H)\,dH] - R^* \right] - \left[\int_0^{H_0} [D(H)\,dH] - R_0 \right]$$ (3)

$$= \int_{H_0}^{H^*} [D(H)\,dH] + (R_0 - R^*),$$

where $D(H)$ is the inverse demand function from (1). For example, if the housing demand function is log-linear

$$\ln(H^*) = \ln(K) + a\ln(Y) + b\ln(p_H),$$ (4)

The income compensation is (using (3))

$$IC = \left(\frac{1}{p_H H^*} \right)^{1/b} \left(\frac{b}{b+1} \right) \left[(p_H H^*)^{(b+1)/b} - (p_H H_0)^{(b+1)/b} \right]$$

$$+ R_0 - R^*.$$ (5)

Other demand functions could be analyzed in a similar fashion.

Housing services H in (5) are not readily observable, but must be estimated. The value of the housing services provided by a unit can be measured using a hedonic index, whose value can be interpreted as the average market rent of a unit with given location, size and other physical characteristics.[5]

A hedonic index of housing services is derived by regressing rent or the logarithm of rent on structural and neighborhood characteristics of the

---

[4]Willig [12] demonstrated that in many practical situations the Marshallian and Hicksian measures of income compensation are numerically very close. The distinction is that the Hicksian measure uses a compensated demand curve while the Marshallian measure uses an uncompensated one. For the data used in this paper, the approximation error is under 2%.

[5]See Merrill [7] for an extended discussion of the meaning and use of hedonic indexes.

unit and on conditions of tenure

$$\ln(R) = \alpha + X\beta + Z\gamma + \mu, \tag{6}$$

where

$X =$ a vector of structural and neighborhood characteristics,

$Z =$ a vector of tenure characteristics such as length of the household's residence in the unit and whether the tenant is related to the landlord, and

$\mu =$ a stochastic error.

The logarithm of the dollar value of the amount of housing services consumed by household j in period t, $\ln(p_H H_j^t)$, is then determined by multiplying the vector of housing characteristics, X_j^t, by the vector of estimated hedonic weights, $\hat{\beta}$: $\ln(p_H H_j^t) = \hat{\alpha} + X_j^t\hat{\beta}$. Two factors can thus account for any difference between the value of housing services and rent —a discount or premium due to conditions of tenure $(Z\gamma)$ and a residual (μ).

The term $Z\gamma$ consists mainly of a rental discount associated with long-term occupancy, and this is due to several factors:

> Lease provisions or long-term residence may tend to slow the adjustment of rents to inflation or other changing market conditions. Long-term tenant-landlord relationships may also bring nonmonetary benefits to the landlord or may actually lower the cost of providing housing services. Over long periods, landlords are likely to gain real cost savings from not having to advertise, from not losing rent during temporary vacancies, and possibly from lower maintenance expenditures. [7, p. 51]

The residual, μ, represents the deviation of the unit's rent from the average market rent for a unit with the same characteristics. A unit with $\mu > 0$ can be considered a "bad deal." In this context, shopping for rental housing may be viewed as looking for units with negative μ (bargains).[6] A hedonic index can therefore be used to determine the amount of housing services currently consumed by a household ($p_H H_0$). An equilibrium demand for housing function can be used to estimate a household's desired consumption ($p_H H^*$) and the price elasticity of demand (b). These can then be used in (5) to determine the compensating income variation IC.

---

[6]Competitive market forces tend to reduce the variance of μ (but not to zero). A household with a bad deal may have $\mu < 0$ for reasons other than inefficient shopping. If the availability of units satisfying its particular needs is low, it may be forced to accept a bad deal. Similarly, households may accept bad deals to reduce their search costs. Further, categorizing units as good or bad deals solely on the basis of the hedonic residual ignores the possibility of omitted housing or neighborhood characteristics. To the extent that this residual measures expenditures on omitted components, then the interpretation of the residual as a bad deal is overstated. Tests of the hedonic indexes used in this paper showed that the hedonic residual is not entirely due to omitted quality items but does include some price effects. See [3] for more details.

BENEFIT AND COST MEASUREMENT

The change in household circumstances analyzed here is a change in relative price of housing resulting from rent rebates to low-income renters. These rebates were introduced through a controlled social experiment, the Housing Allowance Demand Experiment, conducted in two large metropolitan areas, Allegheny County, Pennsylvania (Pittsburgh), and Maricopa County, Arizona (Phoenix).

The experiment was aimed at developing and testing alternative programs for helping low-income households improve their housing by direct cash grants to participants. One major type of program testing was a "Percent of Rent" housing allowance. Recipients of the rent rebate received a payment S equal to a fixed fraction "θ" of their gross rental payments (including utilities), $S = \theta R$. The relationship of the household's net to their gross housing expenditures measures the change in the relative price of their housing. This can be seen by expressing rent as the price of housing times the quantity of housing, $R = p_H H$. For the same quantity of housing, the net outlay of those who received rent rebates is $R_n = (1 - \theta)p_H H$. Thus, their price of housing changes from p_H to $(1 - \theta)p_H$. This change in the effective price of housing permitted econometric estimation of the price of elasticity of housing demand (see [2]).

In the experiment, the rebate θ was varied from 0.2 to 0.6 increments of 0.1, in effect reducing the price of housing by between 20 and 60%. In addition, there was a control group that received no rent rebate ($\theta = 0.0$). Households were randomly assigned to either the treatment group or the control group. Altogether, 672 households in Pittsburgh and 513 in Phoenix participated in these treatment and control groups for the first two years of the experiment (late 1973 to early 1975) and for which sufficient data for analysis were collected. (See [3] for additional details.)

The effects of rent rebates on mobility depend on the existence and direction of any pre-experimental housing disequilibrium. Ignoring moving costs for the sake of exposition, in the case of initial underconsumption, actual housing H_0 is less than the desired amount H_0^*. (Likewise, in the case of initial overconsumption, H_0 is larger than H_0^*.) The household's pre-experimental utility gain from moving is $(U_0^* - U_0)$. With the introduction of the experimental price discount, the utility of consuming the new desired level of housing H_e^* becomes U_e^* while the household's intial utility level increases from U_0 to U_e (since payments are received in the initial unit).

The utility gain from moving to the optimal unit $(U_e^* - U_e)$ may be decomposed into three parts:

$$(U_e^* - U_e) = (U_e^* - U_0^*) + (U_0^* - U_0) - (U_e - U_0). \tag{7}$$

$(U_e^* - U_0^*)$ represents the experimentally induced change in equilibrium utility levels, $(U_0^* - U_0)$ represents the pre-experimental disequilibrium, and $(U_e - U_0)$ represents the actual utility gain at the initial position. This decomposition may be relevant because of the limited duration of the experiment (three years). The household might respond differently to an experimentally induced disequilibrium $[(U_e^* - U_0^*) - (U_e - U_0)]$ than to a nonexperimental disequilibrium $(U_0^* - U_0)$.

The compensating income variations of these separate components of utility gain can be computed, allowing hypotheses about their separate effects to be tested.[7] To compute these decomposed compensatory income variations for a log-linear demand function, the following quantities must be determined: the household's initial consumption of housing services $(p_H H_0)$, its preexperimental equilibrium level of housing services $(p_H H_0^*)$, its experimental equilibrium level of housing services $(p_H H_e^*)$, and its expenditure on these housing services (R_0^*, R_e^*); the household's initial expenditure R_0 is known.

Housing services are measured using hedonic indices for the two Demand Experiment sites (see Merrill [7]). The hedonic indices take into account a wide variety of physical and locational characteristics and account for 66 to 80% of the observed variation in rents. Furthermore, tests of their validity support the contention that they measure housing services with a high degree of accuracy.

Equilibrium household consumption of housing services $(p_H H^*)$ was estimates from a log-linear demand function that incorporated demographic characteristics and serially correlated errors.[8] The estimated price elasticities of demand for housing services were -0.12 in Pittsburgh and 0.01 in Phoenix; the estimated income elasticities were 0.22 and 0.34, respectively.[9] Because of the variability of the price elasticity estimates and the possibility of omitted variables, the price elasticity was treated parametrically and was set equal to -0.22 in order to reestimate the demand equations.[10] The most important consequence of low price (and income)

[7]For the log-linear demand function these variations (using (3)) are:

(i) Total disequilibrium $= \int_{H_0^*}^{H_e^*} [D(H)\,dH] - (1-\theta)R_e^* + (1-\theta)R_0 = (1-\theta)\{(b/(b+1))(1/p_H H_e^*)^{1/b}[(p_H H_e^*)^{(b+1)/b} - (p_H H_0)^{(b+1)/b}] - R_e^* + R_0\};$

(ii) Initial disequilibrium $= \int_{H_0}^{H_0^*} [D(H)\,dH] - R_0^* + R_0 = (b/(b+1))(1/p_H H_0^*)^{1/b}[(p_H H_0^*)^{(b+1)/b} - (p_H H_0)^{(b+1)/b}] - R_0^* + R_0;$

(iii) Induced disequilibrium = Total disequilibrium − Initial disequilibrium.

[8]To predict accurately the equilibrium level of housing services, the post-move income used in the prediction equation should be measured net of moving costs. Moving costs when amortized are only a small fraction of income, so that ignoring moving costs in the prediction of $p_H H^*$ should make little difference in the measure of benefits.

[9]See Friedman and Weinberg [3] for more details.

[10]This price elasticity used is the expenditure price elasticity estimated by Friedman and Weinberg [2]. The estimated equations are presented in an appendix available on request from the authors.

elasticities of demand in the context of this analysis is that large changes in income or prices lead to only small changes in demand, and to even smaller changes in the benefits from moving.

Equilibrium household expenditure (R^*) was based directly on the value predicted from the household's demand function for housing services. That is, if households are estimated to demand H housing services, the households are presumed to pay the going market price for those housing services, $\$H$. This assumes in effect that the household surrenders any tenure-related discount that is enjoyed at its previous location, and, in addition, either surrenders any "good deal" beyond the tenure discount or eliminates any "bad deal."[11]

---

[11]An alternative method tested treated the good or bad deal experienced by a household as possibly reproducible, depending on the characteristics of the local housing market. In a tight housing market, such as Pittsburgh with a rental vacancy rate of 5.1% in 1974, households that move are likely to find it difficult to reproduce a good deal and difficult to improve a bad deal. On the other hand, in loose housing markets, such as Phoenix (14.4%), previous bad deals may be easily reversed and good deals reproduced. (Rates are from [11].)

To test these hypotheses, regression equations of the following form were estimated for Control households that moved at each site: $\hat{\mu} = \alpha + \rho\hat{\mu}_0 + \omega$, where $\hat{\mu}$ = estimated hedonic equation residual (good or bad deal) after moving, $\hat{\mu}_0$ = estimated hedonic equation residual before moving, ω = error term.

The results of the estimation tended to support the hypothesis concerning market effects on the reproducibility of good or bad deals at the two sites. These results follow.

Independent variable	Pittsburgh		Phoenix	
	Initial bad deal	Initial good deal	Initial bad deal	Initial good deal
Constant	0.067	0.061	− 0.077	0.071
	(0.051)	(0.051)	(0.051)	(0.058)
Initial deal	0.155	0.194	0.415	1.179
	(0.272)	(0.264)	(0.326)	(0.368)
R^2	0.01	0.02	0.03	0.17
Sample size	48	34	50	52

Note: Standard errors are in parentheses.

An initial bad deal is estimated to persist in Pittsburgh, whereas in Phoenix, it turns into a small good deal, on average, after moving. Similarly, in Pittsburgh, good deals disappear upon moving whereas they are reproduced in part in Phoenix.

In the alternative method, therefore, the observed persistence (or lack of persistence) of good and bad deals as based on the estimated regressions was incorporated into the expected post-move level of expenditures. Thus, rather than threat the entire good or bad deal experienced by a household in its initial unit as a potential cost or benefit from moving as the first method implies, the alternative method of measuring expenditures treats it only partially as a potential cost or benefit.

The specification of several important costs of moving is straightforward. The potential costs of moving included here are out-of-pocket costs of moving, the costs of searching for a new unit, and a proxy for the psychological costs of moving attributable to such factors as neighborhood social attachment. Since the household makes its decision before actually incurring the cost, it is the expected moving costs that matter.

The cost most clearly associated with moving is out-of-pocket costs of moving possessions from one unit to another. Expected out-of-pocket costs were estimated by using a household-specific predicted value of such costs obtained from a regression of actual moving costs on household demographic chararcteristics.[12] Expected search costs also were estimated based on household-specific predicted value of a regression, one relating the time spent searching for the household's initial enrollment to the same household characteristics used to explain out-of-pocket moving costs.[13] The proxy used for the psychological costs of breaking neighborhood attachments is a function of the length of residence, the tenure discount.[14]

Combining the measure of costs and benefits into a single net benefit measure was explicitly avoided. Using such a procedure requires that all costs and benefits be measured in the same units; in addition, it would have required a choice of discount rate and planning horizon (expected length of residence). In short, such a procedure would have imposed untestable restrictions on the model.

[12] The mean out-of-pocket moving cost reported by movers was $54.06 in Pittsburgh and $12.59 in Phoenix. The costs are low in Phoenix because 85% reported moving their belongings using their own or a borrowed vehicle or no vehicle at all (35% in Pittsburgh). In order to get a monthly cost, the expected moving cost should be amortized over the household's estimated tenure in the new unit. Using expected total moving costs as expected from the regression equation directly as an independent variable allows the sample itself to determine simultaneously the amortization rate and its effect on mobility. To the extent that movers tend to be households with lower than average costs, this method underestimates the potential out-of-pocket moving costs of a randomly selected household. The equations predicting both expected out-of-pocket moving costs and expected search costs are available on request from the authors.

[13] The mean search time reported in the baseline interview was 95 days in Pittsburgh and 33 days in Phoenix. Again, when included in the mobility equation, this measure's coefficient could implicitly measure the (amortized) price of search time. Since this measure is reported by all households, no bias is expected.

[14] The discount is expressed as a negative exponential function of the length of residence, where the maximum of about $15 per month in Pittsburgh and $23 per month in Phoenix was reached after about 10 years [7]. While part of the site difference may be explained by generally higher rents in Phoenix, the higher discount in Phoenix may also reflect the generally looser market there, with landlords increasing rents relatively slowly to induce tenants to remain. The loss of the discount is already included in the benefit measure so its inclusion as a cost measure as well as in a sense a misspecification. However, it quantifies the psychological costs in dollar terms, the same metric used for expected out-of-pocket moving costs and for the benefit measures.

TABLE 1
Characteristics of Cost Measures

Measure	Median	Mean	Standard Deviation	Minimum	Maximum
Pittsburgh (sample size = 672)					
Expected out-of-pocket moving cost ($)	58	61	16	0	138
Expected search time (days)	61	59	19	0	105
Current tenure discount ($)	5	6	6	0	15
Phoenix (sample size = 513)					
Expected out-of-pocket moving cost ($)	17	16	5	0	39
Expected search time (days)	37	37	18	0	88
Current tenure discount ($)	5	7	8	0	23

TABLE 2
Characteristics of benefit measures (in Dollars)

Measure	Median	Mean	Standard Deviation	Minimum	Maximum
Pittsburgh					
Experimental households (sample size = 377)					
Initial disequilibrium	10	19	34	− 67	214
Induced disequilibrium	1	− 2	16	− 67	31
Overall disequilibrium	9	18	31	− 55	230
Control households (sample size = 295)					
Initial disequilibrium	9	18	34	− 52	184
Induced disequilibrium	0	0	0	0	0
Overall disequilibrium	9	18	34	− 52	184
Phoenix					
Experimental households (sample size = 264)					
Initial disequilibrium	14	24	36	− 36	191
Induced disequilibrium	4	2	17	− 65	53
Overall disequilibrium	16	26	37	− 27	219
Control households (sample size = 249)					
Initial disequilibrium	16	25	39	− 74	180
Induced disequilibrium	0	0	0	0	0
Overall disequilibrium	16	25	39	− 74	180

The median, mean, standard deviation, and range for each of the measures of costs are represented in Table 1 and for the benefits in Table 2.[15] The tables reveal that the potential benefits of moving that result from the price discounts offered by the Demand Experiment are small, especially in relation to the expected costs of moving. The size of the induced benefit is a direct result of the low price elasticity of housing demand for low-income households. With a low elasticity, the experiment creates neither a large disequilibrium in housing consumption nor a large benefit from moving. Because of both this small disequilibrium and (measured and unmeasured) costs of moving, households would appear to be about as well off not moving (and accepting the rent rebate associated with their initial unit) as they would be if they adjusted all the way to their equilibrium experimental position H_e^*. The modest size of the incremental benefits to be gained from moving thus suggests that households may be unlikely to respond in a major way to the benefit measures, although there should still be a positive relationship between searching and moving and the measures of benefits.

ESTIMATION OF A BENEFIT-COST MODEL OF SEARCH AND MOBILITY

The microeconomic model of search and moving presented in Section I predicted that a household would search for housing if it believed that the present discounted value of search and moving costs (TC) was less than the present discounted value of the disequilibrium that could be eliminated (IC). In other words, if the net expected gain from searching and moving is positive, a household is likely to look for a new unit.

In general, the benefit and cost measures for each household j can be specified as

$$IC_j = \widehat{IC} + \epsilon_{1j},$$
$$TC_j = \widehat{TC} + \epsilon_{2j}, \tag{8}$$

where the benefits and costs are estimated by $\widehat{IC}$ and $\widehat{TC}$, respectively, and ϵ_{1j} and ϵ_{2j} are random prediction errors. The stochastic terms ϵ_1 and ϵ_2 may arise for several reasons. For example, variation in tastes among households and uncertainty about the future affect the valuation of the

---

[15] Benefit measures are presented only for the case in which good and bad deals are assumed not to persist; that is, households are assumed to pay the average market price for a unit when they move. Assuming persistence of the initial good or bad deal influences the benefit measures but does not affect the relationship between the benefit measures and searching or moving.

income compensation associated with eliminating a disequilibrium; imperfect information about the availability of units providing different amounts of housing services affects the costs.

Since ϵ_{1j} and ϵ_{2j} are not observable, the model of searching and moving must be specified in a probablistic framework. Let P_j denote the probability that household j will search or move. Then

$$P_j = \text{prob}(IC_j > TC_j) = \text{prob}(\widehat{IC} - \widehat{TC} > \epsilon_{2j} - \epsilon_{1j}). \quad (9)$$

The probability of searching and moving is positively related to the expected value of the compensating income variation (the benefit from moving) and negatively related to the expected costs.

The housing market affects the relationship between the benefit from and the probability of moving. A household may search for a unit because it expects to increase its utility, but the search may lead the household to realize that housing units with the appropriate housing services are not available. Because a household can move only if its search is successful, the lack of adequate units may attenuate the link between the potential benefits of moving and the probability of moving.

Two specifications of benefit measures were used. Model I includes measures that partition the household's disequilibrium into an initial (that is, pre-experimental) disequilibrium and an experimentally induced disequilibrium, as indicated in Table 2. Households may discount the experimental disequilibrium, so the initial and induced equilibrium may have different impacts on mobility. Model II includes only an overall measure of disequilibrium. Tables 3 and 4 present results of estimating separate benefit-cost models of search and of mobility using logit analysis for the case of benefit measures that do not account for the persistence of good or bad deals.[16] The cost and the benefit measures perform well at both sites. The significant variables have the expected sign in both the search and the mobility models. In the combined site equations almost all the variables have the correct sign and almost all are highly significant.[17]

The benefit measures add significantly to the explantory power in eight of the twelve equations estimated. As expected, the benefit measures are more significant in explaining search than in explaining mobility, although only slightly so. Further, as might be expected, expected search time bears

---

[16]When the benefit measures used in the search and moving equations account for this persistence, the results are basically unchanged from those in Tables 3 and 4 and so are not presented.

[17]Chi-square tests do however indicate that search and mobility behavior in the two sites is different. Only for mobility Model I does the test indicate no significant difference at the 0.05 level, although all·do so at the 0.01 level.

TABLE 3
Logit Model of Housing Search

Independent variables	Pittsburgh		Phoenix		Combined sites	
	Model I	Model II	Model I	Model II	Model I	Model II
Constant	1.285*** (0.401)	1.224*** (0.401)	1.449*** (0.411)	1.449*** (0.413)	1.696*** (0.173)	1.692*** (0.173)
Cost Measures						
Expected out-of-pocket moving costs	-0.009* (0.005)	-0.008 (0.005)	0.029 (0.019)	0.029 (0.019)	-0.009*** (0.002)	-0.009*** (0.003)
Expected search time	-0.001 (0.004)	-0.001 (0.004)	-0.021*** (0.005)	-0.020*** (0.005)	-0.009*** (0.003)	-0.009*** (0.003)
Current tenure discount	-0.089*** (0.014)	-0.085*** (0.014)	-0.066*** (0.013)	-0.068*** (0.013)	-0.079** (0.009)	-0.078*** (0.009)
Benefit Measures[a]						
Initial disequilibrium	0.005* (0.003)	—	0.006** (0.003)	—	0.005*** (0.002)	—
Experimentally induced equilibrium	0.016** (0.007)	—	-0.000 (0.008)	—	0.009* (0.005)	—
Overall disequilibrium	—	0.005* (0.003)	—	0.005* (0.003)	—	0.005** (0.002)
Chi-square of benefit measures (significance)	5.83[b] (0.10)	3.22[c] (0.10)	3.92[b] (NS)	3.42[c] (0.10)	6.97[b] (0.05)	6.25[c] (0.05)
Proportion searching	0.549		0.676		0.604	
Coefficient of determination (ρ^2)	0.05	0.05	0.09	0.09	0.07	0.07
Sample size	672		513		1,185	

Note: Standard errors in parentheses below coefficient.
[a]See text for measurement method.
[b]With two degrees of freedom.
[c]With one degree of freedom.

* t – statistic significant at the 0.10 level.
** t – statistic significant at the 0.05 level.
*** t – statistic significant at the 0.01 level.
NS Not significant at the 0.10 level.

TABLE 4
Logit Model of Residential Mobility

Independent variables	Pittsburgh		Phoenix		Combined sites	
	Model I	Model II	Model I	Model II	Model I	Model II
Constant	0.566 (0.416)	0.522 (0.415)	0.923** (0.376)	0.924*** (0.371)	1.170*** (0.166)	1.167*** (0.168)
Cost Measures						
Expected out-of-pocket moving costs	-0.016*** (0.006)	-0.015*** (0.006)	0.015 (0.018)	0.015 (0.018)	-0.018*** (0.003)	-0.018*** (0.003)
Expected search time	0.005 (0.005)	0.005 (0.005)	-0.013*** (0.005)	-0.013 (0.005)	-0.004 (0.003)	-0.004 (0.003)
Current tenure discount	-0.114*** (0.015)	-0.112*** (0.015)	-0.083*** (0.012)	-0.084*** (0.012)	-0.097*** (0.009)	-0.097*** (0.009)
Benefit Measures[a]						
Initial disequilibrium	0.005* (0.003)	—	0.005* (0.003)	—	0.005*** (0.002)	—
Experimentally induced equilibrium	0.012* (0.007)	—	0.002 (0.007)	—	0.008 (0.005)	—
Overall disequilibrium	—	0.005* (0.003)	—	0.004* (0.003)	—	0.005*** (0.002)
Chi-square of benefit measures (significance)	3.60[b] (NS)	2.51[c] (NS)	3.02[b] (NS)	2.88[c] (0.10)	6.82[b] (0.05)	6.46[c] (0.05)
Proportion moving		0.342		0.548		0.431
Coefficient of determination (ρ^2)	0.07	0.07	0.09	0.09	0.10	0.10
Sample size		672		513		1,185

Note: Standard errors in parentheses below coefficient.
[a]See text for measurement method.
[b]With two degrees of freedom.
[c]With one degree of freedom.

*t-statistic significant at the 0.10 level.
**t-statistic significant at the 0.05 level.
***t-statistic significant at the 0.01 level.
NS Not significant at the 0.10 level.

a stronger relationship to the probability of searching than to the probability of moving. The estimated impacts of both the initial and total disequilibria are comparable in the search and mobility equations and across sites. The estimated impact of the experimentally induced disequilibrium is more than that of the initial disequilibrium although in no equation is there a significant difference between the coefficients of the initial and the induced disequilibrium. An increase of $10 in the total disequilibrium is estimated to increase the probability of search by 1.2 percentage points and the probability of moving by 1.1 percentage points. Despite the significance of the benefit measures, the small average size of the disequilibrium (cf. Table 2) indicates that the overall impacts of housing disequilibrium on search and mobility are small.

CONCLUSION

The model presented in this paper provided a rigorous framework for analyzing residential search and mobility. Despite some tantalizing results concerning the roles of household disequilibrium, transactions costs, and market phenomena in influencing search and moving, there is clearly room for more development of this model. Before describing such new directions, it is worth recapitulating the results.

The major finding of the model is that, for low-income households, the benefits of moving are small. The economics of the housing demand of low-income households is such that relatively large changes in traditional economic variables such as prices and income result in relatively small changes in equilibrium housing demand. Further, because immobile households are partially compensated for any suboptimal housing consumption by increased nonhousing consumption, the potential benefit from moving is further decreased.[18] The conclusions stem directly from observed values of price and income elasticities of housing demand among low-income households and are robust with regard to the range of alternative estimates of such parameters that appear in the literature. That is, even

---

[18] For example, if the price elasticity of housing demand among low-income households is − 0.22 and if a price rebate of 40 percent is given to a household that initially spends $150 per month for housing, equilibrium housing demand would increase by roughly $13 per month, but the compensating income or cash equivalent value of actually moving to the new equilibrium position would be less than $3 per month. (For a price elasticity of − 0.22 and a price reduction of 40%, demand would increase by $0.22 \times 0.40 = 8.8\%$. The compensating income of such a price reduction is approximated by $1/2 \times$ change in price $\times$ change in demand = $2.60.) Thus, what appears to be a sizeable incentive to move, a subsidy of at least $60 per month, actually results in a very modest incentive. Roughly comparable incentives to move would be created by doubling the income of low-income households (using an estimated income elasticity of 0.36).

if the "true" price and income elasticities of housing demand are considerable larger than those used in the analysis, their qualitative implications for moving incentives would be basically unchanged.[19]

By contrast, the costs of moving appear to be highly significant in influencing rates of residential search and mobility. In the models presented here, cost variables consistently explained more variation in search and mobility than did benefit variables, reiterating a finding of Goodman [4].

The costs of search and moving appear to be highly variable from place to place. Although it is obviously inappropriate to generalize from only two sites, households in a fairly loose housing market (Phoenix) had much lower costs and higher mobility than households in a very tight housing market (Pittsburgh). Likewise, variations in the price per unit of housing services among metropolitan areas resulting from variation in factor prices, mismatches between supply and demand, discrimination, and the degree to which good or bad deals can be reproduced may all influence the benefits of moving.

Despite the insights provided by this model, its empirical results are somewhat dissapointing. The explanatory power of the empirical models is smaller than that of models that rely heavily on sociodemographic variables (see [5] for such models estimated for the same sample). A number of extensions of the model could enhance its generality and improve its goodness of fit. Among the most promising extensions are:

- the use of demographically disaggregated demand functions to estimate benefit measures;
- decomposition of the housing bundle into components;
- more rigorous specification of expected costs of search and moving; and
- interactive determination of demand functions and mobility equations.

Part of what is estimated to be housing disequilibrium may really be variation in housing preferences not captured by the housing demand functions. Demand functions disaggregated by demographic characteristics such as household size and composition, age, race, and/or sex would yield more accurate estimates of equilibrium housing demand and consequently better estimates of the benefits to be gained from moving.

A more fundamental reason for the small impact of benefit measures is that disequilibrium in "housing services" may matter relatively little to households. A more significant incentive to move may arise from disequilibrium regarding specific housing features, such as components of the

---

[19] For example, when the model was estimated with a price elasticity of -0.40, the results were qualitatively unchanged.

housing bundle (for example, interior space and quality, neighborhood features, and accessibility). Changes in some household characteristics may have only a modest influence on overall housing services demand but a dramatic impact on the demand for specific housing features. For example, several analyses have shown that housing demand first rises and then falls with increasing household size [6]; thus very small and very large households could demand the same dollar amount of housing services, but a different composition of the housing bundle. Consequently, changes in household size or composition can lead to large disequilibria in the desired housing bundle even though desired expenditure levels can remain nearly constant. It is possible to estimate demand functions for several separate housing components based on the hedonic index used in this analysis. Measures of disequilibrium in such components could then be used to calculate the income compensation associated with moving to eliminate a particular disequilibrium, using a generalized version of the methods presented here.

Two improvements in specifying the cost side of the model may also be useful. Out-of-pocket costs and search costs estimated here from regressions of actual costs on demographic variables, can be disaggregated further according to household demographic characteristics and other variables. In addition, the degree to which good and bad deals are likely to be replicated upon moving could be specified to depend not only on housing market characteristics but also on household characteristics and initial location within a city.

Finally, the model may be estimated interactively rather than in a two stage procedure. In the model as it now stands, housing demand functions are estimated before the equations describing search and mobility. It is possible to estimate demand and mobility parameters simultaneously using maximum likelihood techniques; such a procedure could lead to a more efficient set of parameter estimates describing each kind of behavior.

In sum, this paper represents but an early stage in modeling residential mobility—the introduction of a rigorous framework and a richer view of the determinants of mobility than has been typical of mobility studies. Much remains to be done.

References

Abt Associates Inc. *Experimental Design and Analysis Plan of the Demand Experiment.* Cambridge, Mass.: August 1973*a*.

Abt Associates Inc. *Site Operating Procedures Handbook.* Cambridge, Mass.: April 1973*b*.

Abt Associates Inc. *Summary Evaluation Design.* Cambridge, Mass.: June 1973*c*.

Bailey, Martin. Effects of race and other demographic factors on the value of single-family homes. *Land Economics,* Vol. 42, pp. 215–220, May 1966.

Becker, Gary. *The Economics of Discrimination.* Chicago: University of Chicago Press, 1957.

Bradbury, Katherine L., and Downs, Anthony (Eds.). *Do Housing Allowances Work?.* Washington, D.C.: The Brookings Institution, 1981.

Brown, Lawrence A., and Moore, Eric G. The intra-urban migration process: a perspective. *Geografiska Annaler,* Vol. 52B, pp. 1–13, 1970.

Budding, David. *Housing Deprivation Among Enrollees in the Housing Allowance Demand Experiment.* Revised. Cambridge, Mass.: Abt Associates Inc., 1980.

Burns, Leland S., and Grebler, Leo. *The Housing of Nations.* New York: MacMillan, 1977.

Burtless, Gary, and Greenberg, David. Inappropriate comparisons as a basis for policy: Two recent examples from the social experiments. Technical Analysis Paper No. 21. U.S. Department of Health and Human Services, Office of the Assistant Secretary for Planning and Evaluation, Office of Income Security Policy, July 1980.

Carliner, Geoffrey. Income elasticity of housing demand. *Review of Economics and Statistics,* Vol. 55, No. 4, pp. 528–532, November 1973.

Congressional Budget Office. Measures of housing need: findings from the annual housing survey, in (U.S. House of Representatives, Committee on Banking and Urban Affairs, Subcommittee on Housing and Community Development) *Task Force on Assisted Housing.* Washington, D.C.: U.S. Government Printing Office, 1978. Pp. 1570–1590.

Congressional Budget Office. *The Long Term Costs of Lower Income Housing Assistance Programs.* Washington, D.C.: U.S. Government Printing Office, 1979.

Congressional Budget Office. *Federal Housing Assistance: Alternative Approaches,* Washington, D.C.: U.S. Government Printing Office, 1982.

Court, Andrew. Hedonic price indexes with automotive examples, in *Dynamics of Automobile Demand.* New York: General Motors Corporation, 1939. Pp. 99–117.

DeLeeuw, Frank. The demand for housing—a review of the cross-section evidence. *Review of Economics and Statistics,* Vol. 53, No. 1, pp. 1–10, February 1971.

Drury, Margaret; Lee, Olson; Springer, Michael; and Yap, Lorene. *Lower Income Housing Assistance Program (Section 8); Nationwide Evaluation of the Existing Housing Program.* Washington, D.C.: U.S. Government Printing Office, 1978.

Fenton, Chester. The permanent income hypothesis, source of income and the demand for rental housing, in (Joint Center for Urban Studies) *Analysis of Selected Census and Welfare Program Data to Determine Relationship of Household Characteristics, Housing Market Characteristics, and Administrative Welfare Policies to a Direct Housing Assistance Program.* Cambridge, Mass.: July 1974.

Follain, James R., and Malpezzi, Stephen. *Dissecting Housing Value and Rent: Estimates of Hedonic Indexes for Thirty-Nine Large SMSAs.* Working Paper 249-17. Washington, D.C.: The Urban Institute, February 1979.

Frieden, Bernard J., and Solomon, Arthur P. *The Nation's Housing: 1975 to 1985.* Cambridge, Mass.: Joint Center for Urban Studies, April 1977.

Friedman, Milton. *A Theory of the Consumption Function.* Princeton: Princeton University Press, 1957.

Friedman, Joseph, and Kennedy, Stephen D. *Housing Expenditures and Quality Part 2: Housing Expenditures Under a Housing Gap Housing Allowance.* Cambridge, Mass.: Abt Associates Inc., 1977.

Friedman, Joseph, and Weinberg, Daniel H. *The Demand for Rental Housing: Evidence from a Percent of Rent Housing Allowance.* Cambridge, Mass.: Abt Associates Inc., 1980*a*.

Friedman, Joseph, and Weinberg, Daniel H. *Housing Consumption Under a Constrained Income Transfer: Evidence from a Housing Gap Housing Allowance.* Cambridge, Mass.: Abt Associates Inc. 1980*b*.

Friedman, Joseph, and Weinberg, Daniel H. The demand for rental housing: evidence from the housing allowance demand experiment. *Journal of Urban Economics,* Vol. 9, pp. 311-331, 1981*a*.

Friedman, Joseph, and Weinberg, Daniel H. Ex ante and ex post correction for selection bias with an application to the housing allowance demand experiment. Unpublished manuscript. 1981*b*.

Friedman, Joseph, and Daniel H. Weinberg (Eds.), *The Great Housing Experiments.* Beverly Hills, Calif.: SAGE Publications, 1983.

Gillingham, Robert F. Place-to-place rent comparisons using hedonic quality adjustment techniques. Bureau of Labor Statistics Staff Paper No. 8. Washington, D.C.: U.S. Government Printing Office, 1975.

Goodman, John L., Jr. Housing consumption equilibrium and local residential mobility. *Environment and Housing,* Vol. 8, pp. 855-874, 1976.

Griliches, Zvi. Distributed lags: a survey. *Econometrica,* Vol. 35, No. 1, pp. 16-49, January 1967.

Griliches, Zvi. Hedonic price indices revisited, in Zvi Griliches (Ed.) *Price Indexes and Quality Change.* Cambridge, Mass.: Harvard University Press, 1971. Pp. 3-15.

Hamilton, William L. *A Social Experiment in Program Administration.* Cambridge, Mass.: Abt Books, 1979.

Hanushek, Eric A., and Quigley, John M. The dynamics of the housing market: a stock adjustment model of housing consumption. *Journal of Urban Economics,* Vol. 6, pp. 80-111, 1979.

Hastings, N. A. J., and Peacock, J. B. *Statistical Distributions.* New York: John Wiley and Sons, 1975.

Haugens, Robert, and Heins, A. James. A market separation theory of rent differentials. *Quarterly Journal of Economics,* Vol. 83, pp. 660-672, November 1969.

Hausman, Jerry A., and Wise, David A. Social experimentation, truncated distributions and efficient estimation. *Econometrica*, Vol. 45, No. 4, pp. 919–938, May 1977.

Hausman, Jerry A., and Wise, David A. Attrition bias in experimental and panel data: the Gary income maintenance experiment. *Econometrica*, Vol. 47, No. 2, pp. 455–473, March 1979.

Heilbrun, James. *Urban Economics and Public Policy*. New York: St. Martin's Press, 1981.

Intriligator, Michael D. *Econometric Models, Techniques, and Applications*. Englewood Cliffs, N.J.: Prentice-Hall, 1978.

Johnston, John. *Econometric Methods*. 2nd ed. New York: McGraw-Hill, 1972.

Kain, John, and Quigley, John M. *Housing Markets and Racial Discrimination*. New York: National Bureau of Economic Research, 1975.

Kaluzny, Richard L. Changes in the consumption of housing services: the Gary experiment. *Journal of Human Resources*, Vol. 14, No. 4, pp. 496–506, Fall 1979.

Kennedy, Stephen D. Sample selection and the analysis of constrained income transfers: some evidence from the housing allowance demand experiment. Paper presented at the meetings of the Econometric Society, June 1978.

Kennedy, Stephen D. *Final Report of the Housing Allowance Demand Experiment*. Cambridge, Mass.: Abt Associates Inc., 1980.

Kennedy, Stephen D., and MacMillan, Jean. *Participation Under Alternative Housing Allowance Programs: Evidence from the Housing Allowance Demand Experiment*. Revised. Cambridge, Mass.: Abt Associates Inc., 1980.

Kennedy, Stephen D., and Merrill, Sally R. The use of hedonic indices to distinguish changes in housing expenditures: Evidence from the housing allowance demand experiment. Paper presented at a conference on The Housing Choices of Low-Income Families, March 1979.

King, A. Thomas. Land values and the demand for housing. Unpublished Ph.D. dissertation. Department of Economics, Yale University, 1972.

Lancaster, Kelvin. *Consumer Demand: A New Approach*. New York: Columbia University Press, 1971.

Lane, Terry S. *Origin and Uses of the Conventional Rules of Thumb*. Cambridge, Mass.: Abt Associates Inc., 1977.

Lee, Tong Hun. Housing and permanent income: tests based on a three year re-interview survey. *Review of Economics and Statistics*, Vol. 50, No. 4, pp. 480–490, November 1968.

Lee, Tong Hun, and Kong, Chang Min. Elasticities of housing demand. *Southern Economic Journal*, Vol. 44, No. 2, pp. 298–305, October 1977.

MacMillan, Jean. *Mobility in the Housing Allowance Demand Experiment*. Revised. Cambridge, Mass.: Abt Associates Inc., 1980.

Maisel, Sherman J.; Burnham, James B.; and Austin, John S. The demand for housing: a comment. *Review of Economics and Statistics*, Vol. 53, No. 4, pp. 410–413, November 1971.

Mayo, Stephen K. Welfare and housing, in (Joint Center for Urban Studies) *Analysis of Selected Census and Welfare Program Data to Determine Relationship of Household Characteristics, Housing Market Characteristics, and Administrative Welfare Policies to a Direct Housing Assistance Program*. Cambridge, Mass.: Joint Center for Urban Studies, 1973.

Mayo, Stephen K. *Housing Allowance Demand Experiment: Housing Expenditures and Quality Part 1: Housing Expenditures Under a Percent of Rent Housing Allowance*. Cambridge, Mass.: Abt Associates Inc., 1977.

Mayo, Stephen K. Theory and estimation in the economics of housing demand. *Journal of Urban Economics,* Vol. 10, pp. 95–116, 1981.

Mayo, Stephen K., and Fenton, Chester. *Alternative Mechanisms for Determining the Cost of Standard Housing.* Cambridge, Mass.: Abt Associates Inc., December 1974.

Mayo, Stephen K.; Mansfield, Shirley; Warner, W. David; and Zwetchkenbaum, Richard. *Housing Allowances and Other Rental Assistance Programs—A Comparison Based on the Housing Allowance Demand Experiment, Part 1: Participation, Housing Consumption, Location, and Satisfaction.* Revised. Cambridge, Mass.: Abt Associates. Inc., 1980a.

Mayo, Stephen K.; Mansfield, Shirley; Warner, W. David; and Zwetchkenbaum, Richard. *Housing Allowances and Other Rental Assistance Programs—A Comparison Based on the Housing Allowance Demand Experiment, Part 2: Costs and Efficiency.* Revised. Cambridge, Mass.: Abt Associates Inc., 1980b.

Merrill, Sally R. *Hedonic Indices as a Measure of Housing Quality.* Revised. Cambridge, Mass.: Abt Associates Inc., 1980.

Merrill, Sally R. and Joseph, Catherine A. *Housing Improvements and Upgrading in the Housing Allowance Demand Experiment.* Revised. Cambridge, Mass.: Abt Associates Inc., 1980.

Mieszkowski, Peter. *Studies of Prejudice and Discrimination in Urban Housing Markets.* Boston: Federal Reserve Bank of Boston, December 1979.

Musgrave, Richard A. Policies of housing support: rationale and instruments, in (U.S. Department of Housing and Urban Development), *Housing in the Seventies Working Papers,* Vol. 1. Washington, D.C.: U.S. Government Printing Office, 1976. Pp. 215–233.

Muth, Richard F. *Cities and Housing.* Chicago: University of Chicago Press, 1969.

Muth, Richard F. The derived demand for urban residential land. *Urban Studies,* Vol. 8, No. 3, pp. 243–254, October 1971.

Muth, Richard F. Moving costs and housing expenditures. *Journal of Urban Economics,* Vol. 1, pp. 108–125, 1974.

Nelson, David. Income elasticity of housing demand. Unpublished Ph.D. dissertation. Department of Economics, University of Oregon, 1975.

Ohls, James C., and Thomas, Cynthia. *The Effect of the Seattle and Denver Income Maintenance Experiments on Housing Consumption, Ownership and Mobility.* Denver: Mathematica Policy Research, Inc., January 1979.

Olsen, Edgar O. A competitive theory of the housing market. *American Economic Review,* Vol. 59, No. 4, pp. 612–622, September 1969.

Pascal, Anthony. The analysis of residential segregation, in (John P. Crecine, Ed.) *Financing the Metropolis.* Beverly Hills, Calif.: SAGE Publications, 1970.

Phlips, Louis. *Applied Consumption Analysis.* New York: American Elsevier, 1974.

Pindyck, Robert S., and Rubinfeld, Daniel L. *Econometric Models and Economic Forecasts.* New York: McGraw Hill, 1976.

Polinsky, A. Mitchell. The demand for housing: a study in specification and grouping. *Econometrica,* Vol. 45, No. 2, pp. 447–461, March 1977.

Quigley, John M. Housing demand in the short run: an analysis of polytomous choice. *Explorations in Economic Research,* Vol. 3, No. 1, pp. 76–102, Winter 1976.

Quigley, John M., and Weinberg, Daniel H. Intra-urban residential mobility: a review and synthesis. *International Regional Science Review,* Vol. 2, No. 1, pp. 41–66, 1977.

Rosen, Sherwin. Hedonic prices and implicit markets: product differentiation in pure competition. *Journal of Political Economy,* Vol 82., No. 1, pp. 34–55. January/February 1974.

Rossi, Peter H., and Lyall, Katherine C. *Reforming Public Welfare.* New York: Russell Sage Foundation, 1976.

Rydell, Peter C. *Shortrun Response of Housing Markets to Demand Shifts.* Report R–2453-HUD, Santa Monica, Calif.: Rand Corporation, September 1979.

Rydell, Peter C.; Mulford, John E.; and Kozimor, Lawrence W. Dynamics of participation in a housing allowance program. Working Note 10200-HUD. Santa Monica, Calif.: Rand Corporation, 1978.

Speare, Alden, Jr., Goldstein, Sidney, and Frey, Williams H. *Residential Mobility, Migration, and Metropolitan Change.* Cambridge, Mass.: Ballinger, 1974.

Straszheim, Mahlon. *An Econometric Analysis of the Urban Housing Market.* New York: National Bureau of Economic Research, 1975.

Struyk, Raymond J., and Bendick, Marc, J. (Eds.). *Housing Vouchers for the Poor.* Washington, D.C.: The Urban Institute, 1981.

U.S. Department of Commerce, Bureau of the Census. *Current Housing Reports.* Series H-170-74-13. Washington, D.C.: U.S. Government Printing Office, September 1976.

U.S. Department of Housing and Urban Development. *Housing in the Seventies Working Papers.* Washington, D.C.: U.S. Government Printing Office, 1976.

U.S. President's Commission on Housing. *The Report of the President's Commission on Housing.* Washington, D.C.: U.S. Government Printing Office, 1982.

Vidal, Avis. *The Search Behavior of Black Households in the Housing Allowance Demand Experiment.* Revised. Cambridge, Mass.: Abt Associates Inc., 1980.

Wallace, James E.; Bloom, Susan P.; Holshouser, William L.; Mansfield, Shirley; and Weinberg, Daniel H. *Participation and Benefits in the Urban Section 8 Program: New Construction and Existing Housing.* Cambridge, Mass.: Abt Associates Inc., January 1981.

Weicher, John C. Policy and economic dimensions of "a decent home and a suitable living environment." Paper presented at the American Real Estate and Urban Economics Association meetings, May 1976a.

Weicher, John C. The rationales for government intervention in housing: an overview, in (U.S. Department of Housing and Urban Development) *Housing in the Seventies Working Papers,* Vol. 1. Washington, D.C.: U.S. Government Printing Office, 1976b. Pp. 181–191.

Weinberg, Daniel H. Housing benefits from the urban section 8 program. *Evaluation Review,* Vol. 6, No. 1, pp. 5–24, February 1982.

Weinberg, Daniel H.; Friedman, Joseph; and Mayo, Stephen K. Intraurban residential mobility: the role of transactions costs, market imperfections, and household disequilibrium. *Journal of Urban Economics,* Vol. 9, pp. 332–348, 1981.

Willig, Robert D. Consumer's surplus without apology. *American Economic Review,* Vol. 66, pp. 589–597, 1976.

Zais, James P.; Goedert, Jeanne E.; and Trutko, John W. *Modifying Section 8: Implications From Experiments with Housing Allowances.* Washington, D.C.: The Urban Institute, 1979.

Zellner, Arnold. An efficient method of estimating seemingly unrelated regressions and tests for aggregation bias. *Journal of the American Statistical Association,* Vol. 57, pp. 248–368, June 1962.

Index